THE ENCLOSED GARDEN

THE FRED W. MORRISON
SERIES IN SOUTHERN STUDIES

THE ENCLOSED GARDEN

WOMEN AND COMMUNITY IN THE EVANGELICAL SOUTH, 1830–1900

BY JEAN E. FRIEDMAN

THE UNIVERSITY OF NORTH CAROLINA PRESS

CHAPEL HILL AND LONDON

© 1985 The University of North Carolina Press

All rights reserved

Manufactured in the United States of America

Library of Congress Cataloging in Publication Data

Friedman, Jean E.

The enclosed garden.

(The Fred W. Morrison series in Southern studies)

Bibliography: p.

Includes index.

1. Women—Southern States—Social conditions.

2. Feminism—Southern States—History—19th century.

3. Social structure—Southern States—History—19th

century. 4. Women—Southern States—Religious life—

History—19th century. I. Title. II. Series.

HQ1438.S65F75   1985   305.4′2′0975   84-25831

ISBN 0-8078-1644-2

FOR MARY

and for the recent generations of southern women, especially
Marjorie Bee and her daughter Ann,
Janice Powell, and Wanda Langley

CONTENTS

A section of photographs will be found following page 54.

PREFACE

he Enclosed Garden is the author's search to understand the relationship between the nineteenth-century social structure and the lived experience of southern women. Intrigued by the excellent studies of antebellum northern women by Nancy Cott, Carroll Smith-Rosenberg, and Barbara Berg which suggest that modernization and its attendant sexual segregation prompted women to form independent women's networks that ultimately challenged the patriarchy, I used them as a point of departure. Those studies formulated the basic question of my own study, namely, why did the southern women's reform movement emerge only gradually in the late nineteenth century?

The early stages of my research led me to see the importance of community as a powerful factor in integrating southern women's identity and in preserving their traditional role. The structure of the evangelical community then became the object of study. But it was the point of intersection between community structure and women's psyche that compelled my interest. Gradually it became clear that only a multimethodological approach, one using anthropology, sociology, literary analysis, and psychology, as well as traditional historical methods, would be able to penetrate the layers of reality that have hidden southern women's historic identity. The result was a study of community and its effect on the role and identity of black and white women. But this means that no immediate answer to the original comparative question is at hand because this kind of multidimensional analysis for women of other regions is not presently available. The author hopes this study will challenge historians of women to analyze the problem of community structure and women's psychic response in order to make a comparative work possible.

Writers and scholars are paupers, dependent upon their friends and colleagues for advice and criticism. This list of acknowledgments attests to my own poverty. I am most indebted to Lester D. Stephens, department head, who generously gave his time to edit and criticize the raw first drafts. His patience, tact, and wisdom helped sort out the relevant and irrelevant, the worthy and unworthy. Paul C. Nagel, who believed in supporting the scholarship of the junior faculty, listened intently to my research plans and encouraged me by making available departmental grants. Lester Stephens did the same. In addition the University Patent Fund underwrote part of this research.

Tania Modleski, with enduring good humor and tough-mindedness, edited the later drafts, challenging and criticizing ideas and language. Very simply, her friendship and encouragement made this book possible. Nancy Fraser read the early manuscript, recognized its possibilities, and gave astute suggestions that greatly contributed to the richness of its themes. It was she who supported me through various writer's cramps and crises. Emory Thomas always accepted my work with enthusiasm; he taught me that writing was exciting. Moreover, he defended the work even though he graciously disagreed with parts of it.

Everett Lee offered invaluable help in organizing the quantitative data. His willingness to teach and guide a neophyte was nothing short of inspiring. Susette Talarico patiently schooled me in data gathering and quantitative methods; the successes are hers, the mistakes, mine. Janice Powell, my assistant and consultant who programmed, coded, and clarified data went beyond what was expected of her.

Paul Freeman and Pattie Buice, Jungian analysts, helped considerably in shaping the third chapter. They cannot be held responsible, however, for my tendency to adopt literary and historical methodology rather than a consistent psychological one.

I would like to thank my readers who added their own special critical and editorial talents to the manuscript. They are Nancy Rubin, Fran Teague, Darlene Clarke Hines, Ellen Nolan, Lee Kennett, and Mary Gordon. To Carol Berkin, who read the final draft, and to Iris Hill and Sandra Eisdorfer, who did such superb editorial jobs, I owe a special debt of thanks.

Perhaps, in the order of things my thanks should first have been to Bill Shade, my old adviser, partner, and friend. By unceasing energy he stretched my concept of culture and loosened my imagination.

Many thanks to my hard-working assistants: Tom Richey, Melissa Tufts, Todd Butler, and Bebe Crosby.

The archivists, librarians, and curators of the collections I visited were most helpful and tireless in their efforts to make available pertinent material, and I am grateful to them.

Finally, much credit is due the secretaries who, in a pre-word-processor department, faithfully met the deadlines with accurate and good copy. They were outstanding not only for their efficiency but for their kindness. They are Kathy Coley, Ann Saye, Nancy Heaton, Janice Scarborough.

INTRODUCTION

hy the southern women's reform movement emerged in the late nineteenth-century South is a question answered only by analyzing the subtle and complex roots of southern women's identity. Until the late 1870s southern culture inhibited the formation of women's consciousness, collective identity, and self-assertion and at the same time discouraged female association. Traditionally, historians have attributed the repression of feminism to the institution of slavery. The southern patriarchy, the argument went, demanded the subservience of all dependents including slaves, women, and children in order to retain autocratic power over the slave system. Any challenge to the patriarchy threatened slavery. Certainly, there is truth in this argument. But what social institution supported slavery and was especially threatened by its loss? The families who depended upon slavery for status and the accumulation of property defended the system. Thus southern families and the kinship connections that fostered the southern community need closer analysis if we are to understand the maintenance of traditional attitudes toward women.

The evangelical community, a church-directed, kin-dominated society, linked plantation, farm, and town in the predominantly rural South. As Frank Owsley and, more recently, Robert Kenzer have explained, the coming together of elite and farmer kinsmen and kinswomen in the churches made kin rather than class the principle determining element in social relationships. It would be a mistake to assume that this was the case only for rural society; in fact, kin values pervaded the towns and thus reinforced traditional obligations for urban women as well. However, in the South (as elsewhere) the phenomenon of urbanization was not primarily a movement away from kin ties to the impersonal city; rather, as the southern refugee pattern indicates, migration was part of a complex exchange movement between city and countryside during the war. In addition, recent works, such as Michael Anderson's study of nineteenth-century Lancashire and George S. Rosenberg's and Donald F. Anspach's analysis of contemporary working-class families, show that urban families are sustained by kin connections.[1]

Historians of northern women assume that sex-segregation offered a basis for the formation of independent women's groups. Sex-segregation as a precondition for reform never materialized in the South because in that traditional society the primary association was with kin. Neighborhood kinship groups and the family-centered evangelical church structure and discipline established the model of sexually integrated association. When women congregated together as they occasionally did in quilting parties or on the road to the market such ephemeral meetings were considered socially marginal, that is, not in conformity with the prevailing heterosocial mode. These meetings never developed into consistent, stable patterns of association that held the potential for a reform network. In this way southern traditional society inhibited female autonomy.

Certainly, it is true that some variation of the neighborhood-kinship pattern existed throughout nineteenth-century America and that women everywhere relied on family as well as friends.[2] However, the greater frequency and durability of southern church discipline intensified family unity and control, preserving to a marked degree evangelical notions of sexual role.

Historians Nancy Cott and Barbara Berg trace the evolution of a women's culture to modernization.[3] Modernization proceeds when certain structural changes occur in a society including the emergence of a market system, democratic institutions, urbanization, and industrialization and when these changes promote a "modern" personality capable of recognizing common interests with "strangers" rather than with family.

The advance of the market system, which absorbed male labor and relegated women to household work, gave rise to distinctive spheres where work and sex role merged.[4] Sexual segregation of northern women encouraged gender-identification, a group consciousness of a common vocation and an identification with womanhood as a purposeful social role. According to Cott, gender ruled women's "sentiments, capacities, purpose and potential achievements."[5] Sisterhood is implicit in Cott's definition.[6] Evangelical prescriptive literature that delineated women's sphere and defined the "belle-ideal" encouraged women's self-conscious identification with members of their own sex. In urban areas the quest for identity, community, and self-respect led to the formation of women's associations. Middle and upper-class women who ministered to the poor and the outcast forged an identification with them that transcended the class barrier.[7] In short, women in regions affected by modernization chose relationships not limited by geographic, familial, and class loyalties and appreciated as sisters those women who shared their common interests. A women's culture is the sum of such connections.

In contrast, the traditional rural society experiences no structural changes and adheres to time-bound methods of agrarian production that do not require specialization of role. Individuals in a traditional society are bound one to another by a sense of solidarity derived from a loyalty to family and place. Traditional societies tend to limit women's choices of relationships to neighborhood and kin. A women's culture does not necessarily develop in traditional society because work roles cross over; males and females are not rigidly segregated in farm economies. Group consciousness therefore tends to identify with family and community rather than with sex. Community and not gender bound southern womanhood. Not until the latter part of the nine-

teenth century did southern women begin to perceive themselves as a discrete class and recognize the limitations imposed upon them by the southern
male-dominated community.

Of course, from the most general structural point of view the lag in the
formation of a women's culture may be explained by the slow rate of modernization. But to describe this structural process is only to begin to raise in-
teresting questions. How did the persistence of traditional kin relationship
shape white women's sense of their social and work roles? To what extent did
conversion into the racially mixed evangelical community affect black wom-
en's identity? What was the influence of the Civil War and modernization
upon the ability of the evangelical community to determine women's roles?
This study aims to answer these questions.

The attempt to understand the evolution of Victorian southern women's
identity is an effort that reaches beyond historical analysis. Indeed, such an
understanding demands a multidisciplinary approach. This study organizes
each chapter around an analysis of a separate dimension. Like a fugue and
its variations, community versus female autonomy is played out by different
voices, different dimensions of experience. The theme can be followed in the
experience of black and white women and is manifest in dreams, conversion
testimony, church structure and discipline, domestic and work roles, war
work, and reform activity.

Chapter 1 uses traditional historical sources and quantitative methods
to reconstruct the neighborhood-kinship settlements and establish the residence pattern of church members. Different kinds of data, namely, United
States census records, genealogies, church minutes, church membership
lists, tax lists, estate inventories, diaries, correspondence, and account led-
gers provided the evidence for studying six North Carolina and Georgia
church populations in depth. The conclusions drawn from this study—high
persistence trends, double standard of discipline, the existence of neighborhood kinship groups—may well reflect larger trends. There is little evidence
in studies elsewhere that disputes these conclusions; on the contrary, Court-
land Victor Smith's study of nine North Carolina Baptist churches confirms
the pattern of a double standard of discipline and Robert Kenzer's recent
analysis supports my own finding that local North Carolina populations
shared common characteristics with the stable, rural southern population.[8]

From diaries, private correspondence, slave narratives, and travelers' accounts, Chapter 2 illustrates how the evangelical social structure defined
sexual roles, including domestic, marital, and work roles. Although the
church defined marriage as an equal partnership and women expected men
to share domestic burdens, in reality husbands generally abdicated household responsibilities. The wife was the nurturer of the family and the guard-
ian of the house. In these roles farm women and city women shared the same
structure of dependency, although it expressed itself in different forms. Farm

women's primary responsibility was the household and "dairy." They helped in the field only until the accumulation of property warranted acquiring servants. The rural partnership, rather than equalizing the relationship between husband and wife, demanded an extra burden from the wife without compensatory autonomy. City women, economically dependent upon their husbands, faced the emotional and domestic consequences of that dependence.

The habitual way of relating to one another in southern evangelical culture determined an individual's sense of identity, and it is the purpose of Chapter 3 to translate southern Victorian sociology into an exploration of women's lived interiority. While it may be supposed that only rural women might have integrated the powerful images of community into their unconscious, in fact urban middle-class women found the imagery compelling and recorded it in their diaries.

Again, the strength of this chapter is the depth of the evidence. By means of a close literary analysis of a small number of diaries, it was possible to reconstruct the psychological idiom of southern women with a clarity, vividness, and detail that could not be obtained by more traditional methods. The choice of particular diaries out of a larger sample was guided by the need to find paradigmatic, ideal types that expressed in a coherent, clear way the imagery presented in fragmented sequences in other diaries. Out of approximately thirty unpublished diaries I found eighteen that recorded dreams, and from these I selected three cases. In the sample of eighteen all but one woman dreamed of community-related themes, such as visiting living relatives and exchanging gossip or news, or existing within a community amidst familiar faces. Most women dreamed of death, their own or a relative's; this, however, can be considered community-related if we remember that in the evangelical context death was a prelude to joining a supernatural community. Within the close, communal environment of the evangelical South, unfamiliar terrain or interaction with "strangers" did not dominate the unconscious of southern women.

Although selectivity is inevitable in literary studies, the crucial test here is whether or not this material coheres with evidence obtained from other sources. The examination in previous chapters of diverse sources, such as church records, diaries, and correspondence, which developed the theme of women's preoccupation with community against the demands of autonomy, supports my contention that the literary material manifested the same preoccupation. Of course, this interpretation is only a beginning, a creative attempt to integrate different kinds of sources into a historical analysis, and its validity will have to be borne out by other studies using sources similar to those that I have used in *The Enclosed Garden*.

The continuing theme of autonomy within community is elaborated somewhat differently in the case of black southern women, as Chapter 4 explains.

Black southern women experienced the same discipline and conversion process as did white southern women; they interpreted that experience differently, however, on account of their Afro-American community with its distinct family system and culture. Greater maternal responsibilities devolved upon black women than upon white women because of the frequency of separation from husbands and the fact that women as breeders were highly valued by their slave masters. Black women's self-esteem was reinforced, in contrast to that of black men. This independence and self-esteem encouraged Afro-American women to assert themselves and take social initiative. And because black men and women were equally powerless—a circumstance not replicated among white men and women—black women had more opportunity and more of a tendency to exercise leadership within the black community than white women had in theirs.

The pattern of conversion and acceptance of leadership can be seen in black women's conversion testimony. An analysis of conversion symbolism reveals women's own perception of themselves and the perception of women within the Afro-American community. In order to construct the pattern of recurring imagery that intimates the sense of self and relationship to others, Chapter 4 presents the results of an analysis of published sources of Afro-American conversion testimony through the *God Struck Me Dead* series, the Works Progress Administration's slave narratives, and the "God Struck Me Dead" manuscripts found at the Amistad Research Center. The conversion process suggests that *metanoia*, or change of heart, dramatized the formation of identity as it was experienced by women and men in the Afro-American community. While the number of actual converts was small, the evangelical values precipitating conversion were widely accepted, permeating even the nonconverts. Therefore, the study of conversion testimony may well shed light upon the culture of nonconverts.

The final chapters trace the survival of the family networks and church discipline even in the midst of crisis and change. The Civil War and the modernization period disrupted the habitual life of southern Victorian evangelicals. Nonetheless, social reintegration followed along traditional lines. Refugees fled to family and kin; consequently, forms of dependence and of community described earlier were not seriously eroded by war and urbanization. Domestic reconstruction or women's leadership in rebuilding southern churches, in addition to the decline in church discipline, fostered women's networks. However, the networks drawn from the traditional social source—neighborhood kinship groups—tended to conserve traditional racist and sexist hierarchies.

This study is a journey, an effort to carry the investigation of southern women's identity through various dimensions in order to understand why their autonomy emerged only gradually in the Victorian period. A complex symbol, "the enclosed garden," encompasses the mind, the church, and the community of women and men in the evangelical South. *The Enclosed Garden* is neither a history of suffrage nor a history of the southern women's reform movement, but rather it is an analysis of community and the ways in which the rural evangelical kinship system resisted women's reform even into the twentieth century.

THE ENCLOSED GARDEN

1. E D E N

*There is the mother and her daughter enjoying mutual confidence.
There the father and children; the wife and husband, the sisters, the
cousins, the aunts and nieces, and all are bound one to another, and
as a living chain connected link by link, by the law of consanguinity.*
Mary Ann Cobb to Howell Cobb, 14 December 1843[1]

omplex ties of kinship bound southern women to each other and to men. The importance of kinship cannot be underestimated in the Victorian South: it remained the vital connection, the difference between isolation and security. The South derived its unique identity not only from slavery but from the interdependent kin connections that were reinforced by membership in local evangelical churches. Southern women's identity, then, may be considered in the context of familial and religious expectation and demand.

Strangers who traveled through the South often missed the pathways that connected the folk to their community. Emily P. Burke, a New England schoolteacher, mistook a local church in north Georgia for a barn; it appeared as a deserted building in the middle of a thicket. When she inquired where the worshipers came from, an inhabitant replied, "Oh, out of the woods, all around here." The visitor then observed the little paths that led to habitations.[2]

The isolation of the churches impressed Emily Burke. She supposed that because churches were "few and far between," causing the faithful to travel twenty to forty miles to worship, religious privileges were necessarily limited.[3] The traveler did not see that the meetinghouse defined the boundaries of the evangelical community and linked neighbor, kin, men, and women in the scattered rural settlements. The isolation and expanse of southern settlements made "community" less a village of proximate neighbors than an understanding of the heart among distant kinfolk and neighbors.

Town squares and county seats provided gathering places for the southern population, but southern towns were hardly more than trading centers. Even in such rural outposts, kinship determined identity: urban did not mean impersonal. The grid of personal, kin relationships spread outward from the local Baptist, Methodist or Presbyterian church. Evangelical churches exerted a powerful, often hidden influence on southern culture, sociology, and psychology. The pathways to the church revealed the roles, values, and beliefs of the antebellum southern people.

Those who came down the paths to the church were a mixed lot: planter and farmer, black and white, male and female, child and adult. Yet they traveled in family groups in wagons and on horseback or muleback, and those whom they met were mostly kin. Everyone looked forward to the meeting and the time just to be together. During the break between the services men and women would split into sociable groups and discuss the politics, domestic news, and gossip of interest to their own kind. At the end of the religious exercises, in the clearing the women served a spread of food—meats, pies, and cakes—and everyone partook of the repast. Sometimes the unchurched but hungry invited themselves to eat, and there was not much the women could do about it. At other times, churchgoers visited nearby families and friends for dinner. The women had already prepared the Sunday feast, which allowed families to enjoy the day.[4]

What drew the community to the church was the preaching—the hellfire, damnation, mercy, and salvation of the spoken word that touched an emotional response in the hearers. Individuals lived and duplicated the history of salvation outlined by the preacher; women and men measured their lives by their experience of conversion and the struggle to remain one of the elect. Anne Beale Davis recalled a vivid scene in her church experience: "I was nine years old when I heard of the certainty of the resurrection of the body after death. . . . I felt I had no time to lose in preparing for my maker. I went below the graveyard to a fence all alone and kneeled down, and devoutly prayed that I might be spared."[5] Such early convictions wore off and worldliness set in. Later the sickness and death of loved ones awakened a renewed conviction of sin and desire for salvation. An urgency existed among the stalwart to "get religion." Sermons, catechisms, religious newspapers, and revivals fostered one compelling end for an individual life—salvation.[6]

Most of those found on the mourning bench awaiting a call to conversion were women. In southern correspondence, soul counts, or the number of converts added to membership during a protracted meeting, included a majority of women. Conversion of worldly men constituted a real spectacle. Sara Lamar reported to her cousin John Lamar, "Those who knelt and who wanted the minister and people to pray for them included 'our proud cotton gentlemen.'" Sarah Lamar's reason in writing her cousin was to draw him to the church in the hopes of converting the bachelor planter.[7]

Camp meetings dramatized the conversion experience. Great excitement attached to the meetings; the community reckoned time by such events. Mary Ann Lamar started baking a week ahead of time in order to supply her family with delicacies during the encampment. Her cousin Hessie told Mary Ann Cobb she looked forward to the romantic possibilities at the camp. Most, however, prayed for either personal conversion or the conversions of family members. Families attended in groups and tented together. The excitement of the camp meeting was the excitement of risk. Who would humble themselves and publicly walk to the mourners' bench? How many in the family would hear the call? And aware that drinking, gambling, and dancing took place among the shadows, revivalists wondered which force would prevail, good or evil?[8]

The spectacle of the camp meeting did not overwhelm the private exercises of those in attendance. Anne Beale Davis recorded in October 1838 that "the fire of Divine love was first shed forth in the preacher's tent, it rushed from heart to heart until each one in the tent [was] powerfully blessed; two present experienced the blessing of perfect love."[9] Miss Weisiger's conversion happened while she attended a sick child in the tent. Her peaceful and joyous experience led her to join the Methodist church. She claimed she never doubted her conversion.[10]

The spiritual tendrils, such as those extended by Anne Beale Davis, needed stalwart companionship on which to grow and thrive. Companion souls nurtured the convert within the Christian community; kinswomen and kinsmen supported each other in the spiritual struggle. Louisa McGeher wrote Mary Ann Cobb, "I hope dear cousin you will not be unmindful of the importance of religion."[11] Mary Ann Cobb, in turn, reassured a newly converted cousin, "You ask my heartfelt sympathy and you have the whole of it my dear cousin accompanied with my prayer that you may have God's Holy Spirit to guide, comfort and sustain you in the new life which has opened to your view."[12] Later, Aunt Patsy talked to Andrew Cobb on the improvement of his religious exercises.[13] In short, individuals within the Cobb-Lamar family took responsibility for the salvation of other members; the family covenant bonded members within the evangelical community.

Death in the family only reinforced the family covenant. Members transplanted in an eternal abode forged links to the earthly family and pulled them toward eternal togetherness. A pastor consoled bereaved parents with the idea that "we have indeed a little family forming in heaven, and if earthly ties are allowable, then what a bright circle our little departed ones will form amongst the numerous heavenly hosts."[14] Aggrieved mothers prayed to join their children that there may once again be an unbroken circle. In a memorial to Mathilda Todd DeVan her mother wrote, "God grant that these jewels of the broken circle be reunited."[15]

Evangelical discipline strengthened the earthly family circle. By the use of admonition and church trials, congregations attempted to correct and manage the problems of sin and disorder within the family community. Church members hoped to effect changes in individual behavior or induce repentance through separation or expulsion from the church. Congregations heard each case and although only men voted, women witnessed the proceedings. As a result the entire church became personally involved in the aberration of one member. Annie Darden of North Carolina agonized over the expulsion of a member of her church. She wrote, "Tis a very solemn thing indeed to turn one out of church fellowship. Oh that the Lord may reclaim him by his grace, that he may speedily be brought back to the fold again."[16] Because the family covenant was at stake, human drama entered ordinary lives with judgment upon family and neighbor.

In the South a particular "system of relationships" found meaning and direction in the southern evangelical community. Neighborhood kinship networks defined rural-town settlements throughout the South and preserved the familial evangelical culture of the southern community. And within the evangelical community the church exercised a double standard of discipline that regulated sexual roles as a way of maintaining family stability. The community, a broad analytical concept that includes "plantation," "farm," and "town," provides the key to an understanding of women's struggle for autonomy in traditional culture.

Recent historical scholarship examines women's identity-formation in terms of a "role analysis" confined to northern Victorian culture. Scholars contend that the northern women's reform movement advanced along with the economic and social transformations of the Middle Period. The economy sustained growth in agriculture, commerce, and banking and fostered increased urbanization and industrialization. The social by-products of modernization included decreased fertility, marked class stratification, political democratization, and most significantly, the domestication of women.[17] The Cult of Domesticity emerged as a direct response to modernization; that is, the separation of work roles in the industrialized society relegated women to the home. However, historians suggest sexual segregation in northern evangelical culture also provided opportunity for women's associations—prayer groups, missionary societies, and benevolent organizations—that ultimately challenged patriarchal control.[18] Nancy Cott traces the origin of a New England women's culture to the forces of modernization. Barbara Berg and Carroll Smith-Rosenberg find that women's voluntary associations rose out of complex urban demands.[19] Such female associations demonstrated women's creative reaction to a repressive social system. Donald Mathews's *Religion in the Old South* superimposes Smith-Rosenberg's analysis of homosocial networks onto southern evangelical culture and therefore concludes that the sexually dichotomized culture led to profound changes in social and sexual roles.[20] Thus although the studies of Cott, Berg, and Smith-Rosenberg have greatly enhanced our knowledge of northern women's identity-formation and the origin of the northern women's reform movement, they do not readily transfer to the evangelical discipline in the rural-town economy of the Old South.

Women's reform evolved much later in the South because modernization, with its attendant women's culture, occurred in the latter part of the nineteenth century. Rapid, intense economic growth did not figure in the preindustrial South; gradual self-sufficiency marked southern development. Because the South continued what was essentially an older agrarian and family-oriented structural pattern, homosocial networks, or same-sex interaction, did not evolve and therefore southern antebellum women were deprived of a social basis for reform. Family and kinship bonds, drawn tightly together in the local evangelical church, assumed primary importance in defining human relationships. The evangelical church subscribed to a vision of families united in eternity; thus, its members were disciplined to maintain strict sexual roles as a means of uniting the earthly family.[21]

Evangelicalism, a social process that filled the vacuum left by the eighteenth-century disintegration of the Anglican church, followed the southern settlement pattern. Historian John B. Boles accounts for the origin and nature of southern culture in the spread of the Great Revival, 1787–1805. The growth of evangelicalism was the growth of local communities characterized by a powerfully integrated sociology and theology of conversion and individualism. Converts who shared "born-again" values established independent covenanted churches. External events, politics, and westward migration merely distracted but did not deter the spread of a dominant evangelical culture. When European ethnic groups and migrants from the northern and middle states entered the southern frontier, the appeal of religious intimacy and community found ready response among isolated settlers. Evangelical communities established early in the eighteenth century stabilized the families and encouraged them to populate the valleys, plains, and riverbanks with their own kin and kind. Particular regions encompassed particular ethnic groups, so that family and place in the South were synonymous.[22]

Frank Owsley described two methods of nineteenth-century settlement: chain migration, or movement to areas where kin had already established a homestead, and church settlement, or the migration of an entire congregation to a new area. After arrival migrants might move several times but rarely did they remove themselves far from their church.[23] This meant that the ever-widening neighborhood kinship patterns spread throughout a region could be identified by the church as the point of reference. By the nineteenth century, then, church settlement determined the social order; families identified with a church in a special region or place. An example of the settlement process can be found in the establishment of the Cypress Presbyterian community in Harnett County, North Carolina. Scots migrated to the Upper Cape Fear Valley, thus escaping the ruinous tenantry system of the Highlands. In the mid-eighteenth century a group of Scots followed upon the foray of Neill McNeill, an enterprising sailor, and his friend Archie Buie to the Lower Little River where it joins Upper Cape Fear. Neill's Creek, Buie's Creek, Rockfish, and Barbeque formed the tributaries of settlement. The James Cameron family joined the McNeills and Buies and established holdings in the Cape Fear delta of the Upper and Lower Little rivers. In the next decade, various other Cameron kin entered the area along with members of the McNeill families. The Camerons, the Buies, and the McNeills intermarried and soon

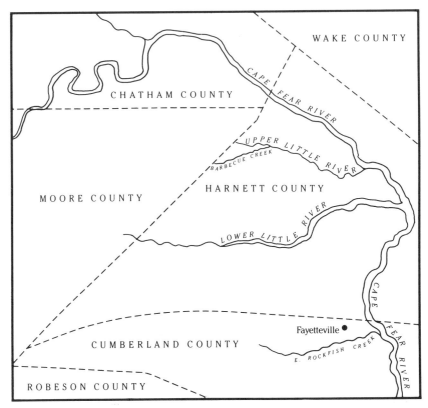

Area of Settlement in Harnett County,
North Carolina, in an 1874 map

controlled the property of the region. Once established, the settlement raised a Presbyterian church at Cypress Creek, the area owned by the Camerons. Thereafter the leading male members of the community managed the church built by their families. Cameron, Buie and McNeill men acted as elders and deacons in the Cypress Presbyterian Church for generations.[24]

At the same time intermarriage drew the congregation together in a complex system of kinship ties. Like tidelines, successive waves of kin imprinted relational patterns on a region. Interrelated nuclear families clustered together in a region and thus formed the evangelical community. Families arranged themselves near kin to form neighborhoods. Sons and daughters lived on family property or worked adjoining acreage. Kin linkages spread into surrounding counties; residences listed in the U.S. census records from 1830 to 1880 suggest that any one church drew kin from great distances. The

kin network established in the settlement period endured well into the twentieth century.[25]

Kin models in the South varied by geographic region. In his study of Alabama white families from 1850 to 1870, William L. Barney delineated four
socioeconomic areas in which responses to political crises differed according to family structure and integration into the market system. Barney identified the mountain population as maintaining the highest density of kin
relations and the least attachment to the market while other regions—the
wiregrass, the rural black belt, and the city of Selma—demonstrated progres-
sively less dependence upon family and kin relationships and greater involvement in the market system. Barney concluded that since each region
held conflicting views of slavery, secession, and reconstruction based upon
its socioeconomic structure, Alabama's geographic diversity obviated cultural or ideological unity.[26] Barney's study suggested that while the high rate
of preference for kin shown in mountain communities cannot be applied
generally in the South, some gradation of kin preference can be. Although
familial and economic structures differed and although political consensus
never existed between the various regions, the familial values of southern
evangelism nevertheless pervaded the culture. In the South separation from
family did not preclude high cultural valuation of kin. When families moved
away it was considered a tragic loss. Catherine Kenan Holmes wrote to her
sister who had moved to West Tennessee, "I often think and give up all hope
of seeing you again in the world."[27] Southern correspondence is filled with
the anguish of separation from kin.

Bertram Wyatt-Brown suggests that nineteenth-century southern culture
was more family-centered, particularistic, and ascriptive than that of other
regions. Southern family connections, according to Wyatt-Brown, were valued
more than education or professional skill. At stake in the Old South was the
social hierarchy, a patriarchy crowned by land-owning dynasties. Family and
property defined power; therefore, family loyalty buttressed the social system
and in turn provided the most powerful basis of self-identity.[28]

The kin networks and church discipline that evolved in the preindustrial
South had two effects upon women's roles. In the first place, the development
of stable family systems rooted women in neighborhood kinship networks
that discouraged the formation of independent *women's* networks. Second,
male control of evangelical family churches insured a double standard of
church discipline which reinforced traditional sexual roles and deterred formation of independent women's organizations.

In southern settlement patterns, the importance of dynasty and family loyalty and the influence of family-centered evangelical churches proved kin
relationships superior to non-kin or friends. In times of health or financial

crisis, southerners relied on kin and very little on friends or neighbors. For example, when Laura Norwood's sister gave birth, Laura tended her along with relatives in the town of Hillsborough, North Carolina. Though the women of Hillsborough offered to help, the sisters hesitated to accept the assistance of "strangers."[29] Usually single young women, such as Lizzie Graves and Julia Picking of North Carolina, acted as traveling nurses among their respective relatives who were ill or confined in childbirth. Kin in financial distress turned to wealthy family members. Mrs. Sara B. Evans, for example, managed a plantation in Louisiana and regularly lent money to relatives or took in family who had no means of support.[30] The correspondence of southern women demonstrates that the most vital friendships were with kin. One young woman became deeply depressed because of her cousin's marriage. She confided to her diary that [Lou's marriage] "would not be half so bad if she could live in the neighborhood, and by degrees cool my ardent confiding love into a common friendship, by the waning light of her own."[31] Martha Foster Crawford believed simply that she "could not live without Cousin Lou."[32] Fannie Page Hume had "five separate cries" when her cousins left after a visit.[33] Mary Telfair, a Savannah planter, deprived of the close relationships of kin, wrote to a New York friend, Mary Few, "I wish I had *a land of Cousins* to go [to], for I have a *large* heart which could contain as much love again as at present fills it."[34] The pain of separation from kin may also be seen in Louisa Lord's correspondence to her cousin Martha. "I am afraid you think I have forgotten you entirely but I have not[.] [A] day never passes but [t]hat I think of you and long to see you again."[35] Thus, the grid of familial relationships sustained the emotional, financial, and social well-being of the rural southern community.

The reason why southerners primarily chose kin had to do with a complex cultural response. According to Wyatt-Brown, class identity and status meant that kinship ties were valued over all others. Michael Anderson theorizes that cost-benefit assumptions, that is, a whole set of mutually beneficial bargains and exchanges, determined why individuals preferred kin.[36] Property and "cost effective" motivations would, in part, explain kin preference; however, since kin ties are social resources, used only as circumstance and culture demand, it is conceivable that affection, religion, and ethical considerations peculiar to the South contributed to valuation of kinship.[37]

Southerners shared American Victorian family values and certainly enjoyed family ties.[38] We have seen that women who often visited together felt great pain upon separation from female kin, but affection existed as only one dimension of the kinship bond. Other dimensions included the social and ethical foundations of the southern evangelical community that rested in Christian principles, most specifically in the Sermon on the Mount. Calvinist, Wesleyan, and Separatist traditions converged in the radical evangelical call to conversion or a new life of perfection. Evangelical conversion, cumulative in its effect upon the individual, implicitly established the ideal Christian community as an intimate union of believers directed toward new communal values.[39] Donald Mathews has effectively demonstrated that "the polarity of 'community' and the 'individual' simply did not exist for Evangelicals."[40]

The church reinforced the bonds of kinship, especially since the kindred chain often extended into an entire geographical region. In addition, evangelical churches linked scattered kin by idealizing heavenly reunion. Heaven was a hope that the family would reunite intact, unbroken by the infidelity of even one member. Moreover, conversion was a family affair. At church or campground the "mourner" or potential convert suffered through the rite of passage most often in the company of family.[41] One young woman's anxiety was relieved by the presence of her cousin; only the most intimate associate, preferably a relative, could provide support at such a vulnerable time. Lizzie Graves accompanied her cousin Mary Ann to a camp meeting; the cousin would not allow Lizzie to leave her even "ten minutes at a time until she professed a change of heart."[42] Similarly, Anne Turner supported her son when he converted at Lowe's Campground in September 1856.[43] Lastly, the articles of faith in church covenants were expressed in familial terms. The local community of the Beaver Dam Baptist Church promised to "watch over families under our care,"[44] a serious responsibility that implied the exercise of discipline.

Discipline, the second important factor that inhibited the development of female networks and reinforced traditional sex roles, set the evangelical community apart. Conversion led the initiate into church membership, into a community of believers. Thus elected members of the congregation believed that "from eternity God chose out of the human family a certain definite number unto everlasting life" and that therefore the elect properly disciplined the unholy.[45] Following the precepts of the early church, congregations administered fraternal correction. Sealed for eternity and bound to one another in discretionary discipline the elect pledged "to keep our own appointed meetings, and our own secrets, being taught . . . that the church of Christ is a garden, enclosed, a Spring sealed a fountain shut up."[46]

While American evangelical churches enforced some form of discipline throughout the nineteenth century, northern churches abandoned the practice of control over private sexual activity in the early 1830s.[47] In contrast, the use of church trials, especially in the Baptist church, persisted until much later in the South. Although the number of trials declined during the Civil War and abated to an extent in the postwar years, the practice continued into the twentieth century. Such surveillance of behavior in the rural South maintained a strict definition of sexual roles by enforcing a double standard of discipline.

Exclusion from the closed evangelical community proved humbling. Although the subject may not have lost a place in heaven, the individual lived as an outcast. Articles of discipline reminded congregations that

> when a member is turned out of church if he still continues in a state of impenitentance [*sic*], persists in his sin . . . it is of the utmost consequence that every member should act a uniform part towards him. We may it is true, continue our ordinary course with him as a man, in the concerns of this life; but there must be no familiarity, no social intercourse, no visitings to, or from him, nothing in short, that is expressive of ignorance at his conduct.[48]

Church trials and hearings operated as the chief instrument of church discipline. Trial procedure is found in evangelical tradition and in church codes of discipline. Methodist churches, North and South, shared the *Form of Doctrine and Discipline* adopted in 1784. Though periodically modified, the *Discipline* remained substantially the same throughout the Victorian era. Even when the South split from the General Conference in 1845, the South adhered to the *Discipline*. Baptist congregational policy accepted local church autonomy on the matter of discipline; therefore, no book of discipline was generally accepted. American Presbyterians inherited the first *Book of Discipline* adopted by the reformed church in Scotland and revised it in 1818 and 1839 as the *Constitution of the Presbyterian Church*.[49]

In addition to the books of discipline, the Rules of Decorum of each church laid down the standards of fairness. For example, the Beaver Run Baptist Church, Isle of Wight County, permitted only one person at a time to speak and while speaking the individual could not be interrupted except by the moderator. No member was "privileged to laugh or whisper" during a speech. And to insure a familial regard for one another during the proceedings members addressed each other with the title of brother or sister.[50]

Men managed church discipline both at the investigative and at the trial stages. Evangelical churches generally followed disciplinary procedure, which provided a pretrial investigation, a statement of the charge in writing, a citation of witnesses, and preparation time for the accused. The churches also allowed the accused the right to cross-examine witnesses. Moderators and elders who presided over the trial were male and generally they appointed male committees to investigate rumors or charges. In the Baptist and Methodist churches male elders presented the case to the congregation, while in the Presbyterian church the accused appeared before a board of elders. Evangelical congregations debated and discussed the case after which they voted upon it. In the Presbyterian church the accused occasionally appealed the elders' decision to the congregation. More often the case was appealed to the district presbytery. From the presbytery, the case could be appealed to the synod and the General Conference. In contrast, the congregational system of the Baptist church maintained the independence of individual churches, and thus no review system existed. Baptist associations acted only in an advisory capacity.[51] The Methodist Church's Quarterly Meeting acted as a review board, but it was a local association to which the pastor belonged and in which he had influence.[52] Since ministers presided in evangelical churches and retained influence in the local review boards, church discipline remained largely in the hands of the clergy. However, only a unanimous vote by the congregation or in some cases a majority vote expelled a member.[53]

The male-dominated trials all but excluded women from the proceedings. Women voted in the more lay-oriented churches, such as the Primitive Baptist church.[54] However, in those churches where women had the vote, a quorum was determined by the presence of male members. Thus judgment by female peers was offset by the guarantee of male presence and authority. Women did not vote in the evangelical church trials although they were present in the congregation during the hearings. Baptist supporters of the right of women to vote in the church argued that the principle of equality demanded it. Furthermore, church suffragists believed that if women were denied the vote they would not then be responsible for the purity of the church. The latter argument hit at the crux of female church membership. If women did not participate in the exercise of discipline, how could they constitute a church?[55]

Opponents argued that women's incompetence made them unfit to vote. It was claimed that women were by nature emotional and prejudiced and therefore could not maintain church purity. The right of women to vote raised the specter of the "unnatural" rule of women, and it was feared that voting in church would lead to national or state franchise. Participation in the exercise of discipline meant stepping out of women's "natural" domestic sphere. Antisuffragists claimed support for their position in the Pauline and Petrine injunctions against women speaking in the churches. Did women have the right to constitute a church? Opponents of the vote for women argued that the "whole church" was a figure of speech which referred to men who voted and to women who acquiesced "in feeling" to the vote.[56] Women's responsibility for the purity of the church was limited to the exercise of influence, pious example, and conversation.

There are a few indications, however, that women challenged the rule of silence. For example, in the Pleasant Union Christian Church of North Carolina and the Broad Run Baptist Church of Virginia, women constituted a majority of the dissidents who withdrew.[57] Often dissident groups formed in opposition to a disciplinary decision. In breaking from the churches, women exercised de facto votes against the disciplinary rulings. Nonetheless, in stable churches the codes of discipline allowed male management to enforce a double standard of church discipline. No significant distinction existed between county and town church discipline, probably because towns were rural outposts, centers of social and commercial exchange. (See Appendix, Table 1.1.)

The sexual double standard is clearly evident in the cases brought before six churches: in North Carolina, Mount Olive Baptist Church, Alamance County, and Cypress Presbyterian Church, Harnett County, and in Georgia, Beaverdam Baptist Church, Wilkes County, Bark Camp Baptist Church, Burke County, Cabin Creek Baptist Church, Jackson County, and First Presbyterian Church, Athens. In addition, a study of C. V. Smith's data on nine North Carolina churches confirms the double standard of judgment. (See Appendix, Table 1.2.) Located in two distinct economic and slave-holding regions, the upper and the lower South, the church congregations nonetheless demonstrated similar patterns of behavior. This suggests that the culture of the evangelical community remained constant throughout the South in the nineteenth century. Despite differences between the regions, both are representative of the Victorian South because of their rural, stable population.[58]

The evangelical social order disciplined both sexes, but of those accused of offenses men substantially outnumbered women. The North Carolina and Georgia congregations brought to trial almost three times as many men as women. (See Appendix, Table 1.2.) Moreover, evangelical churches accused almost twice as many men of multiple offenses. (See Appendix, Table 1.3.) It was as if men were expected to fail. Such expectations predisposed congregations to leniency for men and they forgave or acquitted male offenders with greater frequency than female miscreants. (See Appendix, Table 1.4.)

Furthermore, men were more likely to be charged with lesser offenses—drinking, dancing, or disorderly conduct. Nearly all accused men faced minor allegations while only about half the females were so accused. Women, more often than men, were charged with serious trangressions, usually with sexual offenses such as adultery, abortion, fornication, and illegitimacy. Only 6 percent of the male offenders were accused of sexual misconduct in contrast to 44 percent of the females. (See Appendix, Table 1.2.) Female church members were probably accused of sexual offenses more often because illegitimacy and adultery were included in the category of sexual misconduct. But the very fact that illegitimacy and adultery were considered serious offenses is proof that a double standard existed. Such a standard enabled the church community to blame women for sexual conduct that involved men. In the fifteen churches examined only two cases of bastardy (male responsibility for illegitimate birth) occur, one of which involved a black man. The white male offender was acquitted.

The church's response to the punishment of accused women was more severe than its reaction to male offenders. Here, too, the double standard operated—for although men were more often charged than women, a woman once charged was more likely to suffer the full consequence of church discipline. Of those charged with sexual misconduct more women than men suffered suspension or exclusion. (See Appendix, Table 1.5.)

Evangelical church custom provided for restoration once a period of time elapsed after conviction and punishment. In North Carolina and Georgia churches, however, the percentage of male petitioners who had their punishment revoked was nearly twice that of female petitioners. Few women petitioned for restoration; perhaps they lacked confidence that they would be forgiven for their serious offenses and felt that their sin was great and their punishment deserved. (See Appendix, Table 1.6.)

In the intimate, interrelated culture of southern evangelical communities sexual offenses and disorderly conduct posed the most dangerous threats to social order. The church trials offered the community the only measure of satisfaction in an atmosphere of concerned, involved kinfolk and friends. Adjudication of domestic disputes would have been impossible in an impersonal, legal context. Disordered private relations affected all members united in the grid of community relationships. Church discipline, then, ultimately achieved an evangelical social order, but it was one that discriminated against women. However, within limits, many women resisted church control. In cases of disorderly conduct some women remained independent of the church while others refused to submit to its discipline. Even those reconciled to the church first had their say and did so in no uncertain terms. Within the context of the evangelical community southern women demonstrated remarkable audacity.

Those who refused to repent or accept the friendly intervention of the church risked expulsion. Some women chose this independent course. Such was the case of Abba Mathews of Broad Run Baptist Church, Fauquier County, Virginia. On 12 July 1828 a rumor reached Brother Wright, a member of the church, that she had been acting disorderly. A committee of two men—Brother Wright, who heard the rumor, and Brother Biggs—were appointed to cite her to appear at the next monthly meeting. The men apprised her of the charges and attempted to discuss them with her, but she refused to attend the meeting. Five months later when cited again she not only refused to come to the church but rebuffed the committee with "improper language." The church voted to exclude Abba Mathews. Another woman, Sally Cornwall, had not attended the Occoquam Baptist Church in Virginia in three years and when cited for drunkenness she simply ignored the church summons. Rachael Coatney, who often got drunk with her servant Nelly, also did not repent and remained indifferent to exclusion. In addition, a Mrs. Thornton wrote "a contemptuous letter" to the Cabin Creek Baptist Church in Georgia in which she refused to pay a debt another woman claimed she owed her. When cited by the church Mrs. Thornton challenged the disorderly charge against her.[59] Clearly, these women would not submit to evangelical discipline.

Church discipline, however, allowed some women to defend their case and be reconciled to the church. When Brother Walker of the Pleasant Grove Primitive Baptist Church, Reidsville, North Carolina, charged Sister Cobb of withholding fifty cents in church funds, Sister Cobb, after several months of disputing the case, made him admit it might be a mistake. In another case, when Brothers Shadren and Walker were involved in a dispute, Sister Walker stood in the Pleasant Grove Primitive Baptist Church and said she was hurt at Brother Shadren's remarks about her children. Later the whole matter was dropped.[60]

Women guilty of the charge against them sometimes displayed anger and aggression before a reconciliation with the church took place. The Cabin Creek Baptist Church cited Rachael S. Duncan for improper language when she was heard to say that "if she could kill Mr. Sharp she would be willing to land in the bottomless pit of eternity." The church later forgave the repentant Rachael Duncan her anger.[61]

In Wheeler's Primitive Baptist Church, North Carolina, a vituperative exchange occurred in September 1839 between Sally Margis and Sister Polly Blalock. Sister Margis accused Sister Blalock of keeping a disorderly house and of allowing fiddling and dancing. Polly Blalock admitted her wrong but countercharged that Sister Margis kept "a *bass* house," or a house of ill-repute. In spite of their mutual contempt the church reconciled the pair and made them shake hands before the congregation.[62] In this way the church resolved explosive neighborhood quarrels.

Mavey Walker demonstrated outright hostility to her neighborly committee. It happened that members of the Pleasant Grove Primitive Baptist Church saw Mavey Walker drunk and reported it to the congregation. Sister Walker appeared at the church and "gave satisfaction." She was angry when a committee investigated her conduct a second time and openly wished that church members John Summers and James Walker could be "put belly to belly and a ball shot through them." Only the timely intervention of Brothers Smithy and Davis settled the affair.[63] In a second case Brother Larkin Smithy accused Sister Tina Smithy of burning his house, barn, and fence rails in a dispute over rent. After church mediation Sister Smithy agreed to pay damages.[64]

Although lesser charges of disorderly conduct provided women with an opportunity to speak out, more serious charges prevented any outspoken defense. Women who were accused of sexual offenses were suspended from the church if they were contrite, excluded if they were not, but they were reconciled with the church only after they were punished. C. V. Smith noted that "the only offense for which both confession and defense were ruled out was adultery," but he allowed that this practice was not universal.[65] Nevertheless, this widespread practice effected a double standard because more women than men were accused of sexual offenses and denied a defense. The operation of a double standard may be seen in a number of cases taken from church records. In one case, rumors reached the Byrd Presbyterian Church in Goochland County, Virginia, that Mrs. Martha Cole had committed adultery. The proof lay in her "having a child born within less than six months after marriage."[66] Technically, the charge should have been fornication but congregations were often imprecise in defining charges. The congregation served a citation upon Mrs. Elizabeth Key, her mother, whose responsibility it was to counsel her daughter and bring her to repentance. The mother informed the church of her daughter's contrition:

> I received your letter [and] have conversed with my unfortunate daughter, M. Cole. She acknowledges her guilt in tears—lamenting over the wound her conduct has given the church with which she has connected herself. As you have been so kind as to afford her the privilege of communicating through me, she requests me to tell you she considers the offense so great that she wishes you and the session to deal with her as our church discipline requires. She hopes time will convince [the church] of her sincere penitence. Notwithstanding the inexpressible distress I have felt on the occasion, I have the satisfaction now of seeing her seriously regarded in a religious concern.[67]

Despite the mother's assurance, the congregation voted to suspend Martha Cole until "she exhibit[s] ample evidence of the sincerity of her repentance."[68] In the evangelical culture the church chose to work through a close relative and to suspend rather than exclude the young woman. Although repentance was exacted from Martha, the congregation took no action against her male partner. Church minutes also suggest that sexual offenses generally met with a preemptory response from congregations. The Bark Camp Baptist Church recorded that Rachael Sconeirs was "charged with sin of having a bastard child. Excommunicated."[69] The Beaverdam Baptist Church noted the expulsion of Sister Mary E. Darricot for "leaving her mother's home without provocation and leading a Lewd or Obscene life."[70] A Jackson County Baptist church removed Sister Elizabeth Spurlock from the congregation "for disorder—fornication."[71]

Because women carried the burden of proof, the closed evangelical society regarded any provocation by females as serious. The Mount Olive Baptist Church excluded Mary Bivin because she was "too thick with young men."[72] Wheeler's Primitive Baptist Church reprimanded Sister Polly Murdock because she became "too intimate with Mr. Lashley."[73] Any attempt to facilitate intimacy between the sexes met with prompt discipline. For instance, when a neighbor claimed that she saw Sally Sarting "cover her daughter and a young man together on a bed,"[74] the church excommunicated her.

Although evangelical assumptions about the dark side of human sexuality presupposed female provocation, the churches considered aggression a male disorder. Such beliefs constituted the basis for the double standard. Thus the churches believed that they exercised discipline to protect women against male aggression. Several cases indicate this type of social control. Brothers Nichols, O'Brien, and Summer were cited by congregations because they abused their wives. And when Brother Eli J. Hester swore at a free black woman for testifying against his friend for abusing her, the Wheeler's congregation called him before the church.[75] Such protection of women functioned well within the accepted values of the double standard.

The male-dominated church and the kin-oriented society interfered with the development of separate women's groups within the church structure. With few exceptions, religious association in the antebellum South followed either a sexually integrated or a male-segregated pattern. The two exceptions to this pattern can be found among the Methodists, who generally segregated their congregation by sex. And in the 1840s *The Doctrines and Discipline of the Methodist Episcopal Church* advised the formation of band societies, small groups of three or four Christians who would freely confess their weaknesses to one another. That much soul searching and holy abuse could be expected from such groups may be judged by the question directed to seekers before admittance to the band: "Do you desire to be told of *all* your faults, and that plain and home?" The disciplinary guide suggested questions to be asked of band members: "What known sins have you committed since our last meeting? What particular temptations have you met with? How were you delivered?" Given the frank nature of the exchange, the *Discipline* suggested that the bands be segregated according to sex and marital status.[76] There is no indication, however, that these bands gained common support. Both sexes participated in other Methodist associations such as prayer groups and classes. Methodists, like other evangelicals, considered female prayer groups improper, antithetical to family values and culture.[77]

The difficulties of organizing female prayer groups in southern evangelical culture can be seen in a few examples. Martha Foster Crawford was able to recruit other wives of southern missionaries into a female prayer group only after two years of effort. The women resisted meeting without their husbands. Reports of scant attendance at prayer meetings provide further evidence that women were reluctant to join prayer groups.[78] The women who did meet together, however, learned leadership skills and enjoyed the society of other religious-minded women. Miss Weisiger, convinced of the positive nature of the prayer meetings, believed that "it is good for us to meet together although few in number."[79] However profitable, little evidence survives of the numbers or persistence of female prayer meetings.[80]

Methodist classes, attended by mixed groups of men and women, received religious testimony and held intense discussions of individual spiritual problems. Women's classes were uncommon, but all classes were presided over by a male.[81] Such an arrangement was quite uncomfortable for any woman who might have wished to speak of dissatisfaction with her religious, familial, or marital role. Ella Thomas expressed evidence of this painful frustration: "There are thoughts, doubts, suggestions which present themselves to my mind. If I could only *talk of them*. I think of our class leaders but there is in old Mr. Mann no appreciation of the trials of a woman's nature."[82] Miss Weisiger shyly hesitated to speak in a class meeting where so many joined in the discussion yet felt guilty about not speaking up.[83]

Although they were aware of the problems of mixed religious associations, southern women had few alternatives. Antebellum reform associations were largely male. In North Carolina, the Sons of Temperance gained wide influence. In Georgia and Virginia, temperance groups were male associations, although women attended lectures and signed petitions.[84]

There is scattered evidence of the existence of women's missionary societies, but no general pattern of organization emerges despite the American Home Missionary Society's encouragement of the formation of male and female home missionary societies in every congregation. For example, no female counterpart to the male Domestic Missionary Society of the Athens First Presbyterian Church existed.[85]

Female benevolent societies were more characteristic of urban areas, however. Leisure and proximity to other women enabled southern city women to form religious and charitable associations. However, even urban women risked community disapproval because activism competed with women's domestic sphere. A young preacher, the Reverend T. Carleton Henry of Charleston, described community reaction to women's activism: "If there be neither husband nor father to complain, *community* will."[86] Nevertheless, the Reverend Henry defended women's organized efforts. He preached that to sneer at "one actively engaged in God's work while no domestic duty was omitted" was shameful.[87]

Despite community antagonism urban women joined charity efforts. The Female Bible Society of Lexington, Kentucky, responsible for the distribution of testaments, met with great success in their door-to-door campaign. Women's institutes in southern towns organized benevolent societies, and Charleston, South Carolina, supported many women's charity organizations. Traveler Anne Royall was impressed by two very active women's groups in Charleston, the Ladies' Benevolent Society and the Female Charitable Society. Other cities boasted of women's groups. The wealthy Mary Telfair generously supported the women's group of the Independent Presbyterian Church of Savannah in its campaign to raise money for a parsonage. And Lynchburg, Virginia, boasted that its Women's Missionary Society, established in June of 1832, lasted for nearly twenty years. Church historian Stella Wyatt Brummitt blamed the breakup of the still solvent society in 1851 not on the women but on the fighting between ministers of the church.[88]

Women's religious societies did not penetrate much beyond the perimeter of the South, except for the port cities and a few scattered towns in the interior.[89] With the exception of urban societies then, evangelical influence prevented southern antebellum benevolent associations from moving toward organized women's reform.

Without women's networks, independent groups committed to reform had no chance to emerge. Nevertheless, women found opportunities in which to develop their managerial skills, and they exercised those skills in the evangelical family culture. Women served as Sunday school teachers, supervisors, and administrators of infant schools and orphanages, and their ad hoc working societies often raised money for church projects by sewing, holding fairs, and selling domestic handicrafts. Women were also responsible for the solicitation of church funds, but the disposition of those funds was left entirely in the hands of male trustees who dispersed them in conjunction with other males in the congregation.[90]

Obviously, women's involvement in charity management did not lay a foundation for women's reform. The southern women's reform movement arose along with the organization of church groups in the late nineteenth century. Reform was eventually the product of secular or modernizing trends, which altered the southern perception of church discipline. Moreover, "domestic reconstruction," or women's participation in rebuilding churches after the war, supported reform. In the meantime, sexual roles generally followed a distinctly traditional rural pattern. In the rural South, however, the economic position of women did allow them opportunity for initiative and household management.

Because the household remained the administrative center for farm and domestic affairs, gender boundaries overlapped. Women helped in the fields and, in the absence of their spouses, wives acted as deputy husbands. Although rural southern women experienced some latitude in role definition, only sheer necessity occasioned women's expedient labor, and their responsibility was proportionate to their status and their husbands' presence.

Attached to the household in the neighborhood-kinship society of the rural South, women formed few bonds based upon acquaintance; rather, they relied on the older, sustaining ties of marriage and family. Even when their economic and social obligations multiplied, southern women looked to family support, which implied dependence, not to a women's network, which fostered independence. Within this context a women's culture was slow to coalesce in the premodern South.

2. MAN AND WOMAN

Unto the woman he said, I will greatly multiply thy sorrow and thy conception; in sorrow thou shalt bring forth children; and thy desire shall be to thy husband, and he shall rule over thee.
Genesis 3:16

raditional gender-defined roles characterized the rural-town economy of the South despite historians' assumptions that the agrarian partnership encouraged equality and fostered women's autonomy. Historians contend that a more equal domestic partnership existed because work roles tended to cross over; women worked in the field and managed the estate or farm in the husband's absence.[1] Although a less strict definition of work role applied in the country, still what was women's work was clearly understood. Men rarely helped with housework or domestic chores; southern men and women accepted traditional sex-role behavior with one exception. Urban middle-class women formed associations because of the availability of greater leisure in the cities and proximity to women neighbors. Urban associations later became the basis for the women's reforms that adjusted sex roles.

The agrarian partnership in which women shared economic production with men and assumed dual work roles in the household and the field was as much a product of southern self-sufficiency as it was a consequence of the lack of an integrated regional market system. The premodern economy of the Old South witnessed the development of gradual self-sufficiency and diversification. Although regional specialization insured the successful production of cash crops, most farms diversified their output. Generally, livestock and corn provided a food supply on southern farms.[2] Men and women, therefore, could depend upon their own productivity for subsistence. The necessity of such self-sufficiency can be seen also in the sheer isolation of southern farms.

The scarcity of railroads and waterways in the interior precluded development of an integrated market system and instead fostered yeomanry. Neighbor traded with neighbor except in small market towns such as Athens, Macon, and Columbus, which served a minor but vital backcountry trade. Highly developed market systems existed only on the rim of the South in the port cities of Charleston, Savannah, New Orleans, and Mobile. Scattered railways linked the food supply of some country areas with nearby cities. In areas dominated by cotton production, however, the planters controlled the trade system and ignored the backcountry exchange.[3]

Southern self-sufficiency also deterred modernization, a key requisite for the development of a woman's culture. Without the effect of modernization, sexual segregation was less likely to occur in the South. Low population density and the availability of land practically guaranteed farm ownership, thus making migration to urban areas less attractive.[4] Furthermore, the growth of cities traditionally depended upon a cheap labor supply. One recent theory contended that since the South had a longer growing season, the wages of agrarian workers were high. In order to attract rural labor, urban employers were forced to pay "a transfer wage that exceeded the value of urban labor's marginal product." Thus the expansion of southern urban centers was frustrated by the lack of a marginal labor force.[5]

The southern economy, a result of rural isolation, distance from markets, and the availability of slave and family laborers, placed a premium on women's labor both black and white. Throughout the major part of the nineteenth century semi-frontier conditions prevailed in the interior. Women, mostly black slaves, provided heavy labor for ploughing and planting. In addition, women were responsible for the full complement of household manufacture. This was necessary because few areas established fulling and spinning mills. By the eighteenth century, for example, North Carolina had only twenty mills and Virginia had fifty-five. Even though the number of mills doubled between 1840 and 1860, southern production continued to lag behind that of the North. The lack of southern manufacture thus necessitated a cottage industry. Household manufacture added to the duties of women already burdened by the domestic chores of cooking, cleaning, dairying, minding children, and tending the garden. The contribution of rural women to household maintenance, with the exception of candle-making, brewing, hunting, and the rounding up and slaughter of cattle, had not appreciably changed since the colonial period.[6]

Julia Cherry Spruill, historian of colonial southern women's roles, described the frontier partnership:

> With broadaxe and jacknife, he made his cabin, furniture and many of the farming implements and kitchen utensils; and with spinning wheel, loom and dye-pots she made all the clothing of the family, the household linen, blankets, quilts, coverlets, curtains, rugs, and other such furnishings. She made her own soap and candles, and . . . had to be doctor and apothecary to her family. . . . She needed also to understand the use of firearms that she might protect her home from wild beasts and Indians, and kill wild animals for food.[7]

Both Julia Spruill and Frank Owsley, author of *Plain Folk of the Old South*, maintain, however, that the dual nature of women's work, at times, placed an unequal burden on the women. Spruill noted that "the backwoods women had the reputation of being more given to labor than their husbands."[8] And social historian Frank Owsley relished his portrait of the dynamic woman among "shiftless" poor whites. He wrote: "While the men were taking their ease, the women hoed the corn, cooked the dinner, or plied the loom, or even came out and took up the ax and cut wood with which to cook the dinner."[9] Women's work, so essential to the farm, substituted for servant labor in the field and the household. On servantless farms men expected women to help in the field. And without women's household labor men would have been forced to sacrifice time needed in cultivation and harvesting.[10]

The necessity of women's labor resulted in a working partnership that included both sexes and races. Emily P. Burke, a traveler, observed that in the low country "all work in the field together[,] white men and black men, white women and black women without distinction. I have been told it is not an uncommon occurrence to see a white woman holding the plough."[11] The rural partnership, however, was not directed toward women's independence. In the first place, farmers who owned a number of slaves preferred not to have their wives and daughters in the field. When servants were available, white women returned to domestic pursuits.[12]

Frederick Law Olmsted, traveler and writer, noted that on one farm two daughters cooked the supper and the black servant prepared only the breakfast because her services were demanded in the field.[13] In the initial phase of farm enterprise, nonetheless, white women's labor was indispensable. Emily Burke spoke of poor South Carolina farm women, "obliged to take a part" along with men in the cultivation of their few acres.[14] White women may have performed heavy labor regardless of their personal inclinations. Olmsted encountered a sullen farm wife who complained, "Been cuttin' brush in the cotton this afternoon. Knewe't would bring on my headache. Told him [her husband] so when I begun."[15] And Mary Carr, a farm wife, wearily reported the monotony of her days, rising early, scraping cotton, and planting corn.[16]

Besides doing fieldwork, the farm wife maintained a household industry. Farm women manufactured cloth, a long and laborious process involving six stages of preparation from seeding to weaving. After cultivating the cotton crop and ginning, women then carded and rolled the cotton prior to spinning. The spun cotton thread was then dyed and woven. Most women considered a day's work spinning six cuts or 960 yards of thread.[17]

Country women devoted a considerable part of their time to spinning. In the Mississippi backcountry Olmsted noticed mistress and servants in their various cabins "spinning at old-fashioned great wheels and weaving at ancient rude hand looms."[18] Clothing and all the towels, tablecloths, curtains, and bed linens were made by hand. Until spinning mills became a more common industry in the later nineteenth century, homespun remained the typical backcountry fashion.[19] Emily Burke inquired of one woman whether it would not be cheaper to purchase than to manufacture cloth. The woman replied that "she could if her time was worth any thing, but there was no

labor she could perform that would bring her any money."[20] Olmsted recounted the plight of a young cottage weaver who wove thread for bagging
yarn. The woman was paid in yarn which she traded off at a store for goods.
Her visitor calculated that by working steadily from dawn to dusk she earned
sixteen cents a day. The lot of country girls who worked in the cotton mills
was not much better; they earned from forty to sixty cents a day if the work
was steady. By the 1830s only the more prosperous plantations found it
cheaper to buy than to manufacture material. Mary Telfair, a Savannah
planter, discovered that fact when advised by her overseer that assigning
spinning tasks to good female field hands was inefficient and only added to
the plantation's debt.[21]

In areas where factories did not exist women sold surpluses of homespun
and food at the nearest city market.[22] Women's trade, in the colonial tradition, maintained the family and only rarely established an independent business.[23] Furthermore, the occasional trips to market because they fulfilled a
family purpose did not sustain a stable, independent women's network. Nevertheless, such a "minor" trade exacted from the women considerable effort.
Required to market the surplus, some women traveled over a hundred miles
in mule-drawn carts loaded with cloth, produce, chickens, ducks, and geese.
Hogs and occasionally wild deer were tied to the carts and taken along to be
sold. In Savannah, women traveled together and provisioned themselves with
hominy and coffee so that they could camp along the way. Usually, they tried
to arrive in Savannah at nightfall in order to sell at the morning market. Upon
arrival they stayed on the outskirts of the market where they ate and slept on
the bricks.[24]

The sight of women going to market did not strike southerners as unusual.
Olmsted left a vivid picture of one of these dauntless women:

> I shall not soon forget the figure of a little old white woman, wearing a
> man's hat, smoking a pipe, driving a little black bull with reins; sitting,
> herself bolt upright, upon the axle-tree of a little truck, on which she
> was returning from market. I was riding with a gentleman of the town at
> the time, and as she bowed to him with an expression of ineffable self-
> satisfaction, I asked if he knew her. He had known her for twenty years,
> he said, and until lately she had always come into town about once a
> week, on foot, bringing fowls, eggs, potatoes, or herbs, for sale in a
> basket. The bull she had probably picked up astray, when a calf, and
> reared and broken it herself; and the cart and harness she made her-
> self; but he did not think any body in the land felt richer than she did
> now, or prouder of her establishment.[25]

For some like the "little old white woman" marketing may have provided
a subsistence income. Most women contributed the marketing profits to
family maintenance. Only a few wives—like Mrs. Bullitt of Louisville who

sold butter, turnips, and ham—considered the money personal income.[26] Domestic conditions of rural women were such that extra income went to household support.

Southern households rarely provided domestic advantages and this added to women's burdens. Among the poorest squatter families in the sandhills of South Carolina, for example, women endured lack of fireplaces and were forced to cook in Dutch ovens out of doors. The more settled poor used Dutch ovens in their fireplaces and baked bread in earthenware before the fire. Brick ovens were quite rare and only prosperous farmers had kitchens. Kitchens, built separate from the house to prevent fires, seemed to undiscriminating visitors to be "shanties" behind the cabins. One traveler described a plantation kitchen as rough-hewn with a low chimney and a roof built of sticks and mud. On one side a large opening functioned as window and door. The kitchen, fully supplied, measured no more than fifteen square feet. Preparations for cooking included gathering wood and hauling water.[27] Existing regardless of class, these conditions suggest the sheer labor that cooking involved and therefore the heavy responsibility that women's dual work role necessitated.

Equally laborious was the task of washing clothes. Consuming many hours of effort, laundering required soaping, boiling, beating, and hand rubbing until the clothes became reasonably clean. Women conducted the entire laundry operation out of doors and suffered exposure in the cold weather.[28] One woman, Polly Summey of North Carolina, found an alternative to the bone-numbing exposure and work that doing the laundry entailed. She purchased a washing machine from an enterprising salesman named Poindexter. Polly enthusiastically endorsed Poindexter's washing machine because it protected her from exposure and saved work. Although two servants were needed to operate the machine, one to crank it and the other to soap the clothes, still Polly Summey preferred the machine:

> [It] supercedes the necessity of boiling anything unless tis very greasy clothes and does not take so much soap in the usual way of washing. . . . [You] can wash in the house on a cold day better than in a tub and what is still better it does not wear out clothes like rubbing them in that it takes the dirt and grease out better than tubs which [leak and] must be kept out of the sun. . . . Washers are excellent for bags, carpets, negro clothes which you know is the hardest kind of washing.[29]

Sometimes women's community efforts enlivened the drudgery of domestic work. Quilting parties provided bedding for the winter. And periodically neighboring women got together for the work of spinning and weaving. Also nursing one's relatives and neighbors sometimes demanded a communal effort. Working together broke the monotony of farm life and reinforced local ties while at the same time it insured family survival.[30] Sporadic social occasions, however, could not compete with the demands of family and farm. Without a self-conscious women's culture such informal meetings remained social or functional.

Women, after all, were entrusted with the care of the family. When not in the fields or spinning women tended to the needs of family members. Fredrika Bremer, a Swedish traveler, noted as she visited a poor isolated cabin that the "mother kept her eyes very much fixed on her children."[31] In addition to the children, women looked after their husbands' needs. One North Carolina farm woman apologized in a lighthearted vein for making her husband serve himself while she wrote a letter. She greeted a friend with the words: "I know you will excuse me for leaving my Old Man to wait upon himself when I tell you no place to me is like home."[32]

In addition to being economic partners with their husbands, durable farm wives filled traditional domestic roles; they accommodated their husbands, supported the maintenance of the farm, and managed household affairs. Like their colonial forebears, southern rural women worked to improve the family property in order that they might move not toward independence but toward dependence as a leisured class.[33] If hard work did not bring prosperity, southern migrants, men and women, moved westward in the hopes of improving their lot.[34] One farm woman, hearing of a western friend's good fortune in selling butter for 37½ cents a pound, dreamed of getting rich herself. She shared her idea with the ubiquitous visitor, Frederick Olmsted. "I'd like to be rich," she said. "Not so rich as Wade Hampton, but so rich I needn't do any more work."[35] Not every woman migrant experienced success. A man who traveled with his family to the Oregon Territory told of hard times and how it affected his wife and daughters. He described unemployment, declining wages, and rising prices. In a letter he revealed how the women supported the family: "Ann and the girls take in washing and make pies to sell. We get 25 cents for washing large things; 12½ for small; we have done about $5.50 this week."[36] Despite the hard-luck cases, southern men and women moved west to advance their status.

Farm women envied the gentry their leisurely life. Although planters' wives took on habits of leisure, they also bore the burden of the agrarian partnership.[37] Historians Anne F. Scott and Catherine Clinton document the extraordinary workload of plantation mistresses. Anne Scott details their life as follows:

> No matter how large or wealthy the establishment, the mistress was expected to understand not only the skill of spinning, weaving, and sewing but also gardening, care of poultry, care of the sick, and all aspects of food preparation from the sowing of seed to the appearance of the final product on the table. Fine ladies thought nothing of supervising hog butchering on the first cold days in fall, or of drying fruits

and vegetables for the winter. They made their own yeast, lard, and soap, set their own hens, and were expected to be able to make with equal skill a rough dress for a slave or a ball gown for themselves. It was customary for the mistress to rise at five or six, and to be in the kitchen when the cook arrived, to "overlook" all the arrangements for the day.[38]

More recently, Catherine Clinton enlarged upon the household duties of the southern matron. "Like her New England counterpart, the planter's wife managed the household budget, dealt with local merchants, and handled all internal matters of finance. Even without the work created by their husbands' slaveowning, the numerous tasks of antebellum housekeeping kept plantation mistresses busy."[39] As mistress of the household the planter's wife supervised a large sprawling establishment, which, in addition to the "Big House," consisted of dairies, smokehouses, henhouses, and barnyards. The domestic complex supplied the staples and provisions needed for the work force although bondmen and bondwomen supplemented their rations.[40]

The plantation mistress did indeed perform the work Scott and Clinton claimed for them, yet a good deal of their work was supervisory and their heaviest labor cyclical. For instance, women supervised hog butchering and processed pork during the autumn months and supervised planting the garden in the spring. Fall and spring, plantation mistresses cut out and sewed slaves' clothing for distribution in the winter and summer, but on larger plantations these tasks were also delegated to female slaves. Candle-making, carpet-weaving, or mattress-making were not routine tasks, and few mistresses ventured upon such undertakings in the middle and late Victorian period.[41]

That planters' wives reserved some leisure time may be found in comparing the work schedule and private diary of Mrs. William B. Taliaferro, the former Sally Nivison Lyons, of Gloucester, Virginia. A memorandum for 1861 itemized her monthly household production:

MEMORANDA
1861

January 4—Cut out two pairs of flannel drawers for Mr. Taliaferro. 3 shirts for Jimmie.

January 10—Cut out six pairs of drawers for Leah, six for Fannie. Three aprons for Leah, two for the boys, six nightgowns for Jimmie and Warner, two new petticoats for Leah. Two new pairs of stockings for self. Two for Leah. Knit two pairs of socks for Mr. Taliaferro, jacket for Warner. Cloth jacket for Wellington. Four calico dresses for little Georgie. Another nightgown.

January 22—Made 6 lbs. grease in soap by Mrs. Randolph's recipe—13 lbs.

of soap. Two bodices for Fannie. Two chemises for self. [illegible] panta-
loons for Jimmie and Warner.

January 30—Two nightgowns for self. February 14- Commenced six shorts
for Mr. Taliaferro. G. jacket for Warner.

February 20—14 pounds of soap. 5 pounds of grease.

April—Cut out two calico jackets each for Lyons and Warner. 2 more jackets
each for Lyons and Warner. 3 gingham jackets for Warner, 3 pair panta-
loons for Warner.

May—Mouselaine and Calico dress and sack for Leah. Cambric dress for
Fannie. Calico dress for self. G. apron for self. 2 white bonnets for Leah.
One for Fannie. Calico dress for Georgie. 14 little shirts for children,
cotton.

July & August—2 winter dresses for Fannie, 3 flannel petticoats for Fannie
Booth. 3 bodices for Lyons. Double gown for Georgie. 2 inside handker-
chiefs for self. One pair of winter pants for Lyons. 2 for Warner. Jacket
each for Lyons and Warner. Gingham apron for Leah. 3 flannel shirts for
Warner, 3 for F.B., 4 flannel petticoats for George Wythe. 2 cotton skirts for
self. A quantity of wool spun and prepared for knitting.

October—Knit 18 pairs of socks for soldiers.

November—Made 2 comforts for soldiers. Four aprons for F.B. Five for
George Wythe, 1 for Leah. Pants for Lyons and Warner. Poplin dress for
Leah. Sam's, Abram's, and Manx's clothes.[42]

Sally Taliaferro's daily diary entries for February 1861, however, note the flexibility within the work schedule:

Feb. 15, 1861—Very busy all day cutting out shirts.

Feb. 16, 1861—Dined at Elmington. Very busy all morning in my garden.
Visit from Neal in the evening.

Feb. 17, 1861—Sunday

Feb. 18, 1861—Mr. T. and I drove around Islehorn and spent the day.

Feb. 19, 1861—Visitors all day. Opened a barrel of flour.

Feb. 20, 1861—Visit to Mr. Dabney's and Waverly. Planted Potatoes.

Feb. 21, 1861—Bright day.

Feb. 22, 1861—Took Miss Fonent to stage. Visit from John T.

Feb. 23, 1861—Beautiful day, Tremendous wind, prevented from going to
Auburn.

Feb. 24, 1861—Sunday.[43]

In a ten-day schedule, Mrs. Taliaferro worked one day preparing slave clothing and part of two days working in her garden. The rest of her time was
spent visiting and enjoying her leisure.

Catherine Edmondston kept a record of important events in her life in the summer of 1860. Visiting occupied the majority of her time although she did make blackberry wine and also put up brandy peaches and preserves. The latter she accomplished while a neighbor read a John Wilson essay to her.[44] Most planters' wives balanced work and leisure. For instance, Annie Darden, who quilted, also made sausages, sowed beets and carrots, had the sheep sheared, and still reserved time for writing.[45] Those women who may have found leisure wanting in their schedule generally assumed supervisory authority as well. For example, Meta Morris Grimball, who maintained that "a plantation life is an active one," described what were essentially supervisory duties. She recorded her day as follows:

> This morning I got up late having been disturbed in the night, hurried down to have something arranged for breakfast, ham and eggs. [W]rote a letter to Charles. . . . Had prayers, got off the boys to town. Had work cut out, gave orders about dinner, had the horses feed fixed in hot water, had the box filled with cork. [W]ent to see about the carpenters working at the negro houses, where there are men mending chimneys, white washing . . . now I have to cut out flannel jackets, and alter some work.[46]

Though demanding, the southern mistress's job of supervision was almost a luxury compared with the work of the farmers' wives, who cut brush and planted corn.

The management of the household enterprise made the planter's wife at best a junior partner in the plantation business. The husband maintained the plantation's "business," which included complex financial matters, crop decisions and field management, market assessments, and political responsibilities. And because the planter controlled the finances and overall management, mistresses at times considered themselves "slaves" on the plantation.[47] Full domestic responsibilities devolved upon the women.

Little of an equal partnership is evident in the work roles of planter-politician Howell Cobb and his wife, Mary Ann Cobb. She found her life as a plantation mistress fatiguing. She complained to her husband that all of the cooking, cleaning, and baking for her large family, guests, and retinue was excessively demanding. "You have no idea," she said, "how busy I am. I walk and stand during the day so much that my feet are sore."[48] Later she gave her husband the particulars of her day: "This morning I was up before daylight . . . beat batter and [made] sausage balls . . . saw the milk poured into the churn and set Sabina to work."[49]

His wife's complaints aroused some guilt in Howell Cobb, for he wrote, "I promised to take more interest in domestic affairs. . . . I indulge the hope that I shall prove to be a better housekeeper or rather gardner than my past exploits would induce one to anticipate."[50] However much Cobb, active in congressional politics, felt obliged to share in domestic work, he rarely visited his home and therefore abrogated his domestic responsibilities. But not only did Mary Ann Cobb expect Howell to perform his share of the household duties, Cobb assumed that he *owed* his wife assistance.

That women expected men to help with household chores can also be seen in the view of Catherine Edmondston. She and her husband, Patrick, had a discussion one day as he dropped sticks and straw into a stream and compared them to two men starting out in life together. Patrick spoke enthusiastically about the man of "energy and decision" who succeeds in life and "leaves his companion far behind." "No," said she, pointing to the stick that remained near the shore, "*this* is the man occupied at *home* by a round of *home* duties. See how faithfully he performs them all, not so brilliant as the first but more useful and to my mind happier." Patrick reluctantly agreed but shortly thereafter rejoined his Confederate corps and left the "home circle."[51] The relationship between the planter and his wife was not an equal one despite the expectations of the domestic partnership. Because men controlled the finances, they made the ultimate decisions concerning the household.

Women acted in the time-bound tradition as "deputy husbands," a term applied to colonial wives of northern New England.[52] As heads of households men incorporated their wives' points of view, but they represented the family in all external matters. When absence or incapacity prevented men from fulfilling their administrative responsibility women substituted for their husbands, as "deputy husbands." Lucilla McCorkle dutifully copied in her journal, "a Good Wife" [is a woman who] "in her husband's absence is wife and deputy husband."[53] No matter now actively or judiciously a woman responded to this role, she maintained a wifely diffidence. As historian Laurel Thatcher Ulrich emphasized, "A woman became a wife by virtue of her dependence, her solemnly vowed commitment to her husband."[54] As "deputy husband," Mary Ann Cobb in May 1846 carried out her husband's decision to build servant houses. He sent money and instructions, and she hired the laborers and supervised their work. At other times she smoothed over Howell's misunderstanding with the overseer, kept his railroad stock in safekeeping, and collected his debts. All the while, however, Mary Ann Cobb depended upon Howell's allotments to run the household.[55]

In fact, women were totally dependent upon their husbands' allowances to run the household and moreover were answerable to their husbands for all financial decisions made in their capacity as deputies. By her husband's leave Anne DeWolf Middleton handled the financial negotiations for the purchase of a farm and farming implements for her father, but she hesitated before the closing and wrote to her husband, "Mr. V[augh] now demands an immediate decision. I shall (acting on the liberty you gave me) close the business by purchasing, but if he says nothing I shall leave it until I hear from you."[56] And Mary Ann Cobb spoke defensively and sometimes fearfully about the financial decisions she made in Howell's absence. An extraordinary expense moved her to write to him: "I know you will as usual say all is right to what I have done—but perhaps you may conjecture what has induced me to go to this expense . . . remembering all my . . . talks of economy—Well, I have a good reason for it."[57] She refused to discuss her "reason" in her letter but promised to talk with him about it when he returned. A few months later she nearly despaired waiting for her husband to approve her decision. She complained, "As to this world . . . I am accountable in a great degree to you—and when necessity compels me to act without your advice I am miserable until I can lay the matter before you. . . . I live upon your approbation—even reproof would be preferable to the suspense I sometimes endure."[58]

While plantation wives struggled with their role as "deputy husbands," widows and unmarried women exercised complete control over their plantations. Nancy Pinson, Sarah B. Evans, Mary Telfair, and Mary Elizabeth Rives were examples of women who skillfully operated their plantations at a profit. Prior to the panic of 1837 Nancy Pinson's accounts showed a balance of $2,500 a month.[59] Sarah B. Evans of Louisiana, who managed both her own and her son-in-law's estate, averaged $1,000 a month.[60] Such women directed planting, harvesting, shipping and purchasing operations, and all matters regarding animal husbandry and the care of slaves, their maintenance, purchase and sale, and work schedule. In addition, women supervised auxiliary businesses—such as lumber mills—that were connected to the plantation. As conservative investors, women managers often placed their profit in slaves and in bank and railroad stock.[61]

The leisured life of urban upper-middle-class women contrasted with the work routine of women in the rural community. Proximity to a market relieved most city women of tedious farm chores, although some women managed virtual farms within city limits. But since husbands usually did the routine buying, city women largely confined their duties to household supervision and the tending of children.[62]

The calm "motherly demeanor" of one urban wife impressed Fredrika Bremer. The writer noted that a Charleston matron's table arrangements, hospitality, kindness to servants, attention to her children, and personal care of a flower garden marked her not only as a responsible housewife but as a social ornament as well.[63] The balance between leisure and duty set this class of women apart from farm wives. Bremer noted, however, that middle-class women indulged their daughters. She observed that "parents, from mistaken kindness, seem not to wish their daughters to do anything except amuse themselves and enjoy liberty and life as much as possible. I believe that they would be happier if they made themselves more useful."[64]

Perhaps not without some regional prejudice, the New York book trader, Miss Mendell, observed the same female role pattern among mothers and daughters as did Fredrika Bremer. In an editorial comment, the young writer opined: "If woman was created only to be admired and petted for her beauty, her childlike and tender form, to be loved for her dependence, the Southern woman must receive the palm."[65] Urban mothers expected their daughters to assume the same dependent role, and it was this heritage that Miss Mendell criticized. She wrote: "I would ask mothers, as one who loves or suffers, to make their daughters self-reliant—if only in one thing. . . . Does it not rend the heart of mothers to see their daughters marry for a home? Can they not see that it is for want of some real interest in something else, that they resort to marriage?"[66] Miss Mendell implicitly blamed the marriage market for the plight of southern women. The marriage market dictated marriage as women's only "career," a consequence of fixed sex roles and women's economic dependency.[67] While southern women suffered painful consequences and restricted lives because of the marital "economy," nonetheless these traditional values operated nationally.

Daughters of the middle and upper classes whose only ambition was marriage led more "leisured" lives than their mothers. Correspondence and diaries, however, demonstrate how sudden the transformation was from frivolous girl into sober matron, responsible for the management of a household. Urban households needed fewer slaves than country estates. The market replaced domestic industry because it provided foodstuffs, dry goods, and household items. However, women were still responsible for food preparation and washing, ironing, cleaning, and sewing. Preserving and processing meat remained a seasonal chore for urban women also. But the smaller household and the less onerous chores gave city women more leisure than rural women.[68]

The availability of leisure time and the concentration of the female population in the cities encouraged association between women. Because female association tended to follow the development of the market system, women's societies did not penetrate much beyond the port cities of the South and a few scattered towns in its interior. Even within the cities community disapproval, as well as anti-abolition attitudes associated with feminism, limited the advance of systematic organization. For the most part, rural evangelical discipline controlled the role, attitude, and behavior of southern women.

Outside the cities, the absence of an organized female network made women even more vulnerable to the frustrations and demands of traditional sex roles. Anxiety concerning marriage and family plagued the younger generation of southern women. These tensions are reflected in the journal of an unwed farm girl who recorded her dilemma:

> I know not what to do; I can't leave here, it seems unless I marry, and there is the difficulty, I cannot find any body to marry, and I have no

right to stay here in the others way, nothing but an old maidish fool as I am; O that I died before I lived to see such a time as this.[69]

Self-hatred inherent in the single status tore at the vitals of Victorian women's self-respect. The deep importance that attached to marriage sometimes engendered a fear of marriage, especially in the case of women accustomed to the relative independence of single life. Martha Foster Crawford, a young woman who later became a missionary to China, suffered at the thought of her impending marriage. She confided to her diary: "I have the blues—I can't help it. And Why? I am continually haunted with the idea of *being married*. I feel like a prisoner . . . I formerly felt free . . . but now I feel I have my part to act—that I am no longer independent."[70] Doubts did not disappear even when a woman got married, as is demonstrated by the offhand remarks of Mary Ann Cobb. When the newly married Mary Ann Cobb anticipated the burdens of motherhood, she joked with her husband: "What will become of me when I am surrounded by the dozen little squalling brats (that our kind friends have prophesized unto us), all their little wants to be supplied then baking, mending, patching to be done?"[71]

Largely traditional ideas of marriage and of women's economic and emotional dependence were, as we have seen, only in part counterbalanced by shared responsibility in the home. Women participated in decisions about the children's education, and men sometimes relieved wives of the burdens of tending to infants. Nonetheless, traditional attitudes toward marriage found universal acceptance in the South. The full responsibility for running the household devolved upon the wife, and almost certainly her doubts about marriage were in proportion to the enormity of her domestic task. Mary Ann Cobb warned a cousin about to be married, "After a week or two of *housekeeping* and *children tending alone*—you can judge of how you will like a state of *celibacy*."[72] Husbands expected their wives to sacrifice their own interests and create a haven for them. That men attached importance to a well-run home can be seen in Waddy Butler's anxiety regarding his marriage. He wrote to his bride: "I am becoming very impatient for our marriage for I am wearied, tired at times almost to madness, of my present mode of life; I long for a home of my own and some one, to whom I can give my whole confidence and my whole heart, to preside over it."[73] Sidney Bumpas's letter to his fiancée, Frances Moore Webb, demonstrates that he believed that marriage was an institution designed for male comfort and support:

I believe that our dispositions and tastes are alike, that our views and determinations are the same—our interests are identified and we shall soon be one. In short, dear Frances, I am fully satisfied that there is no one on earth so well calculated to make me happy and useful as yourself.[74]

Baldly stated by men such as Sidney Bumpas and Waddy Butler, the Victorian ideal of True Womanhood suggested that women's submission, purity, and piety served male domestic interests.[75] But Victorian women believed that the powerless held a formidable weapon in the *example* of self-sacrifice. Implicit in the female ideology was the hope that the man could be converted to a holy union, a relationship modeled upon the spiritual union of Christ and the church. The Methodist church solemnized marriage vows with the familiar injunction that the joining together of the man and the woman signified "the mystical union that is between Christ and his Church."[76] In the tradition of the mystical union the sacrifice of self paradoxically led to knowledge of self. When Elizabeth Lindsay Lomax reviewed the first years of her marriage, she noted they were unhappy because she "had yet to learn to relinquish *self* and live for another."[77] Knowledge of self lay in the struggle to understand the other. She added:

> It has ever been my opinion that the *first* year of a woman's married life is one of trial and the traits of character hitherto lying dormant, are now developing themselves by the force of circumstances. Deeply impressed on my memory are some of the events of that year! I desire *never* to forget them, but cherish them with gratitude as being the means of knowing myself.[78]

The struggle forged the partnership, which was all the more stable and lasting because of its spiritual basis.

Theoretically, marriage united two individuals who were to perform gender-related roles, but mutual support was to lead to the true spiritual union. Although the marriage ceremony enjoined obedience on the wife but not on the husband, ministers still stressed mutuality of responsibility. The couple vowed to keep

> a high esteem and mutual love for one another; bearing with each other's infirmities and weaknesses . . . to encourage each other . . . to comfort one another . . . in honesty and industry to provide for each other's temporal support; to pray for and encourage one another in the things that pertain to God, and to their immortal souls.[79]

Anne Turner replicated these sentiments in her diary when she wrote of her hopes for her newly engaged daughter and her fiancé. She wished her daughter to be kind, sympathetic, submissive, charitable, forgiving, pleasant, in short, "a good housewife." Her example, Anne Turner hoped, would induce him to flee to the only sure refuge [God]. . . . His conversion from "worldly glory" might lead to a union where both partners might be "benevolent kind and courteous—pious, resigned and submissive . . . [and so] bring up their household in the fear of God . . . [so that] their duties to God predominate over every feeling of a worldly nature."[80]

Walter Lewis Nugent fulfilled his marital promise when he encouraged his sixteen-year-old bride, Eleanor Fulkerson Smith Nugent, to develop as a woman and a writer. "You are not exactly just to your own capabilities when you think you fail in descriptive powers," he wrote to her. "[H]ad you less diffidence of your own ability, you would have given me an essay that might have found its way *incognito* to some journal." Later when Eleanor Nugent confided fully to her husband, he exulted, "In this letter I have the *woman*, not the diffident and retiring girl which you have hitherto persisted in being."[81]

Both men and women committed themselves to a spiritual union that implied mutual support, obligation, and responsibility. However, evangelical tradition assumed that women possessed a greater spiritual capacity than men who engaged in worldly pursuits. Women took their spiritual superiority seriously and used it to attempt to build an equal partnership, but husbands resisted their wives' efforts. The marital union then was a struggle to reconcile these perspectives.

Fear of idolatry, or love of an individual above God, served to check a too dependent marital relationship. Women especially felt the danger of overweening dependency. Cornelia Christian's response to Walter Lenoir's passionate love letters was to tell him that although she thought of him day and night she hoped God would keep them from idolatry.[82] Catherine Edmondston, deeply attached to her husband, prayed, "Keep me, O God, from Idols!"[83] And a sister church member warned Frances (Fannie) Moore Webb Bumpas of loving her spouse too much lest his death ruin her.[84] Distance from an inordinate attachment served to reinforce the woman's position and elevate her to an equal plane of struggle. Anne DeWolf Middleton explained to her husband, Nathaniel Russell Middleton, that she loved her home because there she led "a *pilgrim's* life" with him.[85] The struggle to develop a union remained a consistent theme in women's correspondence. Julia Jones's cousin complained that, although she wished to go to Alabama, "as usual my plans were not seconded. Unless I force myself upon him and make him take me I verily believe I would stay here a hundred years for anything he cares."[86] Even the efficient mistress Lucilla McCorkle, who dutifully copied into her diary "a good wife never crosseth her husband," noted that her husband's "mind and mine have past [*sic*] through a crisis . . . passion has too often swept us away."[87] And Mary Ann Cobb, never at a loss to express her displeasure, reminded Howell Cobb, newly elected Speaker of the House, "You are more than *the peoples' servant* my demands upon your attention will be more exacting in proportion."[88]

Women struggled in marriage for a true union, but men consistently retained a dominant role in the marriage. Women acting as deputy husbands deferred to their husbands in management and business matters. Wives also submitted to spouses in domestic concerns and in the care and training of children. Although women expressed an educational preference for their children, fathers made the ultimate decision concerning the children's education. Howell and Mary Ann Cobb debated sending their boys away to school; Mary Ann feared the effects of worldly influences upon the boys. Howell argued strongly, however, that the boys "must come in contact with the wickedness of the world," and he insisted that protectiveness would lead to their dissipation.[89] Howell won his point and the boys were sent away to school. Planters also assumed responsibility for educating their daughters although it meant considerable expense. But because the daughter's education reflected family status, the planter could not ignore that matter. Usually a father or a male relative accompanied a young woman to inspect a school's facilities.[90]

The deferential model of the marital partnership naturally encouraged traditional sex roles for their children. Sex typing is clearly seen in Lucilla McCorkle's organization of her household. A North Carolina minister-planter's wife and an inveterate listmaker, Mrs. McCorkle outlined the duties of her children. Little boys, she maintained, carried wood, made fires, chopped, hoed, raked, swept the yard, cleaned shoes, watered the horse, shelled corn, and fed the cow and pigs. In contrast, Mrs. McCorkle directed girls toward household and service responsibilities: sewing, knitting, sweeping and dusting, making beds, and making doll clothing. Above all, she stressed, daughters were trained to "think of other's comfort and sit straight."[91] In her estimation, then, girls were to remain sensitive to interpersonal relationships while boys were to deal with active pursuits. Another example of the strength of sex typing can be seen in Mary Ann Cobb's experiment. Once, Mary Ann Cobb made her boys sew for their grandmother. While the sight amused their mother, the boys resented the work and the grandmother disapproved.[92]

In the unequal domestic partnership, responsibility for the training and discipline of sons and daughters largely devolved upon the mother since she was regarded as the nurturer of the young. However, women expected husbands to support their disciplinary measures. Such insistence upon a husband's cooperation led Anne DeWolf Middleton to reprove her husband. She wrote him, "I, without the support and *aid* in the training of our children, which I have a right to expect from you—[have been] left with half my time in a kind of widowhood which keeps me low in spite of every advantage."[93] Another record of parental concern for children can be seen in the Howell Cobb correspondence. Because her husband remained in Washington, Mary Ann Cobb had full responsibility for disciplining the children; Howell relinquished his role. He offered little support to his beleaguered wife, because he regarded his sons' rebellious nature as natural.[94] Mary Ann Cobb, however, lectured Howell about proper discipline for the children. "[T]hey must be disciplined—and with system in it—and when you return—we must be cooperated—if we desire success."[95] Still Cobb found amusement in the boys' recalcitrance and regarded their behavior as part of their "independence of spirit."[96] Thereafter, however, Howell was careful to reinforce Mary Ann's role as disciplinarian. To his sons he wrote: "Tell them all to be good boys to love each other and to obey their mama in everything that she says to them."[97] And later, he took his son John directly to task for his tardiness.[98]

Wives could also expect support from their husbands in tending to infants. Evidence of a husband's generous help can be seen in Cornelia Lenoir's acknowledgment to her husband. She reported that during his absence the baby awakened four or five times during the night but, fortunately, she was relieved by a servant's assistance. However, she reported, "Mame is so good, comes nearer filling your place than anyone."[99] In this case the husband was more useful than a servant. And Mary Ann Cobb regretted her husband's absence, because he had left her with a colicky baby. She missed his help and told him, "If you had been at home on monday night, I think you would have had to have repeated your very successful attempt at nursing, for he kept me awake for nearly two hours."[100]

But although men may have assisted wives in the care of infants, they did not take on the full burden of training and disciplining children. In the South a woman's traditional role was only occasionally alleviated by her husband's assistance in disciplining the children and tending to them. The domestic partnership strove for mutual emotional support at the expense of domestic help from the husband. Women expected men to help them in the household. Anne DeWolf Middleton, for one, claimed her husband's support as a right. Yet, in general, the response by husbands was either sporadic or expedient.

The evangelical community survived because women adopted traditional work roles that oriented them toward family concerns. In the self-sufficient economy of the Old South, women's industry fostered not independence but rather the commitment to family, spouse, and household.

Survival in the southern preindustrial economy, however, overburdened the partnership, encouraging women to invest in it all their emotional, productive, and social energies. Women struggled to uphold a true union, but since the partnership was an unequal one women functioned as dependents, emotionally and economically. Without the support of a women's culture, women's frustrations, anxieties, and resentments became internalized in a struggle directed against themselves and only occasionally against the community that structured unequal relations between men and women.

The extent to which traditional roles conflicted with individual desires and attitudes can only be understood if womens' interior lives are examined. The spiritual, psychological, and emotional response of southern women is most often found in diaries, but at the deepest level their frustration and satisfaction reveals itself in the diaries' accounts of dreams. It is there that they recorded unconscious fears and hopes.

3.   A   GARDEN   ENCLOSED

A garden enclosed is my sister, my spouse;
a spring shut up, a fountain sealed.
Song of Solomon 4:12

nity of kin, common religious assumptions, and identifica-
tion with place marked the southern evangelical commu-
nity as distinctive and set apart. It was a commonality in
which the ritual of discipline communicated to each person standards of right by which men and women acted.
Religion, kinship, and place gave meaning to the lives of
individuals and bound them one to another. Nonetheless,
however suggestive, role, culture, and community are static terms that cannot be understood unless inquiry is made into the unconscious process that
shaped and interpreted them.[1]

Women accepted evangelical forms in their unconscious minds and fash-
ioned their experience through common structures.[2] But doubt and trust,
anxiety and security, ambivalence and certainty transmuted the unconscious
elements into positive forces for women's identity. For example, the persis-
tent theme of kinship and community is evident in diaries and church records; however, within that context women made their own choices and
accepted community definitions of behavior and relationships only after adjusting them to their own needs. Women thought in common symbols and
acted according to common values, but within the spring of the unconscious
a mature, autonomous self emerged.

Historically southern women are unknown; culture, myth, and place super-
seded their individual identity leaving their interior being—emotion, judgment, will, the unconscious—obscure and irrelevant. The Old South promoted images of "belle" or "mistress" while the New South boasted of the
"New Woman." Neither typology captures the struggles with family and community that carried the Victorian generations of southern women through
anguish and maturity.

Southern Victorian women perceived themselves and their relationships to
others in terms of a distinct symbol pattern. But that pattern will be recogniz-
able to historians only if they penetrate the symbolic system and the language of culture and capture "the inward conceptual rhythm" of the interior dialectic between local and universal, between element and pattern.[3] In
short, southern women were inseparable from their culture and from the
symbols that they used to define themselves.

In the antebellum and post–Civil War era the social demands of integrated kinship networks, church discipline, and farm labor compressed southern women's experience into the confines of a rural, kin-dominated, church-related community. Skillful manipulation of familial and religious symbols, however, enabled some women to loose the bonds of kin and church. Such personal victories did not translate into a social consciousness, an attempt to remove cultural obstacles to women's self-determination. No women's association emerged to consolidate an independent women's position until late in the century; family dependence, the double standard of church discipline, and the patriarchal ethos prevailed. Scholars, then, may follow the history of southern women along parallel lines: the external adjustment to evangelical social and religious control and the internal struggle toward self-definition.

In nineteenth-century culture, maternity, domesticity, self-sacrifice, and religious conversion were expected of women. These expectations initiated powerful internal conflicts in southern women who struggled to resolve them in religious terms. Evidence of their psychic struggle can be found in women's dreams.

Dreams reveal psychic conflict or resolution in symbolic personal and cultural associations that derive their meaning from the individual life. The tools of psychoanalysis did not exist for southern women, but they had a repertoire of symbols available to them, namely, those of the evangelical Christian. These symbols were attached to specific religious experience— conversion, church membership, and mystical-transcendent identification with God. Each stage of this religious experience had both positive and negative consequences for women.[4] Acceptance of personal limits, social integration, and the inner detachment from social constraint through identification with the Divine comprised its advantages; outward conformity to traditional sex roles with its suggestion of female inferiority and the limitations of personal freedom constituted its disadvantages.

The struggle for individual women's identity, which manifested itself in dreams, was set in the context of religious symbolism. Thus interpretation of the religious dream imagery can give scholars some clue as to the nature and process of southern women's self-definition.

The relationship between an individual woman's dream and Christian symbolism is necessarily implicit. It cannot be proved that every woman adapted the concept of evangelical community to her own psychological integration. But because women accepted church discipline and prescribed cultural roles and because they were expected to do so and were rewarded if they followed the evangelical community code, it can be argued that Christian symbols undoubtedly informed women's conscious and unconscious behavior.[5]

Analysis of the dreams of women in the South suggests that on the deepest level community remained a leading symbol of self-definition. Each dream representation of community selected for this study actually revealed the extent to which the woman did or did not differentiate herself from the community. The process of differentiation was sometimes able to occur because of the psychic conflict that existed between southern women and the evangelical community. The resolution of that conflict in the lives of individual women tells us that despite the cultural constraints of a family-centered, church-dominated community, women matured and grew in confidence. The structure of the evangelical community, however, prevented the association of women and the formation of a woman's movement in the South.

The women's dreams studied here represent three possible responses to the evangelical community—rejection, acceptance, or compromise. Anna Maria Akehurst's dreams provide insight into the conflict independent women encountered in the evangelical South. Her marginal social existence and its psychological impact upon her make evident the nature of the community pressures that forced her to reject its demands and maintain her singular identity. In contrast to Anna Maria Akehurst, Frances Ann Bernard Capps, from the time of her early conversion, remained within the evangelical community and interpreted her conscious and unconscious experience largely according to community religious precepts. Amanda Virginia Edmonds Chappelear resisted commitment to the evangelical church. She joined only when confident that she did so on her own spiritual terms, and her conversion occurred in her unconscious struggle for personal identity. Whatever the outcome the interaction between women and the evangelical community had a profound effect upon women's lives.

Anna Maria Akehurst lived as a stranger in the South. Lame, orphaned, widowed, displaced, she endured a tortured, lonely life. A native of New York, she lost her mother in early adolescence. She was married in 1847 to Joseph Akehurst, but her husband died soon after the honeymoon. Within a decade of his death, Anna Maria immigrated to Georgia. Like many single northern women, she was attracted to the South by the prospect of higher wages for teaching. However, teaching positions were difficult to obtain, and so to support herself Anna Maria opened a millinery shop. Later, she secured positions as a governess—first with the Shelman family, who made extraordinary demands on her, and then with Colonel Harris, who proposed marriage. She rejected Colonel Harris and worked thereafter as a matron in orphan asylums.[6] She described her life in this period as "wandering, looking for a home."[7]

During the Civil War she lived and worked in an orphan asylum in Columbus, Georgia. It was in that city that she met Mr. Cady and soon thereafter married him. Although suffering from poor health, Cady was a planter and business agent who traveled for the Confederacy. Anna Maria described the relationship between herself and her husband as insular and cold, but after his death she remembered him as gentle and kind. Happy as a wife, she was less appreciative of her role as a mistress. She believed servants invaded her privacy and resented relatives who visited according to the Victorian custom—for weeks at a time. During the Civil War, in what must have been a difficult period, her former sister-in-law, Jenny Akehurst Lines, and her family took refuge with the Cadys, who apparently gave them shelter in the asylum.[8]

Anna Maria Akehurst's personal history began in the North, which may have accounted for her detachment from the South. Jennie Lines explained that Anna Maria rejected Colonel Harris's suit because "she [was] not partial to southerners."[9] Anna Maria Akehurst's ambivalence toward the South is revealed also in the fact that she wrote tongue-in-cheek observations of relations between mistresses and slaves. But she married a planter, valued her southern relatives, and chose to remain in the South during the Civil War. Thus her indeterminate position as an independent northern woman meant that she was not wholly inside the southern community and so suffered a lonely crisis of personal integration. Nonetheless, her struggle to adjust to social and community claims gives insight into the development of female identity within southern culture.

Postwar economic instability adversely affected the Cady plantation, and in 1866 Cady dissolved his partnership and moved into town where he continued his business full-time. For Anna Maria it meant loss of yet another home. But she suffered an even greater loss in 1867 when her second husband died. Ulcer-ridden and depressed, she took to her bed for an entire year. Meanwhile her husband's partner and debtor nursed her back to health. When fully recovered, she opened a school in Girard, Alabama, with the proceeds from her husband's estate and finally settled into a home of her own.[10]

Beset by loneliness, Anna Maria took in a boarder, John Healy, who shared expenses with her. Still, she longed for more satisfying companionship and in that frame of mind she sent for her niece, Fannie Cady, to live with her. Fannie Cady's father had financial difficulties and Anna Maria may have relieved her brother-in-law of supporting Fannie. While living with her aunt, Fannie became engaged to John Healy. Wishing to provide for their happiness, Anna Maria gave the couple her home, which meant that she had to leave her school. She then took a position in Montgomery, Alabama, as matron of an orphan asylum.[11] Secretly, Anna Maria reproached herself for the sacrifice of her home. She wrote:

> John and Fannie are married! They can never know how much of a sacrifice I made when I worked them *into* and *myself out* of a *home.* They have it, and I am sincere in wishing them happiness for I *love them* both, and I dont blame them[.] I am only confessing to my book my own causes of trouble—or more correctly, how I always manage to work myself out of everything that is comfortable or profitable. Well I am making this cheerless place seem something like home, by working

very hard, I wonder if I wont manage, or let someone manage it out of my hands.[12]

It is clear that what Anna Maria desired was a home. Victorian America made a cult of domesticity, and the market system segregated the sexes based on separate roles. This was especially true in the industrial North where the home complemented the business world. As refuge and as a pillar of the social order, the home remained a compelling image for nineteenth-century women.[13] Anna Maria's need for a home, however, conflicted with her impulse toward self-sacrifice. Self-sacrifice in the Victorian ethos was most clearly identified with maternity and with the woman's lot to suffer, especially in childbirth.[14]

Increased self-recrimination and irascibility characterized Anna Maria Akehurst's personality especially after her husband's death. Always detached and critical of others, she found herself in a nasty and humiliating family quarrel. John and her brother-in-law accused her of being meddlesome about a debt the couple owed. The quarrel subsequently alienated her from the Cadys.

The external aspects of Anna Maria Akehurst's life coexisted with unconscious internal conflict, the tension and resolution of which expressed itself in her dreams. In the period after the death of her husband when she lived in Girard she recorded her initial, recurring dream:

last night I dreamed of Aunt Huldah's place and the sweet apple tree over the spring. All seemed pleasant in the house but it seemed to rain too hard for me to go out in the orchard although I had a great desire to do so, looked from the window and saw the sweet apple tree with no leaves or apples on it, thought it was *not quite dead*, wished for some of its apples, Strange dream! because it has been dreamed over so many times.[15]

Although the nature of Anna Maria's relationship to her aunt is not known, still the dream itself conveys the sense of a very familiar, intimate, feminine place. Perhaps this is a childhood memory and Aunt Huldah was a maternal, affectionate presence in the life of Anna Maria, a motherless child.

The symbol that evokes such longing in Anna Maria—the tree—is often a symbol of self-definition for women and may also be identified with the mother or giver of life.[16] Anna Maria worked among orphans for the greater part of her life and was deeply attached to the children. She confessed missing a baby so much she was beside herself. And once when she was accused of selfishness, Anna Maria maintained that her adoption of Fannie sprang from maternal, self-sacrificing motives.[17] Perhaps for Anna Maria Akehurst the tension of dealing with maternity may have had to do with the nature of her own life-giving propensity. In biblical terms the fruitful tree is associated with the just who avoid temptation and withstand adversity by their trust in

Psalm One

Blessed is the man that walketh not in the counsel of the ungodly, nor standeth in the way of sinners, nor sitteth in the seat of the scornful.

But his delight is in the law of the Lord; and in his law doth he meditate day and night.

And he shall be like a tree planted by the rivers of water, that bringeth forth his fruit in his season; his leaf also shall not wither; and whatsoever he doeth shall prosper.

The ungodly are not so; but are like the chaff which the wind driveth away.

Therefore the ungodly shall not stand in the judgment, nor sinners in the congregation of the righteous.

For the Lord knoweth the way of the righteous: but the way of the ungodly shall perish.

And of the vineyard in Isaiah's Canticle the Lord says:[18]

I the Lord do keep it; I will water it every moment; lest any hurt it, I will keep it night and day.

And again, Jeremiah confirms the fruitfulness of the just:

Blessed is the man that trusteth in the Lord, and whose hope the Lord is.

For he shall be as a tree planted by the waters, and that spreadeth out her roots by the river, and shall not see when heat cometh, but her leaf shall be green; and shall not be careful in the year of drought, neither shall cease from yielding fruit.[19]

Like a tree planted near a spring, Anna Maria longs for the fruit of the just nourished by the water of wisdom. In her motherlessness she also longs for the consolation of the just—she longs to be cared for as the Lord kept the vineyard and the trusting man. Although Anna Maria regarded her own existence as barren because it was devoid of either children or virtue, she nonetheless knew the tree "was not quite dead." In spite of her sterility, Anna Maria believes she can live and bear fruit. In Victorian America all the virtues of true womanhood—piety, purity, domesticity, submissiveness— apotheosized in motherhood. But Anna Maria's hope survives despite nineteenth-century cultural perceptions of childless women as barren and socially marginal.

A dissolving medium, the rain, suggests the possibility of change, but in this dream Anna Maria hesitates to enter the rain and, instead, remains defensively inside. The rain is the means of resolving personal contradictions, and in this case the conflict is between self-preservation and self-sacrifice, or between domestic dependence and sacrificial independence. The rain that fertilizes self-knowledge impedes the dreamer's conscious awareness of this contradiction because the emotion of it is too "hard to bear." Apparently, however, she is trying to let some disagreeable knowledge of herself into this dream.

Whatever self-knowledge Anna Maria repressed, it made her feel guilty. In the same entry as the dream she recorded that she had received news from Fannie that her father was lame and unable to work. Anna Maria's response— "I am very anxious about him. Will divide my salary with him"—was a heroic gesture, perhaps even an effort to convince herself that hers was not a sterile personality.[20] This action reinforced her image of herself. But she had the recurring desire to move beyond mere image.

This is clearly seen in a second dream wherein she attempted to come to terms with her psychic tension. The dream occurred at a time when she keenly felt loss. On 27 February 1871 she was visited by her friend Emma Pierce, an attractive, talented, intelligent widow and mother of two children. The visit reminded Anna Maria of her distance from old friends. "O why must such separations be," lamented Anna Maria.[21] She was equally depressed by a second visit on that day, when she heard Fannie talk of moving to Ohio in the spring.[22]

In her next diary entry Anna Maria told of her dream, which happened after their visits. It was a dream that she could not express, even to Fannie who slept with her that night.[23] As she recorded her experience Anna Maria insisted that "it was no common dream":

> Seemed that I was compelled to cross a river, but there was a large covered bridge which appeared quite unsafe to cross on yet I must go on it in some car or something similar, the bridge being so far above the water which was very shallow there was no escape from a dreadful death in the event of the bridge breaking, which did and I was grasping broken timbers to prevent my falling yet the timbers themselves gave way or were already in motion, so I fell and did not for some minutes try to move or open my eyes, but when I did I discovered a light which I thought was the cars on fire, yet looking again it appeared like the red sky at sunset or a large partition of spinglass with a fire behind it. I past behind this partition, how I dont remember

Every thing there appeared so pleasant and I felt so perfectly happy, every one looked happy, every face like the face of a pleased friend, I talked with several, on the pleasantness of the place dont remember as there were any houses, but nice smooth roads, fine horses, but what particularly struck my fancy, was the happy faces, old people looked so good that they were handsome, and big fat men looked as happy as the young, and as pretty, all seemed dressed with perfect taste except one large man who I seemed quite anxious about, and questioned him on the subject, he said he was only there for a short time that he should be dressed when he came again. I looked at my own cloths and they had been changed to black velvet with bright stars for trimming. All or nearly all had bright glittering trimming on their dresses mostly tincel stars. I seemed to be given the charge of a child or a childs cloths which were beautiful, I remarked that they must have excellent washers. My own dress appeared rather short for one lame like myself but as I looked at my feet they were very pretty and I could walk with so much ease. The only deformity that I noticed was some powder marks that were in a ladies face, but it seemed rather to add to her beauty as it looked some like some little pieces of court plaster. It came from a burn by powder's exploding but she said she didn't think it showed. I dont remember as I saw the little owner of the baby cloths yet there were many children of every age. I know that I have never been as happy in my life as I was in that dream.[24]

Pressure from her unconscious "compelled" Anna Maria to cross the river or face a transition. The bridge and river beneath are a common symbol for the ego and the unconscious. Taken together the bridge and river form a cross at the center of which lies the core of self.[25] Anna Maria noted the distance between the two and expressed the fact that she was fragile; she is aware that entering the water means death to her former self.

Nevertheless, the bridge breaks, and she tries to grasp the usual supports (her defenses), but as she said they "gave way" or "were already in motion" as she falls into her unconscious and turns toward the light. The glow emitted from the car on fire indicates the purging process in which the individual frees the shadowy aspects of her or his personality. Like a sunset, her conscious position is dying, but will perhaps be reborn.[26]

Somehow she simply avoided the barrier to her transformation and entered into paradise, a place full of possibilities, of "smooth roads" and happy friendly people. There were no houses in which to hide. The only disturbing element in paradise was "one large man" about whom she was anxious. The large man said he would remain only for a short time but that he would be dressed when he came back, meaning he would change. The possibility that the last destructive element will be transformed enables Anna Maria to see herself as transformed. The center of her being (the star) and her image of herself (clothes) are transfigured. She appears in a black velvet dress with bright stars for trimming and thus is given a new life. It is a moment of sublime harmony in the dream.

Anna Maria's dream compensated for her alienation and suffering; compensatory elements are manifested in the appearance of children and in the miraculous cure of her lameness. She may have identified lameness, a physical deformity, with her own personality, but in her dream she accepted her weakness and in spite of it she moved freely. "I looked at my feet they were very pretty and I could walk with so much ease," she remembered of her dream. Other deformities and weaknesses suddenly appear as strengths or they do not show, meaning that the ugliness in personal explosions and personal encounters are reduced to a minimum. Finally, the child and the clothes disappear and many children "of every age" are seen in a metaphor of the dreamer's personal reintegration. The dream culminates in a vision of paradise that replicates the earthly evangelical community—a spiritual union where there are no barriers to understanding. Paradise is harmony among the members of the heavenly community; Anna Maria's personal integration sought an inner harmony in order to join the wider community.

But the incongruence between Anna Maria's dream life and reality underscored the powerful conflict within her as she attempted to deal with her weaknesses. Her ordinary life became a "disagreeable reality" when she was drawn into a destructive family quarrel.[27] Fannie and John had borrowed money from Mr. Cady's brother, and they believed that Anna Maria had told the brother that John taunted Fannie about it. Accused of being meddlesome and stung by remorse, Anna Maria confided to her diary: "O my da[r]ling husband, you was taken from the evil to come, for you would have been distressed to have learned that your wife was a mischief maker."[28] Anna Maria accepted responsibility for her part in the incident but not without rationalization and self-pity: "I have been to blame, suppose others do wrong! that does not make my sins any less."[29] Later she defended herself: "But my journal I will tell you what I shall not say to any, John & Fannie *have* said *much* more *than* I told about that debt, and I talked to brother, about it at Fannie's suggestion, I *did* say John talked about it, And he *did* although he has forgotten it. But I did not say he was always taunting her about it."[30]

The same embarrassment forced Anna Maria into a protective withdrawal: "And may I *never* make another confidential friend. . . . may I always feel my utter isolation, and never for one moment be any thing but the cold polite woman, unbending as the mountain and freezing as the frigid zone."[31] Nonetheless, self-disgust moved her to cry, "O that I might tear myself from my self, and think only for the comfort of others! God help me! I am weak!"[32] Here is an admission of conflicting natures and of a desire to eradicate the darker tendencies of manipulation and power. As a solution she determined to act independently and with disinterest. She resolved to mind her own business but more importantly she prayed, "God be merciful to me and give me business of my own."[33]

Anna Maria Akehurst's strength lay in the clarification of her weakness. Her third dream acknowledged the intensity of her struggle. In the week following the family argument, she dreamed she was surrounded by friends. As she walks with them, she talks about "a house in a pleasant grove." Everyone admires the house that belongs to her and she "remark[s] that it was such a comfort to have such a nice home after all the wandering life that I had been subjected too! [sic]."[34] Even her Father approves as he appears among the crowd. She understands that everyone in the crowd had died. When she asks how she died, her Father replies that she had been struck by lightning.

Finally at home in a more integrated self, surrounded by father and friends, who represent the harmonized aspects of her being, Anna Maria learns that her pleasant circumstance is the result of a fiery purge. Beyond her control, lightning struck and caused her death-transformation. Consequently, Anna Maria is given a new image of herself.

Despite the progressive integration of Anna Maria's unconscious life, her childlessness remained a discordant element in her consciousness. Resolution of this conflict coincided with the death of one of Anna Maria's charges, an orphan recently reunited with her grandmother. Grieving, Anna Maria wrote that she wished she were with the child.

Anna Maria's last recorded dream occurred sometime after the death of the orphan. At Christmastime she dreamed that she was reunited with her mother and told her that she "did not look as old as I did."[35] In this moving dream episode, Anna Maria encounters her mother, the one person with whom she most closely identified. She is, in a sense, reunited with her own maternity with all of its disappointments, which is probably why she perceived herself as older than her mother.

The dream sequence revealed to Anna Maria the possibilities that lay in her acceptance of limitations. The extent to which unconscious forces influenced her ordinary behavior is not known, but a hint appears in her diary. In early spring Anna Maria recorded that she underwent a "mortifying experience," "a severe discipline," but she gave no details. On the same day she had answered an invitation to visit a sister-in-law; the invitation had made Anna Maria think that her sister-in-law would be better off not seeing her. In her diary she mused, "When I reflect on the disappointment she would be likely to undergo, I am thankful she is saved that privilege."[36]

After two marriages and the loss of family and friends, Anna Maria Akehurst had succumbed to guilt and a sense of worthlessness. But, in the midst of desolation, she held to her independence. Just before she married for the third time she wrote: "I . . . am separated from my kin by distance, and from my relatives by est[r]angement but I am bless[ed] in my lonely life by having employment which keep[s] me from being beholden to either friend, relative or kin. . . . God has been so kind to me in giving me independence."[37] Independence, like a refractory, withstood the fire of her personal ordeal and enabled Anna Maria Akehurst to enter a third marriage with a more resilient sense of self.

The resolution of conflict in Anna Maria Akehurst's life allowed her a margin of freedom to maintain her personal identity apart from her marital identity. Most women viewed marriage as the sole opportunity for emotional support and cultural identity. Anna Maria Akehurst's status as an educated self-supporting woman with few relational ties was something of an anomaly in the South. Her independent position provided few possibilities for female association in this kin-oriented society and her struggle remained a solitary one.

For younger unmarried southern women whose lives centered about family, friendships, romance, and conversion, integration into the church community raised personal conflicts that were repeated in dreams. Frances Ann Bernard Capps's early religious conversion at age fourteen and subsequent struggle against doubt compelled her to seek religion as consolation. Not only did her otherworldly life assuage doubt about her course, but the evangelical community with whom she shared her doubts gave her a sense of security. On 15 August 1840 she attended a camp meeting where the Reverend Langhorne preached "on the terrors of the damned."[38] Deeply affected by the preaching, Frances, a "mourner," suffered distress and consternation until eleven p.m. on 16 August when she shouted "the praises of redeeming grace and dying love before the assembled multitude."[39] The next day she claimed her mind was relieved of all its doubts. Nonetheless, a week later doubts about her conversion disturbed her, so she sought instruction and advice from the church. Encouraged by a "born-again" sermon preached on 30 August, Frances joined the church.[40] After attendance at a class meeting she wrote, "[H]ow christian-like it seems when we can open our hearts to each other, lay all our trials open and be comforted."[41] It is within the context of evangelical consolation and security that Frances suffered the loss of her sister.

When her sister lay dying in 1841, the young girl sang "Coming Home"; the scene made a deep impression on Frances Capps. The evening that her sister died Frances dreamed that "Margaret Jane went to live at her place" and that she returned to tell Frances about a beautiful place where a kindly gentleman took care of her. Margaret Jane said she loved him "as well as my own father." The sister begged Frances to go back to where there was "so much company." Frances was awakened from her dream by her mother to learn that her sister had died.[42] The concept of heavenly community, a replication of the evangelical church community, comforted Frances. With her heavenly place assured, Frances let her sister go, but she also knew that she would eventually be with her again.

In the meantime the evangelical community sustained her. The memory of her conversion remained sacred to Frances Capps. She considered the camp ground, Hampton, her spiritual birthplace and Reverend Langhorne her "spiritual father." Her sister's conversion at Hampton made the place "doubly dear to her." And she remembered the hospitality of friends at the camp ground.[43] Although her conversion was a dramatic and compelling incident in her life, she accepted it as an initial stage of sanctification and gradually developed spiritual confidence. She renewed her convenant with God on the first day of 1843 and continued to perform works of charity and attend revivals.[44] During the preaching at a camp meeting on 24 August 1845, a storm arose, and lightning struck the camp killing two horses. In the confusion, as Frances related the incident, people panicked and "pleaded not to be cut down in their sins." However, she remained calm, willing to submit to "whatever God disposes." She found her faith strengthened by the incident.[45]

Several years later, in her mid-twenties, Frances experienced a test of faith because of an unhappy love affair. Crushed by the knowledge that the man she cared for loved another, she resolved to withdraw from him. Frances decided not to tell her friends how much she loved him because they would consider her "unmaidenly." Instead she prayed for divine guidance "to give up all."[46] Despite her wishes she discovered her feelings "obstinately attached to an object which has been too blindly loved."[47] A year later, however, Frances rallied and married Mr. Capps after her parents rejected his initial suit.

In her loss, Frances found detachment the basis of religious consolation. When her sister died and she lost a lover, she exercised greater religious discipline and found in it the means of emotional release. Frances Ann Bernard Capps held to a wholly religious perspective, which integrated crises within that view.

Amanda Virginia Edmonds Chappelear, a Virginia planter's daughter, in her late teens before the war, made her decision to convert the creative substance of her personal identity. She socialized in the company of school friends associated with the local Methodist church, but the tension and strain of her life stemmed from the death of her father in 1857 and the pressure from family and friends to seek conversion.[48] It was not until 1861 that Amanda joined the church, although a young minister had tried to persuade her to be converted in 1858. Amanda refused to accompany him to church and he reported her action to the congregation. Despite public exposure she maintained her own religious integrity: "I feared if I went to the altar I might be deceived into believing, so let me pray to be called in secret and solitude."[49]

Before Amanda was finally converted, she recorded "a remarkably strange dream" on 6 February 1859:

> Nannie Bettie were on horseback. Mr. Newman and myself were walking to church, I ran to keep up with the girls . . . [and] came very near running over a horrid rusty looking snake. When I was out of danger, I turned to see what had become of the ugly looking thing, when I turned I beheld a brilliant light in the western sky.

Amanda further related how a cloud obscured the light, but when it rolled away, a large pillar appeared and on top of it "a house or temple and every window [was] illumed with lights." In her dream she continued toward the church, climbing a flight of steep steps to reach her destination. Servants crowded on the steps, and one called to have her sit with them and "watch the gaily dressed people." But Amanda "heeded them not" and went to a large room and began to sing.[50]

Amanda's interpretation of the dream focused upon the snake and the servant: "I have an enemy in the snake and while I have been writing it occured, that the darky that tried to stop me was the evil one tempting me, but I would not heed him, such is my interpretation."[51] The image of the snake has a double meaning. In the Judeo-Christian tradition, the serpent in the Garden of Eden is associated with both sin and higher consciousness. The brazen serpent also represents Christ, an antidote to the venom of sin: "The Son of Man must be lifted up as Moses lifted up the serpent in the desert" (John 3:14).[52] It may be that this dream contains Amanda's potential spiritual transformation. She could not "keep up with the girls" who rode ahead of her on *their* way to church. Amanda is distracted by the snake, but it set her on her own way toward the light. Amanda believed that "the darky" was a temptation, perhaps some failing of hers that would deter her from changing her life. Because Amanda "would not heed him," she demonstrated that she could potentially reach her destination, the large room.[53]

In this dream Amanda began to accept the mystical paradox that the approach to the light of illumination is through utter darkness. In Christian symbolism Christ is the light: "I am the Way, the Truth and the Light" (John 14:6). Baptismal symbolism uses the paradox in its ceremony of rebirth; for example, the descent into the baptismal waters leads to ascent toward the light. Therefore, rebirth symbolism, a description of the union of opposites, of conscious and unconscious, performs a transcendent function. Since conversion or baptism increases consciousness by absorbing formerly unconscious elements, the new state effects even greater insight or light.[54] Amanda saw light in the sky; suddenly obscured, the light reappeared in the church and illumined all the windows of consciousness. She found the source of light within the church and its revelation compelled her toward conversion, yet she hesitated until she could respond from her own unique nature.

Amanda's ultimate conversion was not a capitulation to evangelical pressure, because for her it meant an authentic choice. Amanda did not convert
until her unconscious conflicts set in motion a direction for her conscious
choice. Then her conversion represented a harmony of her conscious and
unconscious life.

These cases suggest that women's dreams consisted of struggles at the
center of their being and that often community emerged as a leading symbol
in that struggle. For Frances Ann Bernard Capps heaven was desirable because it was a community where kin lived in peace. On the deepest psychic
level women struggled toward self-definition and for them the church community was a compelling symbol of integration. The heavenly community
represented Anna Maria Akehurst's image of personal integration, and for
Amanda Virginia Edmonds Chappelear the illuminated church symbolized
her potential for growth and maturity.

In an inner dialectic southern women weighed and shifted the balance
between personal autonomy and the demands of community. Within the
limits of the evangelical community those who recognized the potential for
freedom in divine unity and detachment experienced a sense of worth and
purpose that was personal and unique. However, the barriers to an individual
woman's autonomy in southern evangelical culture are clearly evident in the
cases of Anna Maria Akehurst and Amanda Chappelear. Anna Maria Akehurst
suffered personal alienation when her maternal tendencies conflicted with
her desire for self-sufficiency; the church community made a public example
of Amanda Virginia Edmonds Chappelear because she chose not to attend a
revival. Both of these cases suggest that evangelical control often obscured
the liberating potential of this religious culture.

For those women who sought a varied experience, whose own maturity
and independence welcomed a wider association, little opportunity existed
in evangelical culture. Personal freedom did not translate into variety of
choice because rural isolation and evangelical emphasis upon community
limited the kind of relationships available. Women hammered out their lives
within an all-embracing structure—the community, the powerful symbol of
fulfillment, earthly and divine, of security, assurance, and harmony. But the
nature of this community produced enormous struggles in a woman's interior
being. Unconscious forces resisted, accepted, and adapted cultural forms
that then guided the conscious choice of southern women to determine their
lives.

Both white and black women struggled for self-definition. The clash of
mistress and slave was often the conflict of two developing personalities.
Mistress and slave, bound together by mutual obligations and responsibilities, nevertheless acted out of distinct cultural and communal contexts.
Nineteenth-century Afro-American religious symbolism indicates that black
women's values, attitudes, and roles differed from white women's in some

important ways. Black women exercised religious leadership, as they testified to their spiritual experiences and taught by example and exhortation. And as shouters, their great enthusiasm swelled meetings to a fervid pitch. In addition, communal values determined that each was responsible for all; slave men and especially slave women assumed the care of family and non-kin. Moreover, family members attempted to secure their cohesion by teaching work and survival skills. An examination of black women's experience in slavery reveals that actual behavior remained consistent with symbolic expression.

Path to a once-prosperous church, Savannah, Georgia
(William E. Wilson Collection, Special Collections Division,
University of Georgia Libraries)

Ordinary folk usually seen on southern by-ways
(William E. Wilson Collection, Special Collections Division,
University of Georgia Libraries)

A country couple poses for photographer
(William E. Wilson Collection, Special Collections Division,
University of Georgia Libraries)

The J. M. Dease Family Portrait
(Special Collections Division, University of Georgia Libraries)

Baptism, an intense religious experience
(William E. Wilson Collection, Special Collections Division,
University of Georgia Libraries)

"Old Sarah," nurse to three generations of her master's family
(Vanishing Georgia Collection, Georgia Department of Archives and History)

Boiling and scrubbing the laundry
(Robert E. Williams Collection, Special Collections Division,
University of Georgia Libraries)

Carrying cotton from the gin
(William E. Wilson Collection, Special Collections Division,
University of Georgia Libraries)

*Men, women, and children working in the cotton field
(Robert E. Williams Collection, Special Collections Division,
University of Georgia Libraries)*

Several generations of a family on the Smith plantation,
Beaufort, South Carolina
(Library of Congress)

A slave pen, Alexandria, Virginia
(Mathew Brady Collection, Library of Congress)

Refugees fleeing before Sherman's march
(Library of Congress)

Eliza Frances Andrews, Civil War diarist
(Special Collections Division, University of Georgia Libraries)

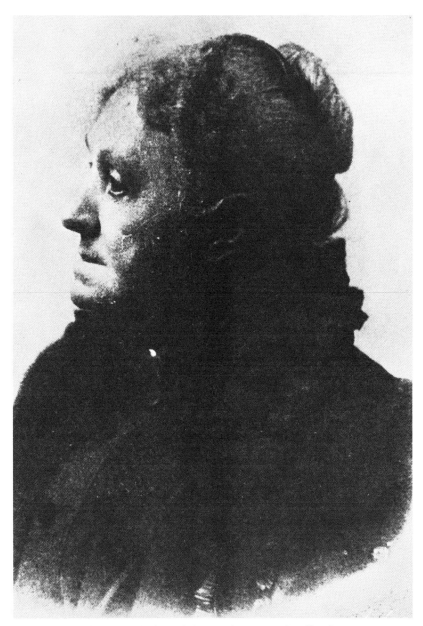

Rebecca Latimer Felton, reformer and suffragist
(Special Collections Division, University of Georgia Libraries)

4.   H E L L

"Yes, in them days it was Hell without fires."
May's testimony, Johnson, *God Struck Me Dead*[1]

ay, a former slave, said she was born in a log cabin "long before the Civil War." Her mother bore nineteen children but only four survived. Her father was sold and while separated from the family he remarried. Then the master gave May's family—her mother, her brother, and her sisters—to his son, who moved them to Culleoka.

May vividly recalled two things about slavery, the work and the ill treatment. She said:

> When I was little I used to work around the big house, cleaning floors, polishing silver, wiping floors, waiting on the table, and everything. My mother was the cook. My mistress was awful mean and exacting. I had better not do anything wrong. She used to beat me like I was a dog—hit me across the head with tongs or poker or anything.[2]

But always there was the presence of her mother who tried to undo the worst of it. May continued: "Sometimes when the snow was on the ground my mother used to stand at the cellar door to slip me a pair of dry moccasins to put on. My feet were so frostbitten that you could track me everywhere I went through the snow."[3] Despite adversity, her "mother used to pray and sing and shout all the time," but May was not particularly religious. "While I was little," she explained, "I did about everything but say my prayers." She did, however, see "haunts." At various times she "saw" Mars Bill, her departed master, and later in life experienced a vision of a friend who had died.[4]

After her marriage she "became an elect in the house of God," and it was then she put her pattern of fear, the haunts and the terror, behind her. She explained to her interviewer, "[God] has taken the fear out of me."[5] Assurances replaced May's fear so that even in her worldly ignorance she felt she could teach. She claimed:

> I often wish I did know how to read but since I didn't have the chance to learn—being fearsome to be seen with a book when I was a slave— God has seen my need and made me satisfied. He has taken me, a fool—for sometimes my head was beat so I thought I was foolish—and hidden with me the secret of eternal life. He has made me to stand up on my feet and teach the world-wise out of his wisdom that comes from on high.[6]

May testified to a faith in a wise and all-knowing "time-God." A time-God, she explained, was a

> being all wise and seeing and knowing all things, having looked down through time before time, [who] foresaw every creeping thing and poured out his spirit on the earth. The earth brought forth fruits in due season. In the very beginning every race and every creature was in the mind of God, and we are here, not ahead of time, not behind time, but just on time. It was time that brought us here, and time will carry us away.[7]

For May it was the "time-God" that steadied her life and brought her to maturity. Family and faith enabled May to endure the pain of bondage.

May's memory retained the texture of slave culture in which families who had suffered separation regrouped and survived. Although kin remained important in the Afro-American community, the mother assumed a large share of the responsibility for the family's well-being. In addition to family, an evangelical faith aided the development of a mature personality. Slavery tested one's faith as the discipline of field and household threatened to undermine confidence and hasten despair. But identification with Afro-American family and cultural values reinforced confidence and allowed women to define themselves apart from white authority. Such self-definition led to tensions between white and black women.

The Afro-American community replicated the evangelical kin society of white southerners. Intermarriage among the black population confined to plantations or farms within a specific region tended to develop stable kin networks. Slaves, like their masters, often lived, married, and died in the same neighborhood where they had been born. The breakup of an estate, however, threatened a sale of slaves out of the neighborhood, but, more likely, the white family heirs retained the servants in their nearby households.[8] In addition, as in white society, the evangelical church provided an ideology and discipline that reinforced social norms. Although few blacks were church members, evangelicalism most probably penetrated Afro-American folk beliefs and ecstatic behavior.[9] The evangelical appeal carried weight beyond mere numbers.

But although community forms remained the same, the distinct Afro-American culture and family systems allowed individuals to interpret their experience within the southern evangelical community differently. For example, maternity in Afro-American culture carried with it greater responsibilities and social consequences than it did in white evangelical culture, and this forced black women to develop initiative and make demands upon white authority for themselves and their family. In slave society where men and women were equally powerless, women's leadership potential was seen in such assertiveness. Although women "preached" and led prayer meetings, their religious leadership did not translate into an autonomous women's culture. Rather, the slave system and Afro-American culture circumscribed relationships beyond the family, and the subordinate position of women became clear in family culture and evangelical religious symbolism.

In ritual—the symbolic rites of conversion—black bondwomen expressed the most significant aspects of their being. The similarity of the images that they used in their conversion testimony reveals the dependence of women upon their family and female kin. This suggests that black women had a corporate identity—an Afro-American identity—distinct from that of the white evangelical family system. Moreover, the conversion process, which grew out of the shared experience of bondage, expressed a religious ideology that enabled women to resist a repressive system.[10]

In his analysis of Afro-American religion, Marxist historian Eugene Genovese claims that slave resistance was essentially political. He argues that "since religion expressed the antagonisms between the life of the individual and that of society and between the life of civil society and that of political society, it cannot escape being profoundly political."[11] However, the Afro-American religious consciousness may have been only indirectly political in the sense that Genovese defined religious expression. It may be argued that most Afro-American women and men acted out of an implicit evangelical consciousness. Moreover, since religion expresses the unity of human experience, and Afro-American religion fused humanity, nature, and God as "inseparable aspects of a sacred whole," slaves' resistance or accommodation to bondage cannot be interpreted as political but rather as salvific—as a religious response rooted in history.[12] Salvation is interpreted here to mean an ultimate responsibility for the self within limits, the limits imposed by the condition of servitude, of being at the disposal of others.[13]

The contradiction between freedom and servitude does not make religious ideology "politically ambiguous," in the sense that Genovese uses the term. Genovese acknowledges that Christianity is socially conservative, that it originated in a patriarchal tribal culture that was adapted to slave and feudal society. He contrasts such conservatism with the revolutionary implication of Christianity: its radical individualism, identification with the collective, opposition to class relations, and millennialism.[14]

These "ambiguous" aspects of Christianity, however, form a cogent religious ideology because, it may be argued, at its heart the religious message is not revolt, but creation—the power to change continuously. Thus, the slaves' creative response to patriarchal domination was continuous self-definition, both individually and collectively. The converted, transformed individual functioned in an inclusive system and interpreted all attitudes, relationships, and behavior according to a religious system of values and acted upon them. Simply stated, although religious behavior may have political implications because religion is by nature social, nevertheless religious ideology does not presuppose a political ideology.

Conversion testimony exposes the levels of religious interpretation of self, community, and ideology. The testimonies of black women's conversion found in Works Progress Administration interviews and in the published and unpublished accounts of Clifton H. Johnson's *God Struck Me Dead* illustrate anthropologist Aylward Shorter's contention that ritual symbolism contains the key to understanding "the essential constitution of human societies."[15] According to Shorter, "Symbolism, and especially ritual symbolism, is the means by which [an individual] shares his [or her] inmost experiences with other[s]. Through ritual [an individual] is able to express values which are otherwise inexpressible and to experience them as shared."[16] The ritual process allowed the transformed self an individual and social expression of the values that gave meaning and coherence to Afro-American culture.

The conversion experience deeply influenced the psychological, social, and spiritual development of black evangelical women. Women as well as men measured their spiritual development by personal insight, commitment to community, and intensity of the initial conversion. In at least one respect, however, women's witness differed from that of men. Women evoked maternal imagery in their testimony. In one case God's insistent call seemed to come from the woman's child. She said, "I went home and took my baby in my arms. The voice inside cried, 'Mercy! Mercy! Lord!' I laid the baby down for I thought the child was talking."[17] Later, having endured a series of trials in her vision, she traveled on a "safe path." "I looked to the south," she claimed, "and saw a beautiful green pasture, and the sheep there were grazing. They turned their heads in the same direction and continued eating and began to bleat, saying, 'Mama! Mama!' Then a voice on the inside answered me in the same tone."[18] Deep maternal ties also led to a midwife's conversion. As she told it, "I had to get down on my knees and stay there for several days, until the Lord freed my soul from the gates of hell. He did that because I asked him to show me my mother, who had been dead about twenty years. That he did."[19] Heavenly choirs of angels called to another ecstatic woman convert: "Mama, Mama, you must help carry the world."[20] And in one version of a celestial visitation, a woman's soul was dressed by "the mother." The woman described her vision as follows:

> We came finally to Heaven. My guide put me down and said "I leave you in the hands of the mother." She arose—a very tall woman—and began to dress me. She had on a long white robe, and she dressed me the same way, and when she was through she said, "Everything just fits." I then began to shout and praise God with the rest of the angels.[21]

Women's use of symbolism suggests that maternity helped to define the converted black woman's concept of herself. The relationships described in conversion testimony are maternal; the Afro-American woman perceives and is perceived as a mother.

Historic factors help to explain the importance of maternity in the Afro-American experience. Two of these factors were grounded in custom, while the third was imposed by the slavocracy. In traditional African religion, power over time was attributed to motherhood because, by bearing children, women established the link between generations.[22] The African spiritual code perceived women as representative of a vital present—the ones who made life and therefore, religion, possible. Like the Creator, a woman contained within her all the primordial elements of creation—knowledge, energy, and life.[23] In addition, child-rearing remained a central concern of Afro-American women. Even while mothers worked in the field or in the white household, older women tended to the children. The importance of the black woman's role as mother becomes clear when we realize that mammies cared for both black and white children. Moreover, wives, separated from husbands by sale or death, retained custody of the children and handled the burdens of child-rearing.[24] A third element that contributed to the valuation of Afro-American motherhood was its economic importance to the white slave master. The mother, so essential to the slave economy as a reproductive resource, gained some privileges, such as extra clothing or food for the children, or, often, three weeks respite after childbirth.[25]

Maternal imagery constituted the one element that distinguished female from male testimony. The remaining elements of conversion stories, like the dynamic of a ring shout, derived from the group vision of Afro-American Christianity and the need to accommodate the authenticity of the individual within that group vision.[26] This need applied equally to male and female converts, but it had different implications for behavior since male and female experience varied considerably.

The group vision appears in conversion testimony as a narrative schema of damnation, acceptance, and rebirth.[27] Although the conversion process follows explicit evangelical assumptions about salvation, the experience also reveals the Afro-American woman's sense of self and her relationship to the community. The desire of some women to identify with evangelical Afro-American cultural values determined their resistance to the demands of white authority.

The vision served as part of an initiation rite. When a female child expressed a desire to be converted, her father told her she "had better not come home unless [she had] seen something."[28] The vision was repeated in various motifs, but it was known to all. What the slaves "saw" and experienced were cultural variants of Christian symbols for creation, freedom, and salvation. The convert proceeded from a creaturely state of dependence to an anguished sense of sin. Finally, the conversion transformed the individual into a responsible being, committed to leading others on the path to salvation.

In the primary stage a "time-God" directed the creature toward conversion. We have already seen how May described a "time-God." Others experienced the "time-God" as a inner voice that said, "Follow me and I will lead you. It was time that brought you into this world and time will carry you away. It is through my grace that ye are saved."[29] To another, the voice spoke inwardly, "I am a time-God working after the counsel of my own will. In due time I will bring all things to you. Remember and cause your heart to sing."[30] One convert confirmed that "He is a time-God and He won't make haste."[31] Converts thus endured religious anguish by being compelled to trust in the mercy of a "time-God." As one woman testified, "It looked like the more I prayed the worse off I got. But the God I serve is a time God. He don't come before time; he don't come after time. He comes just on time."[32]

In the hands of a "time-God" conversion was a developmental sequence that began with the beginning of time. Conversion was therefore not simply a discrete experience but part of the entire creation history. This is seen in the testimony of an aged woman who said, "I am as old as God for He carried me in His mind from the beginning. He started to work with me when I was a little girl."[33] Another woman convert insisted, "I was created and cut out and born in the world for heaven. . . . God started on me when I wasn't but ten years old."[34] Personal conversion histories began in the subteens, the typical age of accountability in the eyes of evangelicals. At the age of twelve, for example, one young girl began to cry uncontrollably when someone said, "You never shall die a sinner."[35] A similar experience happened to a twelve-year-old girl, Amy Perry, who dreamed that she was in "a large green field" when an act of forgiveness toward a friend assured her conversion.[36]

The call to change completely often came in the form of a terrifying command: "You must die."[37] Or "You got to die and can't live again."[38] In fact, some converts felt that they actually did experience death. One woman testified that "when God struck me dead with his power, . . . I declare unto you . . . I died. I fell out on the floor flat on my back. I could neither speak nor move, for my tongue stuck to the roof of my mouth; my jaws were locked and my limbs were stiff."[39] Yet another woman who recalled her childhood experience claimed, "I felt myself dying. It started in my feet and came on up over my body. As it crept over me it looked like I was coming unjointed."[40]

Such experiences of the soul's disjuncture revealed two beings. One female convert exclaimed, "I looked, and lo and behold, there were two marys! There is a being in a being, a man in a man. Little Mary was standing looking down on old Mary on this temple, my body, and it lay on the very brink of hell."[41] The same kind of vision occurred when another woman observed herself and "saw . . . a little body, pure white, and flying along a beautiful stream that flowed from the east."[42] Following this disjuncture, the pilgrim soul then entered on a journey that included a view of hell. But a guide appeared at the brink of hell to lead the soul to heaven. So real were these visions that the subjects were left with a vivid view of the horrors of hell and the bliss of heaven. Their descriptions of hell told "of ravenous beasts," of souls "piled up like timber," and of the "gloom and sadness" of everything. Eventually, however, a path opened, and the guide reappeared. The guide was typically a diminutive person, "a little man, very small with waxen hair. His eyes were like fire, his feet as burnished brass." He led the chosen soul to heaven where, face to face with God, the female convert was surrounded by multitudes of angels, lush pastures, and celestial mansions.[43]

The vision resulted ultimately in a transformation, a new personality. "After I passed through this experience," said one spiritual sojourner, "I lost all worldly cares. . . . I am a new creature in Jesus. . . . I was a chosen vessel before the wind ever blew or before the sun ever shined."[44] The transformation included a commission: "Go into yonder world and tell them what a dear savior you have found. . . . Speak and I will speak through you."[45] A woman who heard "the loveliest singing in the world" believed a voice inside of her intoned, "I call you to preach the gospel."[46] In another vision a damned soul warned a woman, "Oh, go tell the people! Don't come here." The divine command, according to the women called, filled them with a confidence that enabled the women to act on the godly initiative. Filled with new trust in divine guidance, one woman claimed that she was "an instrument in God's hands. . . . when he speaks to me now in the spirit I move and move with certainty."[47]

Emboldened by a spirit of confidence, women preached—that is, testified—at meetings and taught those with whom they came in contact by giving witness. Reluctant to act even though converted, one woman claimed a voice said to her: "Before you shall hold your peace the very rocks and mountains shall cry out against you."[48] The woman explained that from that moment she praised God as the spirit moved her, that is, she publicly testified to the movements of the spirit within her. In a vision a young wife heard God command her to teach, "Go tell your husband that the wages of sin is death."[49] And hearing "the Loveliest Singing in the world," a woman received a commission to "go in peace and fear not for a teacher and preacher shalt thou be and many shall hear thee and believe."[50] A thirteen-year-old girl who received the call to preach and teach protested, "Lord, they won't believe what I say." But an inner voice reassured her, "Open your mouth and I will speak through you."[51]

Once converted, women assumed prominent roles in the Afro-American evangelical community. One man remembered, "At the close of preaching Uncle called on Mama to pray, and she sent up a petition that moved every heart."[52] Fredrika Bremer witnessed "an elderly, sickly black woman" who led a meeting in prayer and who attested to the consoling power of the Gospel in her life. And Charlotte Brooks claimed that she "got religion" through Aunt Jane, who conducted prayer meetings and bible readings on the plantation.[53]

The shouters, enthusiasts who responded vocally to preaching, testimony, or their own spirit, included women. Their participation in the meeting, which was often responsible for moving congregations to an emotional climax, earned women shouters much respect. A man proudly recounted the women members of his family known for their "shouts." He said:

> There was Aunt Bellow, a heavy, brownskinned woman. She was a great shouter. Aunt Charlotte used to cry most all the time when she got happy. Aunt Kate was a tall, portly woman and a shouter. It took some good ones to hold her down when she got started. Any time Uncle Link or any other preacher touched along the path she had traveled she would jump and holler. It took some good ones to hold her. The old ones in them times walked over benches and boxes with their eyes fixed on heaven. God was in the midst of them.[54]

By their shouts black women demonstrated their presence and their indispensability as spiritual catalysts.

Assurance convinced women of their freedom to act. At the climax of a woman's conversion she was consoled by a voice that said, "Ye are freed and free indeed. My son set you free."[55] Even a less intense conversion left the individual with a sense of freedom. "When I 'fessed 'ligion, I didn't see nothin; I just felt that I was free," said a former bondwoman.[56] Afro-Americans experienced a spiritual freedom that naturally reinforced a desire for freedom from bondage. Charlotte Brooks reported that when Aunt Jane and Aunt Sallie led the prayers, they prayed to Daniel's God for deliverance.[57] Rachael Adams of Georgia and Victoria Perry of South Carolina remembered their mothers' praying for the freedom of all slaves. "Some day we are going to be free; the Good Lord won't let this thing go on all the time," Victoria Perry's mother prophesied.[58] Rachael Adams testified, "My mudder said she pray to de Lord not to let niggers be slaves all deir lifes."[59] When Miss Abby, a unionist, came upon Aunt Cherry, an aged bondwoman, one spring day after the Civil War had started, Miss Abby asked her if she would leave her master. The elderly servant answered her by recalling an early faith: "[We] black folks is going to be free—the Bible says so—and I think the time is mighty near. Why, my old father and mother told us when they was about to die—children remember what I tell you. You will be freed from bondage—when we are in our graves—and we die in this faith."[60] Attachment to the divine assured detachment from the unjust and corrupting expectations of the slave world.

The conversion process that forged an Afro-American evangelical identity thus set the individual apart. Women who recognized in the creation theme the essence of their being discovered their own unique nature. The same process that transformed women's identity also invested them with social responsibility and, in many cases, a special commission to "preach and teach."

The idea of the Creator as "time-God" appears in both Christian—especially Augustinian—and in African thought. The Swiss philosopher and theologian, Hans Ur von Balthasar, interpreted Augustine's study of Genesis and its meaning in the context of "the fragmentary nature of time," maintaining that in the Augustinian premise, "God created everything at once. . . . God was able to place in the beginning the basis of everything's being, which lay in matter at first invisible, potential according to their causes . . . , in order to come to the light of realization 'in due succession of time.'"[61] In the Augustinian version, the consolation of a "time-God" is that one's being is rooted in a past and that its meaning will be resolved and revealed in the present. It contains an affirmation of the soundness of human personality, which can support the convert's sense of identity and direct her awareness to the present, the worldly.

Traditional African ideas of time also convey the sense that identity is rooted in the past. Because African thought contains no idea of linear progression, time is experienced in the present and moves backward. The distant future thus holds no meaning. Therefore, as John Mbiti explains, time is experienced by the individual in the present or through generations in the community.[62] It is a process that connects the individual with her true self and with preceding generations. Afro-American women looked also to past generations of women and family for meaning in the present.

Traditional African thought considered women the mediators between past and present, life and death. Dominique Zahan gives an eloquent account of this concept in the African worldview:

> She [the woman] is above all a mediator, since the child perched on her hips is none other than an ancestor returned to the world of men through her. Thus everything occurs as if woman were the crossroad when future and past, death and life intersect. She results from ambiguity, from that which is at once tomb and resurrection, decay and vitality. But she incarnates the junctions, the beginnings and the end of the cycle of human existence.[63]

This notion of woman as temporal juncture takes on special significance in the experience of evangelical conversion. Conversion, after all, is the point of change. The subject encounters a rupture in the process of becoming. It is as if the experience of death and rebirth releases a new and purified woman in whom time itself is transformed. Mbiti argues that in temporal matters both African and Christian systems of thought converge in the idea of resurrection, or tranformation. Because the resurrection restores a person's entire being, which the past had obscured, and because it achieves in the present what was before only a hope, the resurrection brings together both dimensions of past and future.[64]

Balthazar expresses a similar idea in his discussion of a convert's ability to distinguish a new sense of time:

> the whole person, turned away from God and turned sinfully towards creation, experiences in itself in its nothingness and vanity as something belonging totally (together with its present and future) to the past. And the whole of the present time offered by God's grace to the convert comes in and takes the place of this time, which has passed away, as a true continuously arriving present. . . . This is the point at which Paul (and, following him, Augustine) distinguishes between the "old" and the "new," the "flesh" and the "spirit," the "outer" and the "inner" man. "Though our outer nature is wasting away, our inner nature is being renewed every day." (2 Cor. 4:16) [65]

Thus, the "renewed" woman's inner direction set her upon a purposeful course, a path that was goal-directed. As the testimonies reveal, the goal was not reached in Afro-American conversions without a view of hell; such a view was both a warning and, perhaps, a preview of earthly travail. The threat of hell, however, only presaged an encounter with the divine, an encounter that strengthened the woman's confidence and increased her mission to preach and teach. With confidence and direction, the Afro-American evangelical woman tested her new freedom in slavery.

The heart of Afro-American evangelicalism remained in the slave community, where secret prayer meetings took place in which women had an active role. Yet for some black women conversion meant acceptance into racially mixed, albeit segregated congregations. In the mixed evangelical community black women were treated as equals in several respects. For example, white members addressed black women communicants as "sister." Black women as well as white women were accorded the title of sister after their faith was examined in public. The Chapel Hill Presbyterian Church, impressed by the testimony of Jinny, a slave, recorded that "she was examined concerning her faith and hope, and love—and on her rendering an intelligent and satisfactory account of her experience and of her aims, she was then admitted into the church family."[66] Another evidence of equal treatment included the extension of transfer papers to blacks who moved to another congregation. Letters of transferral certified the holder as a church member in good standing. Moreover, black members of the church received charity when indigent or sick.[67] And most significantly, Afro-American women were subjected to the same double standard of discipline as were white women.

Evangelical churches tried few black men and women, but when they were accused the double standard applied. (See Appendix, Table 4.1.) Several factors may account for the fact that accusations were exceptional among the black population. First of all, the seriousness with which black women entered church initiation rites transformed their behavior, especially their sexual behavior, according to Herbert Gutman.[68] Their long retreat into prayer and change of dress indicated the ways "in which slaves managed the difficult transition to adulthood and from prenuptial sexual freedom to postmarital fidelity."[69] Therefore, the few among black women converts who violated evangelical sexual standards would have been obvious candidates for church discipline. Second, the master, rather than the church, dealt directly with most black misconduct. A third consideration involves the structure of authority in separate black conferences. Whites initiated "colored conferences" to review cases of black misconduct, but white moderators conducted the meetings. The white congregation acted as a review board in selected cases in which questions of black discipline were not resolved. It happened in the Beaverdam Baptist Church on 19 December 1840, when a white elder accused Seala, a slave, of adultery, that "after some deliberation the church appointed a collerd [sic] conference for her benefit."[70] Seala acknowledged her transgression to the black meeting and the church forgave her. However, Sister Harler, a bondwoman, continued to press the charge of adultery against Sister Seala for living with a man, Partriet, who had another wife. The church then appointed Jonathan Davis, a white man, to inquire of Partriet's owner, J. T. Irvin, if he intended to allow Partriet to see his former wife. Jonathan Davis reported to "the regular [white] conference" that Partriet's wife lived two hundred miles away and that Irvin had granted permission to his servant to take another wife. The church then dropped the matter.[71] Although local churches struggled with the issue, separation by sale usually constituted a divorce.[72]

What is significant about the church's procedure is that only in exceptional circumstances did the white church intervene in black meetings. Blacks decided less controversial matters among themselves and may have protected their own from exposure to white discipline. This may also account for the few black cases that came to the attention of the white congregation.

The double standard revealed itself as a clear pattern in North Carolina and Georgia church trials. Black women were accused of sexual offenses twice as often as men, but a greater percentage of black men were charged with disorderly conduct. Racial discrimination also influenced charges against church members. (Compare Appendix, Tables 1.2 and 4.1.) Black women were more often accused of disorderly conduct than white women, thus preserving the hierarchical and social order. Black men were charged with sexual trangressions twice as often as white men. The sexual double standard therefore worked most consistently in favor of the white male. Nevertheless, disorderly conduct, intoxication, profanity, and absence were more often white male offenses. Statutes prohibiting the sale of alcohol to slaves, attempts to control gambling by black men, and black habits of deference discouraged drinking, gambling, and profanity in the presence of whites.[73] White women indulged in dancing and idolatry, which were regarded as sins of improper intimacy by the church; in reality, they were the sins of a leisured class. More importantly, a higher percentage of white women than black was accused of sexual offenses. Perhaps this was true not only because of the greater emphasis on the change of sexual behavior among black women converts but also because there were higher expectations for white women's purity and therefore greater supervision among white southerners.[74]

For the reasons explained above, few instances of punishment for sexual offenses are available. Nevertheless, scattered evidence suggests a double standard applied. The only person excluded for a sexual offense in the six North Carolina and Georgia churches that I studied was a woman, Patsy, who was a member of the Beaverdam Baptist Church. All three men so accused escaped excommunication while one man suffered censure rather than exclusion for sexual misconduct. Furthermore, the one individual restored by the church was a man.

Evangelical discipline reinforced behavioral norms and racial roles, and it tolerated black collectivity in "colored conferences." Such discipline, a force for social integration, together with conversion experience, a source of psychological integration, provided substance for Afro-American identity. Conversion contributed toward the Afro-American evangelical woman's personal maturity and social integration. The maturation process, that is, the development of a willingness to make difficult decisions, endure irrational, ambivalent, even violent circumstances, and maintain a belief that circumstances, no matter how outrageous, were manageable, combined interior conviction and sense of purpose with a pattern of determined behavior.

Many Afro-American forms of expression were evangelical; therefore, it is important to consider evangelical influence in black culture generally. African culture easily adapted Christian concepts, symbols, and images, and thus responded enthusiastically to the evangelical "experience" so similar to African spirit possession, initiation rites, and chants.[75] Thus the permeability of the boundaries of religious and psychological experience made evangelical expression significant in Afro-American culture.

Afro-American religious imagery is not merely indicative of social behavior; it also expresses religious symbolism and social forms that draw their meaning from the same source—the Afro-American community.[76] Specifically, black evangelical imagery explores the cultural dimension of black experience because religious symbolism is rooted in familial and proto-familial relationships of the black community. Consequently, the maternal and familial symbolism of conversion imagery suggests the primacy of family associations. Women who wove, washed, and sewed together did so for the sake of family and community well-being. Supportive female relationships existed, but because of the cultural ambivalence that manifested itself in the sexual segregation, gender identification, and group consciousness of Afro-American women, a stable, consistent, durable women's culture did not evolve.

The complexity of Afro-American women's identity formation previously explored in religious symbolism may also be examined in their work roles and relationships. Maturation of the female slave personality may be indicated by productivity at work, resistance to oppression, and provision for families.

Because work roles crossed over in the fields and sometimes in the slave cabin, a strict sexual division of labor did not exist. Sexual segregation was not consistently applied within Afro-American culture. Women's work, whether in the field or in the slave community, provided for the maintenance of the Afro-American family and community; the community subsumed women's group consciousness, and family identification weakened women's gender identity.

Historians often make the point that owners generally valued female slaves for their reproductive capacity and male slaves for their productive capacity. However, as productive workers, women carried a triple responsibility—as field hands for the master, as household laborers for the mistress, and as domestic workers for their own families. Their productive versatility made them valuable hands.

As manual laborers, bondwomen were assigned tasks from ploughing to road construction. As field hands, they hoed and prepared the fields for cultivation. The former slave Nancy Boudry remembered that she "had to work hard, plow, split wood just like a man." Although the master did not often designate which sex was required to do certain work, as historian Jacqueline Jones points out, black women regarded working like a man uncharacteristic of bondwomen.[77] In winter, women picked, ginned, and packed cotton. They also repaired fences, painted houses, and helped to build roads.[78]

In addition to hard labor, bondwomen performed extra duty for their mistresses. On numerous plantations, after women came in from the field, they had to spin. Muriel Galloway claimed that black women often spun as many as seven cuts, some before and some after dinner. It was often midnight when a bell signaled the end of a day's spinning on one Georgia plantation.[79]

As household servants, bondwomen were often accomplished seamstresses and weavers. Skilled black women served as the family seamstress or cut out and sewed slave clothes.[80] On plantations where there were no skilled bondwomen, sewing tasks fell to the mistress. Generally, however, the entire process from picking cotton to sewing the finished product was accomplished through slave effort.

Such productivity earned a bondwoman two dresses a year and two cotton

shirts for her children. Forced to provide additional clothing for their families, grandmothers sewed for their grandchildren or black women weavers
secretly wove extra cloth for themselves.[81] Other bondwomen adroitly manipulated the mistress in order to obtain more goods. This is shown in the
following vignette written by Anna Maria Akehurst.

According to the story, a newly appointed housekeeper announced to the
servants that the women were entitled to eighteen yards of material. She then
called three women to the storeroom to measure out their allotment. Immedi-
ately, the women complained about the scant allotment of cloth, and one
demanded material for a new coat: "How you spect I can work in de field
when I cant get over de fence widout tearnin my coat?" The housekeeper
replied that she was giving them all she was told to give them. The women
continued to argue and said that their mistress always gave them more than
eighteen yards of cotton and wool. Furthermore, they insisted, since they
always made the cloth in their own homes without supervision, why should it
now be rationed? The housekeeper responded that the master "was not going
to give cloth to servants to waste." Undaunted, the bondwomen devised a
strategy to trick the naive housekeeper. They measured their own cloth using a long measure. Naturally, the women measured out for themselves the
entire stock of cloth. When the hapless young housekeeper challenged their
method, the women chided her and said that they "has alers measured de
cloth and nobody neber cuesed dem cheaten afore, and dat she is alers
fenden fault." Defeated, the housekeeper allowed them to proceed until the
planter's daughter intervened and ended the rout. At stake in this confrontation was the well-being of the black women's families. The insufficient clothing allowance forced the women to use whatever means they could to make
up the difference in the allotment of cloth.[82]

Providing for women's families took considerable effort. It was only after
they had completed their fieldwork and their spinning that bondwomen
could tend to their own families. Some idea of the sacrifice made by these
women can be judged from the testimony of John Goodwin, a former slave
who remembered his mother washing, patching, and cooking late into the
night to be ready for the next day in the fields.[83]

As a result of their productivity, Afro-American women won positions of
trust and confidence and often joined mammies as administrative agents
for their masters and mistresses. Indeed, the former slave Margaret Levine
claimed that her mother actually acted as an overseer: "She hired hands, and
would see about food and everything."[84] In the fields, some black women
had management positions. A Mississippi woman became a "hoe overseer,"
supervising the work of other women field hands, and Lucy Skipwith maintained the master household in John Hartwell Cocke's experimental slave
community. As seamstress, weaver, nurse, and most prominently, teacher,

Lucy Skipwith surveyed all aspects of the community, reported faithfully to her master, and even offered him advice or pleaded a case for the needs of various slaves.[85]

Nevertheless, managerial positions for black women were rare, and in general the white woman assumed authority over the black women in her household. It was inevitable, however, that working relationships would lead to frustration and sometimes punishment, a circumstance most mistresses did not relish. Laura Beecher Comer noted in her diary that she "had to punish a servant. . . . [It was a] terrible duty."[86] Although self-restraint was characteristic of most women owners, mistresses were not considered too delicate to employ forms of violence, and instances of cruelty toward black women occurred not infrequently.

Former slave James Curry of North Carolina related "instances of woman laying heavy stripes upon the back of *woman*, and which was sometimes attended with effects most shocking."[87] One slave narrative devoted to a mistress's abuse is entitled, "I Can't Forgive Her, The Way She Used to Beat Us."[88] Resentment festered in the wake of such treatment. A sense of outrage against her mistress remained with freedwoman Charity Bowery until her death. Interviewed by Lydia Maria Child in New York in 1848, Charity Bowery described how Mistress McKinley had sold all of her children: "One after another—one after another—she sold 'em away from me. Oh, how many times that woman broke my heart." Charity Bowery's desire for retribution plainly expressed itself in her reply to a person who informed her that Mrs. McKinley was visiting in town and asked if she had any messages for her. The former slave replied that the messenger should tell the former mistress: "Prepare to meet poor Charity at the Judgment seat."[89] Some slaves who experienced white women's cruelty merely disguised their contempt for such a mistress. This is evident in the case of the death of a particularly mean mistress. At her funeral the slaves wept and feigned grief, but once they got outside the house they muttered, "Old God damn son-of-a-bitch she gone on down to hell."[90] In another setting, a mistress lay dying but told a black attendant that she was all right. Upon overhearing the mistress a child informed her mother, "Yes, she is all right; all right for hell."[91]

Black women resisted total domination by white women. They did this by feigning ill health or by slowing down their work. Sheer stubbornness and impudence sometimes held the mistress at bay.[92] This is well illustrated in Anna Maria Akehurst's amusing story about a black woman's efforts to undermine her mistress's control. The impatient mistress had instructed a servant, Laura, to tell Aunt Fanny, the cook, to hurry dinner. After waiting some time, the mistress sent another servant, Harriet, to get Laura. Both servants then disappeared and still no dinner was served. Finally, the mistress arose, went to the door and unceremoniously yelled across to the kitchen to tell Aunt

Fanny to hurry with dinner. Fanny replied, "Yes'm I'se commin presenly soon, as I tend to my child." Reprimanded a second time when the dinner still had not appeared, Fanny retorted: "I works all I can, I works more'n all de nigers in de house den you allers finden fault with me, my own mussus nebben done so." Taken by surprise, the mistress threatened, "I'll have your master whip you, who am I if I am not your own mistress?" Defiantly, Fanny insisted, "Well he must whip den case I cant do no more, you is my Masters second wife, and we all mighty sorry our Mis'tus dead." Akehurst's narrative concluded: "Whereupon, [the cook] started for the kitchen to tell her fellow servants how she had used up Miss Bell, and the lady returned to the parlor to weep."[93]

In the contest of wills between black and white women, defiant behavior was understandably risky. Ultimately such behavior pushed women toward confrontation, with the result that black women were either sold or hired out. Few bondwomen escaped punishment, but some of them fought back. Such was the case of a former slave who related the story of how her mother, Nancy Bailey, prevented her mistress from attacking her. Her daughter said, "I seen Mistress come in there with a bucket of water to slo[s]h on my mother, and mother grabbed the bucket and threw it on her, and the old woman hollered murder."[94] A Mississippi woman remembered that it was impossible to hire her mother out because she might "whip the white folks."[95]

Another daughter named Cornelia remembered her mother, Fannie, as "a demon—Ma fussed, fought, and kicked all the time."[96] Fannie's independence, conspicuous on the small farm where they lived in Eden, Tennessee, ran counter to Mistress Jennings's will. Cornelia told an impressive story of her mother's refusal to be broken:

> One day my mother's temper ran wild. For some reason Mistress Jennings struck her with a stick. Ma struck back and a fight followed. . . . For half hour they wrestled in the kitchen. Mistress, seeing that she could not get the better of ma, ran out in the road, with ma right on her heels. In the road, my mother flew into her again. The thought seemed to race across my mother's mind to tear mistress' clothing off her body. She suddenly began to tear Mistress Jennings' clothes off. She caught hold, pulled, ripped and tore. Poor mistress was nearly naked when the storekeeper got to them and pulled ma off. "Why Fannie, what do you mean by that?" he asked. "Why I'll kill her, I'll kill her dead if she ever strikes me again."[97]

Those women who did defy white female authority often left daughters a legacy of resistance. Fannie warned her child: "I'll kill you, gal, if you don't stand up for yourself. Fight, and if you can't fight, kick; if you can't kick, then bite." Fannie's rebellion deeply influenced her daughter and she followed her mother's example. After witnessing abuse on the farm, Cornelia decided to pursue an independent course. She stopped playing with white children and began to scrap with them. When observers said, "Cornelia is the spit of her mother," Cornelia determined to be even more like her mother.[98]

The mother-daughter relationship was a key factor in women's survival. Mothers taught daughters the necessary values and skills of survival and they also tried to protect them. "My mother used to teach me how to listen and hear and keep my mouth shut," said a woman who survived slavery. She explained, "Sometimes she [her mother] would have a little meeting, and some of the slaves from the neighboring farms would come over. We children had better get out, or at least make like we were not listening to what was being said and done." Warned not to tell "the white folks" of the mother's activity, the daughter, though frightened, held fast. When whites asked, "Wasn't so and so over in your mamma's cabin such and such a time, or didn't you see or hear them talking and planning to do this thing or that?," the daughter answered, "I don't know" or "No."[99] The lie put the girl in a dilemma: if caught, the master would whip her, but if she told the truth, her mother would whip her. In a case like this, lying protected family and community. Sometimes, too, maternal manipulation benefited the daughter. Lucy Skipwith wrote to her master, pleading to regain control of her errant daughter who had been hired out to another plantation and was caught stealing. She claimed that since her daughter's employers allowed her to be idle, the young girl was susceptible to the corrupt influence of a fellow servant. Lucy's arguments and skill at rearranging the servant roster to accommodate her daughter wrung support from her master and enabled Lucy Skipwith to bring her daughter back under her own supervision.[100] Some mothers managed to buy their children out of slavery, but more often they failed. When Emily Russel fell into the hands of a well-known slave trader in Alexandria, Virginia, in January 1850, she pleaded with her mother, Nancy Cartwright, to save her from being sold: "Oh Mother! my dear mother! Come now and see your distressed and heartbroken daughter once more. Mother! my dear mother! do not forsake me; for I feel desolate! Please come now."[101] But Joseph Bruin, who interceded on Nancy Cartwright's behalf, was unable to prevent Emily's sale, and the girl was then placed in a coffle traveling south. On 4 May 1850 the *Christian Citizen* reported that Emily Russel had died while passing through Georgia.[102]

Mothers could offer only marginal protection for their children, but they did provide daughters with the tools needed for family survival. They taught them spinning, weaving, and carding. Together they alternated spinning in order to meet the quota set by the mistress. Female kin worked together; cousins wove cloth while sets of sisters tended to domestic work, and along with other relatives mothers and daughters labored side by side as field hands. Occasionally, mothers trained daughters in special skills such as nursing and the care of children.[103]

Black women's primary relationships therefore were with female kin who taught them skills and worked with them in the field and household. Thus Afro-American corporate family values largely determined the woman's attitude toward work, toward the mistress, and toward the manager. On a large plantation, the mistress's job may have been supervisory, but the essential task of teaching and training remained a responsibility of black women. This responsibility, especially toward family members, increased black women's mutual supportiveness.

According to historians Deborah White and Jacqueline Jones, women's work was often indistinguishable from men's; nevertheless, certain domestic chores fell to the lot of women. Such chores as quilting, washing, sewing, and communal cooking encouraged female solidarity and the bonds of sisterhood.[104] However, it may be argued that since the primary function of women's work was the maintenance of family, group consciousness was more likely to be community-centered. Women did the family work on Saturdays, and they rushed through their spinning and weaving tasks to be home with their families by sundown.[105] Jones notes that "in the quarters, group work melded into family responsibilities, for the communal spirit was but a manifestation of primary kin relationships."[106] Even "quiltins," traditionally a sacrosanct female activity, may have become a community effort among Afro-Americans. Emily Burke reported that "the men sew as well as the women." She witnessed a quilting party at which "men and women were seated promiscuously around the frame, very quietly yet as expeditiously plying the needle . . . as if their lives depended upon having the quilt out before midnight. After the work the women and men danced and socialized."[107] Perhaps the life of the community did depend upon the quilt, which both provided warmth for a family and was a source of community entertainment.

When women worked in the fields, communal cooking was necessary on some plantations. Communal cooking, a task that fell to older women, provided a domestic service that benefited the entire community. Certain female roles were skilled—midwives, wet nurses, chambermaids, "doctor women" —but with few exceptions, even skilled women were liable to be assigned to the fields. Thus even skilled roles were not specialized, and skilled women were not set apart.

On the plantations where family and corporate values did not operate, women were sensitive to the lack of female support. One black woman, separated from her husband, complained to him in a letter that on her plantation "the servants are very disagreeable; they do all they can to set my mistress against me."[108] The most destructive female—"the tattlin' woman"— operated outside family constraint. A product of an oppressive system, the informer accommodated authority in order to insure a margin of personal security and, in doing so, disrupted a skein of relationships built upon trust. Black women ostracized any woman who informed on the business of the quarters.[109]

Friendships among black women were hindered by the family-oriented structure of the Afro-American community, by the fear of betrayal, and by personal conflicts. Lack of mobility and freedom to choose work were often responsible for explosive personal conflicts among servants. Adele Allston Vanderhorst witnessed "a temper" fight between her servants, Issabelle and Emma, in which the two women clawed at each other and pulled each other's hair.[110] Incompatibility sometimes operated in an environment of distrust. As one Tennessee freedwoman reminisced, "They [white owners] taught us to be against one another."[111] The slave narratives reveal a certain ambivalence about closeness among black women. For example, Lu, a young nursemaid, complained about her treatment by other slaves on the plantation. "They kept doing me so bad I started cussing. I said, 'I'm getting goddamned tired of your knocking me 'round.'" There was one particularly mean old woman, Ailee, who cursed her and threatened to beat her. When Lu told two other women, Mary Ann and Hanna Bell, about Ailee's threats, they said they would beat up Lu if she did not whip Ailee. Encouraged by the women, Lu waylaid the old servant, Ailee, and they got into a terrible row for which they were both later punished.[112] Lu learned to stand up for herself through the support of friends, but the action was diverted against another bondwoman in the community. In another account, when a fellow captive asked Mattie Griffiths, "Have you no friends?," she replied, "You do not talk like one familiar with slavery, to speak of a slave's having friends."[113] Mattie Griffiths claimed that she had been betrayed by a household slave and beaten nearly to death. However, Mattie Griffiths did eventually find a close friend, Louise, a freedwoman, on whom she relied when her fiancé committed suicide. Mattie Griffith's attachment to Louise may be attributed to the urban environment in which she lived and the fact that her mistress retained few slaves. In an urban household associations were more difficult to form. Rural-slave kin networks and the intimacy of plantation communities were not as easily replicated in southern cities as in the countryside. Consequently, slave association included friendship as a primary relationship in the cities.[114]

However, adaptive kin networks typified slave association far more frequently than friendship between strangers. Afro-Americans valued kinship and, as historians Sidney W. Mintz and Richard Price argue, newly arrived slaves torn from their traditional kin ties continued to regard "kinship as the normal idiom of social relations." And in the absence of blood relations slaves "modeled their new social ties upon those of kinship," borrowing Anglo-American kin terms to label their own relationships as "'bro,' 'uncle,' 'auntie,' 'gran.'" The practice remained part of Afro-American tradition well into the nineteenth century. This suggests that slaves "invested non-kin slave relationships with symbolic kin meanings and functions."[115]

The bond between Charlotte Brooks and Jane Lee illustrates the meaning of Afro-American association. Charlotte Brooks told this story of their relationship to Octavia V. Rogers Albert:

> Four years after I came to Louisiana the speculators brought another woman out here from my old State. She was sold to a man near my master's plantation. I heard of it, and, thinks I, "that might be some of my kinfolks, or somebody that knew my mother." So the first time I got a chance I went to see the woman.

Charlotte Brooks ignored the admonition of her "white folks" not to venture off the plantation to visit and instead traveled quickly down the road to meet the woman. When she arrived, she said:

> I met a man, and I asked him what was the woman's name; he said her name was Jane Lee. I went around to the quarters where all the black people lived, and I found her. I went up to her and said, "Howdy do, Aunt Jane?" She said, "How do you know me child?" I said, "I heard you just came from Virginia; I came from that State too." . . . Aunt Jane was no kin to me, but I felt that she was because she came from my old home. Me and Aunt Jane talked and cried that Sunday evening till nearly dark.[116]

Charlotte Brooks found kinship in Jane Lee. Friendship would hardly express the meaning of her deep attachment to the older woman she called "Aunt Jane."

Adoptive kin often acted with maternal care. In one case, a frightened orphan child who was sold ran away and was later captured. An older slave, Aunt Bet, then spoke to the child and gently said, "Honey, don't do that, Mr. Ellison done bought you, and you must go with him."[117] It was Aunt Bet who gathered the girl's belongings and set her on her course. When Mattie Griffith's mother could not bear to tell her that she had been sold, she asked Kitty, an old servant, to break the news. Aunt Kitty then put her hand on Mattie's shoulder and told her, "Alas, poor chile, you mus' place your trus' in the good God above, you mus' look to Him for help; you are gwine to leave your mother now." And later in her life after Mattie Griffiths suffered a severe beating, Aunt Polly, an ill-tempered woman, took pity on Mattie and tended to her. As a result, Mattie felt a deep maternal affection for Aunt Polly.[118]

The use of the kinship idiom to describe relationships between nonrelatives suggests the intensity of Afro-American group consciousness. Women related to one another as family members rather than as members of a discrete gender-defined subculture. Black women and men accepted non-kin as family and in so doing reinforced individual identity and expanded their sense of community—community separate and distinct from that of whites. The conversion experience initiated converts even more fully into the life of the black evangelical community; many women accepted visible positions in Afro-American religious life. Church discipline differentiated between whites and blacks with regard to charges and punishment. Therefore the church further encouraged black religious unity.

Black solidarity did not exclude ties to the white community, for evangelical social responsibility assumed a mutual set of obligations and duties in the mistress-bondwoman relationship.[119] At great risk, some white women taught servants to read and write, while others, either out of duty or of affection, tended sick and dying women.[120] Elizabeth Lindsay Lomax, for example, recorded on one occasion that she "took a long walk this afternoon to see my old servant, Ailsy, who is sick."[121] When her servant, Daphney, died, Caroline Homassel Thornton worried that she might not have taught her correctly on religious matters.[122]

Even in delicate circumstances, some southern white women acted on behalf of female dependents. For example, Mary Ann Cobb took charge of Pauline, a mulatto child, when she believed that the girl could not be raised in her father-in-law's house without risk to the girl. She then proceeded to raise Pauline in her own home, educating her and providing her with useful skills. Mary Ann Cobb believed the girl's salvation lay in sending her north where the young woman might find a good education and eventually a job. Although Pauline's fate is unknown, Mrs. Cobb did assume full responsibility for her and did not treat her as a servant.[123]

The relationship between mammies and their white charges indicates affectionate ties between black and white women. Amanda Virginia Chappelear wept when she was parted from her old mammy. She wrote:

> though she be a servant, tears gushed from my heart as each said "goodbye." . . . [W]ho was it that took me from my Mother's arms and watched me in my childhood gambols, played with me in the old familiar scenes at her old home . . . who sat by my side when I slumbered in my cradle and watched there[?][124]

And in another home the children begged to go with their mammy when she threatened to leave and join the Yankees.[125]

In spite of instances of black and white women's mutual affection and regard, slavery divided women. The proprietary interest in slaves separated mistress and bondwomen by class, culture, community, and family system. Moreover, the sexual exploitation of slave women by white males produced enmity between black and white women. Anne Scott documented the thousands of divorce cases in which white women contended black women were responsible for their difficulties. And, according to Scott, black mistresses brought as servants into the household by the master treated the mistress "insolently."[126] Thus, except for certain instances, white women related to black women not as oppressed sisters but as sexual rivals, servants, dependents, and inferiors.

Resentment of slavery, however, rarely led to acceptance of abolitionism on the part of white women. The proprietary nature of the relationship undermined any radical discontent white women may have felt with the institution of slavery. As Scott has demonstrated, women did hate their husband's philandering in the slave quarters and the sheer drudgery of supervising slaves. Nevertheless, women made their most damning antislavery statements in their memoirs. Such sentiments may have reflected the general postwar reaction to slavery in the South.[127] In the antebellum South, doubts about slavery were rarely systematic; more often they were repressed or resolved in favor of the institution.

A case in point is Ella Thomas's attempt to resolve her doubts concerning slavery. Educated and a gifted diarist, she turned to fiction to resolve her dilemma. The abolitionist theme of *Uncle Tom's Cabin* impressed her, but she also read *Nellie Norton*, a proslavery apologia that she hoped would convince her that slavery was right. As a slave owner and a devout Methodist, Mrs. Thomas provided for the material and spiritual needs of her servants. Moreover, she respected talented individuals, such as the black preacher Sam Drayton. Nevertheless, her criticism of slavery was based upon its demoralization of white families. "The institution of slavery degrades the white man more than the Negro and exerts a deleterious effect upon our children," she claimed. So she turned to the Bible for a resolution, but she later confessed that she felt "if the Bible was right then slavery *must be*." The postwar reaction against slavery disillusioned Ella Thomas because of her religious belief in the legitimacy of slavery, and she discontinued attending services for five years. She wished to be rid of her slaves and hire servants, yet could not bring herself to emancipate her slaves "for the sake of principle."[128]

Another wartime diarist, Dolly Sumner Lunt, when faced with the impending end of slavery, eased her doubts when she wrote:

> I have never felt that slavery was altogether right, for it is abused by men, and I have often heard Mr. Burge say that if he could see that it was sinful for him to own slaves, if he felt, that it was wrong, he would take them where he would free them. He would not sin for his right hand. The purest and holiest men have owned them, and I can see nothing in the Scripture which forbids it. I have never bought or sold slaves and I have tried to make life easy and pleasant to those that have been bequeathed me by the dead. I have never ceased to work. Many a Northern housekeeper has a much easier time than a Southern matron with her hundred Negroes.[129]

Dolly Sumner Lunt relied upon planter wisdom, biblical justifications, and her attention to duty in order to temper her doubts about "the peculiar institution." The war silenced the doubts of Lucy Wood Butler. She explained her loyal position, even though it meant a defense of the slave trade that she condemned:

> I can never be a disunionist whilst I believe that as soon as it is in the power of the South the slave trade will be reopened, an idea which is to me extremely revolting and, apart from the act itself, I feel that the consequences must be in a few years dreadful. . . . But I have no political opinion, and have a peculiar dislike to all females who discuss such matters. . . . [W]hen the time comes I will act the Southern lady for the sake of the country.[130]

The outspokenness of which Lucy Butler complained referred to women's defense of slavery. Visitors to the prewar South attested to women's spirited, "obstinate" support for slavery. Mrs. Basil Hall, wife of a well-known British traveler and writer, found herself challenged by a group of aroused southern women. Mrs. Hall reported that she "went to a party at Judge DeSaussure's where [she] had as tough an argument regarding slavery with some ladies as ever Basil had on any subject with gentlemen."[131] More politely, Catherine Broun asked her unionist friends why, if they objected to slavery "as a stain upon the nation," did they not allow secession?[132] Fredrika Bremer complained that "women grieve me by being so short-sighted on this subject, and by being still more irritable and violent than the men."[133]

Mistresses may have believed themselves slaves to their plantation duties. One woman remembered, "It was a saying that the mistress of a plantation was the most complete slave on it."[134] Nevertheless, white women's support of slavery prevented all but a few extraordinarily keen individuals from identifying white women's lot with slavery. The perceptive Mary Chesnut observed, "There is no slave, after all, like a wife."[135] Ann Scott sees in this parallel made by a white woman a connection with abolitionism. Scott argues, "Perhaps it was understanding growing from this identification with slaves which led so many southern women to be private abolitionists, and even a few to be public ones."[136]

A few white women were abolitionists.[137] And some black and white women formed extraordinary relationships of affection and mutual respect. Black women's loyalty to white women sometimes transcended regard for their own personal bondage.[138] Yet, white women bought and sold black women, a fact that obviated any possibility of the formation of the "bonds of womanhood" that went beyond race.[139] The proprietary nature of the relationship between white and black women separated the interests of the two groups, even though at times mistresses invoked their power of ownership to protect black women. Southern white women's proprietary interest in slaves was both legal and psychological. Women owned slaves and were legally entitled to dispose of them. Along with their husbands, they cosigned bills of sale or hired their servants out. Legally, bondwomen were property, and southern women accepted their right of title to and expectation of profit from black women as property.

White women obviously had a vested interest in slavery and usually defended it both in principle and in fact. Miss Abby, a unionist, recorded that as Federal forces advanced into Georgia, a woman declared, "I'd just as soon see my children on the cooling board than give up my niggers to the Yankees."[140] White brides showed their appreciation of the economic value of slavery by accepting wedding gifts of black women and children. Pride in ownership led families to show off their acquisitions at camp meetings or boast of a black girl as "my little breeder."[141]

Proprietary interests were often difficult to separate from humanitarian concerns. Sensitive to the plight of a slave woman who suffered during childbirth, Sara Edmondston resolved to make the woman's son a household servant if he survived. She wrote, "If the child lives I intend to bring him up as a table servant, have him in by the time he can talk and walk and never let him be rusty—some time to look forward to, but I have a stout heart and am hopeful."[142] Under Sara Edmondston's protection the boy would receive special care. At the same time, the mistress would gain a well-trained servant. Under the circumstances, hers was a humanitarian gesture. Sometimes, too, the proprietary interest worked in favor of the female slave. Sympathetic mistresses might extend their power of ownership to protect slaves. For example, both Emma Lowran and Hester Hunter, former slaves, testified that their mistresses would not allow their "property" to be punished.[143] In her account, Emma Lowran noted that "sometimes Mr. Smith would go to whip her mother for some reason, but Mrs. Smith wouldn't let him do so, for she told her husband that the woman belonged to her and she was not going to have her whipped."[144]

Unfortunately, class, racial prejudice, and sexual competition proved stronger than the impulse to identify with the unfortunate slave. Harriet Jacobs, a slave woman sexually harassed by her master for over ten years, complained that her mistress might have warned or protected younger slave women against the lecherous planter, but "for them she had no sympathy."[145] Jealous wives may have resented the institution that encouraged husbands' philandering with black women, but white women despised the servant as well and thus could have little sympathy with the bondwoman's circumstance. This was certainly true in the case of Laura Beecher Comer, who led her servants in prayer and concerned herself with their religious progress. Nevertheless, she wrote bitterly:

I won't spend all my days looking after Negroes. It's a terrible life! Who can appreciate or understand anything about such a life but a woman who married a *Bachelor* who has lived with his negroes as *equals*; at bed and board! What a life *many poor wives* have to live in uncomplaining silence. If they say *one* word, censure, without measure is heaped upon them. . . . [W]hat *barbarities* I have suffered . . . what I have endured! And God only knows how much more I am still to endure; from this man and his negroes![146]

In this instance the wife recognized that the slave system protected male privileges, and such a situation did little to bind her to black women. The distance between black and white women made the mistress's identification with the slave nearly impossible. Class and racial prejudice widened the gulf between them. Although Laura Beecher Comer appreciated the young servant, Rena, whom she was raising, she recorded in her diary on an occasion when the servant was bathing her feet: "The Negro is a dark, ignorant being; consequently obstinate as all *ignorant* beings are."[147] In the light of such racism, the Negro then was only fit to remain a servant.

As members of distinct cultures, communities, and family systems (children of mixed parentage were rarely recognized as members of the white family), black and white women were only able to develop exceptional ties. For the most part, racism, ownership, and jealousy separated women by class and race.

Within the Afro-American community a familial relationship often developed between black women not related by blood. Thus, Afro-American family values defined priorities and relationships in the slave community. To some extent, family considerations determined black women's work, because female kin trained young women in household and plantation skills. Furthermore, maternal concern for their families motivated black women to form strategies that would help them obtain more food and clothing and greater security.

Black women's identity emerged out of the struggle for survival, but it was denied by the white community until emancipation gave blacks the right to their own autonomy. Afro-American community and culture therefore provided the basis for change in the relationships between black and white that occurred in the Civil War. The intransigence of the white community, however, limited change in racial relationships.

5. THE BLIGHTED EDEN

*When the blighted beauties of Eden are presented to our eyes, it is not
that our regrets may be excited from contrasting it with its former
glory, but that we may be made to shudder at the guilt of sin, and
tremble at the danger of disobeying the Most High.*
Henry Kollock, *Sermons on Various Subjects*, 1:4

he Civil War uprooted the slave system and devastated the
political and economic order of the Old South. Emancipa-
tion severed former ties of bondage; the war divided plantations into a system of tenancies, and loyalty oaths barred
Confederate leaders from office. Nevertheless, traditional
familial and religious bonds survived the loss of the Confederacy enabling southern communities to revive a racist
system, regain political ascendancy, and rebuild their economy. Ironically,
then, the war for union did not destroy the culture of the South. Indeed,
southern culture survived precisely *because* of its local attachments and its
peculiar community structure. Therefore, in the wake of the Civil War, the
South retained the very structure that had previously limited the social role of
women.

Women who had matured in the years before the Civil War discovered that
the war made exhausting demands on their talents for management and
survival. But although an alternate experience for women and new responsibilities raised expectations about changes in women's roles, the southern
community obstructed any radical shift in women's status.

Psychosocial and historical studies suggest that war does not necessarily
destroy kinship networks. This was especially true in the South. Traditional
kin ties held through the war as is evidenced in demographic recovery, rural
persistence patterns, and refugee movements—that is, temporary residence
with kin. By the 1880s the southern population had returned to nearly normal
prewar levels. Furthermore, the southern population tended to reside longer
in the countryside than in the cities, which is an indication of stable kin
relationships. Nor did low urban persistence patterns mean that southerners
cut off family ties. And, finally, it was mostly to kin that southerners turned
when the occupation forced evacuation.[1] The stability of kin networks, then,
enabled the southern community to survive the war, but family ties also
preserved a largely traditional set of social roles.

Studies of families under wartime conditions indicate that unless severe
trauma is induced by extreme situations, stable family conditions can reduce
psychic damage. Psychologists have noted, for instance, that in World War II

British family psychoses decreased if community bonds were strong. More specifically, children fared better if they were kept in their neighborhood with their families even if the area happened to be a war zone. Violent eruptions in divided communities, such as northern Ireland or the Cherokee Nation after removal, on the other hand, inflicted severe psychological damage upon families and individuals.[2]

Even though prewar unionist sympathies flourished in the border states where traditional family animosities divided loyalties in mountain communities and some disaffected yeoman farmers and nonplanters refused to support planter interests, the South was not a divided community during the war. The presence of some unionist sympathies in southern subregions—mountains and swamps—did lead to polarization, as Philip Paludan's analysis of a divided mountain community shows. However, his study is the exception that proves the rule. Loyalties in North Carolina divided along family lines and men fought to revenge family interests. Persecution only reinforced unionist families' resistance to the Confederacy. Despite instances of violence directed toward unionists after the declaration of war, dissenters most often maintained silence and therefore suffered no greater community pressure than social distance.[3] It may be true, then, that the South, because it remained essentially undivided, retained family cohesion during the war.

In an analysis of the World War I German youth cohort, Peter Loewenberg examined the effects of devastation upon family stability. He concluded that the prolonged absence of both parents, the return of the father in defeat, extreme hunger and privation, and the national defeat and loss of prevailing political authority caused regression and traumatization among the young. The overwhelming consequences of starvation and deprivation—especially the "turnip" winter of 1916–17 in which 750,000 Germans died of starvation—produced feelings of helplessness and anxiety in young people regardless of family conditions.[4]

Conditions in the rural South, on the other hand, mitigated some of the more devastating psychological effects of the war. Southern children aided their mothers in tending to the farms in the absence of fathers and therefore experienced to a large degree a stable family life. And while the South suffered hunger and privation, southern farms provided food. The Federal Blockade, although effective, did not produce massive starvation on the scale suffered by the Germans because the South, unlike Germany, was self-sufficient and did not wholly depend upon imported foodstuffs. Moreover, the Federal occupation, which effected social and political change, nevertheless provided a measure of protection for the southern population. Southern wartime conditions, then, allowed a marginal security for family stability and the maintenance of kin ties.

Historians concentrate on the devastation and change in the old order but neglect the demographic trends that ultimately revived the southern community. First of all, the demographic recovery after the war is evidence of the resilience of the southern family system. The decline in white women's fertility characteristic of the first half of the century was exacerbated by the catastrophic effect of the war on the white male population.[5] Approximately 258,000 southern men were killed out of a white population of 5,500,000. Historian Ellis Paxson Oberholtzer estimated that even if the rate of increase of the white population had continued throughout the South during the war, the births would not have replaced the white adult population due to the high mortality rate.[6] The national prewar fertility decline, which included the South, may be contrasted with the postwar rise in population. Referred to as the "vital revolution," the rising standard of living and improvements in health care caused a decline in death rates in the late nineteenth century.[7] Fon W. Boardman, Jr., has indicated that in the last forty years of the century, farm population increased about 50 percent while nonfarm population increased 400 percent.[8] The rural southern population increased somewhat in the latter part of the century, but population increased more rapidly in the urban Northeast, for example. Gains in the southern population may be attributed to the more balanced sex ratio that had been adjusted prior to 1880. In a study of Orange County, North Carolina, Robert Kenzer suggests that "during the 1870s the annual number of marriages and the age at marriage nearly duplicated the antebellum levels." Couples who had postponed marriages and men eager to marry wealthy war widows accounted for the rush into marriage. And by 1880 boys too young to serve in the army had also married, thus eventually returning the sex ratio to "more traditional levels."[9]

The geographic mobility or rate of persistence of southern populations in urban and rural areas is a second index of the strength of southern community bonds. Although studies of the antebellum South indicate a high level of geographic mobility,[10] analyses of postwar population movement emphasize greater urban mobility and relatively higher persistence rates in the countryside. Richard J. Hopkins's study of Atlanta and Paul B. Worthman's analysis of Birmingham indicate a high percentage of geographic mobility among the white native semiskilled and skilled working population in the latter decades of the nineteenth century.[11] Despite migration to southern cities, the population of the southern countryside demonstrated greater stability than did the population of the urban centers. Frank J. Huffman's study of Athens and Oconee County in Georgia between 1850 and 1880 "reveals that country people were consistently more stable than their town neighbors though never by an extreme margin."[12] And Jonathan M. Wiener's work suggests that wealthy planters with sons willing to manage their plantations tended to remain in postwar rural Alabama.[13] Kenzer noted a decline between 1860 and 1870 in the stability among the younger men of Orange County. Men married women outside their immediate neighborhood and moreover lived farther apart from their parents in this same decade. However, by 1880, the

next generation married within the neighborhood and established households near their parents.[14] Stable kin relationships associated with traditional rural culture therefore characterized southern society during the postwar period.

Moreover, low urban stability in the postwar period did not necessarily
mean alienation of family ties. Recent studies suggest that urban migration
among working-class and middle-class families does not lessen family con-
tacts. These studies perceive urban nuclear families not as isolated units but
as entities connected to a larger kin network. Michael Anderson's study of
nineteenth-century Lancashire demonstrated that the survival of a country
immigrant in an industrial city depended upon the worker's connection to
kin. Anderson concluded that families lived near each other in the city in
order to share information, aid, and assistance.[15] Studies of contemporary
southern and northeastern American families reveal the same pattern of dependency upon kin for help in finding jobs and in taking care of families.[16] In
her study of North Carolina communities, Elmora Matthews maintains that
the kin network represents a symbiotic relationship between town and country. The country migrant brings familial values, attitudes, and information to
the city so that country kin exert as much influence on city relatives as the
latter traditionally exert on the former.[17] Such recent works force scholars to
reexamine the pattern of family relationships that existed between city and
country kin in the nineteenth-century South and to explore the strength of
those ties during the crisis of the Civil War.

Refugees often moved between rural and urban regions during the crisis.
When confronted by forced migration, individual families often chose to
move to the homes of their kin, while others moved in with neighborhood,
church, or community groups that included kin.[18] Thus, further evidence
of the durability of the kinship network can be seen in southern refugee
patterns.

Family considerations greatly added to the burdens of refugees. At the
moment of departure, facing "carpets up, curtains down and rooms without
furniture," women anguished for their families. "I am willing to be poor, but
let, oh, let our family circles be unbroken," Judith McGuire, wife of a Washington, D.C., Episcopalian high school principal, wrote shortly before her
removal.[19]

The majority of the refugees were women who traveled with family and
servants. Fathers and husbands were often absent either because they were
on active duty or because they remained to secure their home and posses-
sions while the family moved on to safety. Susan Middleton's father, for example, stayed home until Federal forces moved into Charleston. From across
the river, he anxiously watched their home expecting to see it shrouded in
flames.[20]

As they were forced to flee, women often turned to their kin. For instance,

Fannie Page Hume and her family moved from the home of one cousin to another. Many of the women grew weary of their endless moving about and took solace in long visits. One young wife, tired of living out of trunks, gladly welcomed the visit of a cousin for a few nights. Mrs. Robert E. Lee, displaced early in the war, depended upon relatives for shelter. And Eliza Frances Andrews began her wartime journey traveling to her sister in southwest Georgia.[21]

At the beginning of the war families often took refuge close to home because they wanted to be near their kin and in their familiar neighborhood, and it was only later that some of them moved out of state.[22] The neighborhood, then, provided lines of support. Judith McGuire, who traveled with her daughters and grandchildren, found many friends along the way. She rejoiced when she arrived at Ashland, Virginia. "It seems marvelous," she said, "that . . . so many of our 'Seminary Hill' circle should be collected within the walls of this little cottage."[23]

Others found refuge among their own religious congregations; often, when the pastor fled, there were those in the church who followed.[24] The McGuires, for example, accompanied their pastor, who could provide hardly more than a blind faith to console his exiled parishioners. When they reached a crossroad, the minister finally spoke: "It makes not the slightest difference which road we take—we might as well drive to the right hand as to the left."[25] Often churches became a refuge for entire communities who fled bombardment. This was especially so for displaced dwellers of beleaguered cities. Many of the residents of Vicksburg, for example, lived in surrounding country churches during the siege. However, those who fled to "strange" churches, that is, congregations that did not include family or friends, complained of cool receptions. Denied pews at these unreceptive churches, some refugees started churches of their own.[26]

Domestic strain added to problems in the churches for refugees. The tension of living together in overcrowded conditions caused resentment and hard feelings. Sidney Harding, a Louisiana refugee, often mentioned that her mother and sisters became irritable because they lived constantly on the move. In the fall of 1863 Sidney wrote, "Ma has been out of sorts last two or three days. Been very cross. She has a very unfortunate temper. We have not patience enough with her. God help us all to live peaceable together." Of her sisters she complained to her diary, "Sisters A and F fuss and dispute so much. Then I never can be alone for a minute." The lack of a private room was very distressing to Sidney Harding; she longed to return to her own room at home, a hope ultimately extinguished by the Federal destruction of the family home in 1864.[27]

The presence of in-laws proved especially trying for the young mother, who found herself in a subservient position during her sojourn in the home of her husband's parents. The voluble northern-born Mrs. Joseph Semmes marooned in Canton, Mississippi, persistently complained to her husband about his cousins with whom she lived. Crowded in with two other families, Mrs. Semmes deplored the lack of privacy, which tended to exacerbate personal difficulties. More seriously, however, she resented the disciplining of her children by "Bena" and "Phonso" Semmes, and she complained that cousin "Phonso" set a poor example by his smoking and drinking habits.[28]

Overcrowding seemed minor when compared to the plight of those who suffered personal losses while on the move. Those who traveled with the aged or infirm risked such tragedy. Louisiana-born Lise Mitchell reported to her cousin Annie that they had camped out while on the road but were able to place her ailing grandmother in a farmhouse. The flight of Lise Mitchell's other cousin, however, proved less fortunate. The health of the cousin's mother declined rapidly while the family was detained on a schooner by a Yankee gunboat, and she died two weeks after their release.[29]

Illness, discomfort, and even the death of family members did not disrupt refugee patterns. Although the plight of the refugees may have strained family resources, causing temporary difficulties, it did not ultimately disrupt the function of the kinship system. Relatives felt a special obligation to shelter their kin whether they had the resources or not.[30] The cousins who moved in with Sidney Harding's family, for instance, upset the household, but the family continued to support them. Sidney Harding wrote privately, "I wish they would go," because she felt ashamed for her mother who cried when she could not provide for the family.[31] Other hosts were more generous under the circumstances, and one beleaguered kinsman wrote a gallant note to yet another cousin who asked for refuge: "Haven't seen you for years but [have] warm affection for you. . . . Trying to get room for Sally and her children, but everything taken by refugees. I will pick up [your] trunk at the Depot."[32]

Refugees moved within established community patterns unless prevented by circumstances, and most of them found safety in churches or among kin and neighbors. Southerners believed their condition most unbearable when forced to remain among "strangers." That the community responded well even during grave crisis indicates the strength of community ties as well as the community's sheer determination to survive. As the war continued, women became preoccupied with the practical business of survival. A young woman of North Carolina, Millie Gwyn, wrote to her aunt, "I think we have nothing to hope for but destruction, misery and poverty. But this is not a time for despair but for action."[33] The correspondence of Julia A. Jones, a young North Carolina mother, reflects the support system that women maintained to survive. Family and friends wrote to Julia Jones and exchanged vital information. Jeannette Levingston wrote to her, "I cannot get cloth till after the soldier's clothes are made."[34] Another woman pleaded, "I dislike to beg but am dependent on my friends for all kinds of garden seeds."[35] And Minerva promised Julia Jones, "I will send you that recipe and try to get the boys hats."[36]

The survival system quite naturally absorbed women's energies and super-seded the effort to build women's reform networks. In addition, the sur-vival network provided psychological security. Women depended upon kin for emotional support. During the war, cousins Harriott Cheeves and Susan Middleton of Charleston kept up a remarkable correspondence in which they spoke of shared losses and the gradual change in their lives. The war trans-formed the very nature of young women's lives. When Susan Middleton's family lost its plantation, Susan remained indifferent because, she con-fessed, plantation life bored her.[37] Still, its absence changed Susan and she remarked to Harriott that she begrudged these changes:

> The realities of my life and the situations in which I have been placed have been so strangely different from what my character and the early promise of my life would have led one to expect. Anxiety, responsibil-ity, and independence of thought or action are what are peculiarly abhorrent to my nature, and what [nonetheless] has been so often required of me.[38]

As the war continued, death and loss became more typical and therefore more disruptive of psychological security. Harriott wrote to Susan about how her life was falling apart, and she lamented the necessity of adapting to a new one:

> I cannot write much—I am afraid tonight—my heart is so full of Mrs. Hobrook. . . . Sally and Lise's mother is near death. . . . I feel as if there was no use for the war to end, or any good thing to happen. So much that made the happiness of our lives is taken beyond our reach, and in our age, it is as if we immigrated to a new country. It is hard to take up a new thread of life.[39]

In addition to the need to discuss personal change, the cousins relied upon each other for support because only to one another did they openly admit fear. Said Susan to Harriott: "You will never persuade me you are courageous. I remember several occasions when you were frightened." Har-riott readily confessed "to a cowardice most unsuitable to my mature time of life."[40]

Southern women's correspondence demonstrates that the kinship connec-tion remained active during the war. Women's reliance upon the kin commu-nity reduced psychic tension and stabilized individuals and families. How-ever, dependence upon traditional community relationships inhibited the development of independent women's networks.

The tenacious community ties that held through the war circumscribed the education of women. Americans in the early national period adapted eighteenth-century English educational philosophy that stressed a "useful" education for women.[41] Thus women's education subordinated association, ambition, and analytic thinking to Christian usefulness or domestic virtue. Hannah More, a British reformer who insisted upon education for women, argued:

> A general capacity for knowledge, and the cultivation of the understanding at large, will always put a woman into the best state for directing her pursuits into those particular channels which her destination in life may afterwards require. But she should be carefully instructed that her talents are only a means to a still higher attainment, and that she is not to rest in them as an end; that merely to exercise them as instruments for the acquisition of fame and the promotion of pleasure, is subversive of her delicacy as a woman, and contrary to the spirit of a Christian.[42]

And Mary Wollstonecraft, the enlightened English feminist who supported coeducation, maintained: "[M]ake women rational creatures, and free citizens, and they will quickly become good wives and mothers."[43]

Because it was basically familial and community controlled, the education of southern women lagged behind the education offered to the women in the North, which gave "Republican Mothers" an education that eventually subverted the traditional system.[44] In many instances, the community carefully refined and adapted education to traditional values. The war-crisis period may then be characterized by the community's attempt to interpret, limit, and channel the alternative experience of southern women, whose understanding and circumstance demanded autonomy. Not until the modernization period, when community control relaxed, did women's education supply the ranks of reformers, missionaries, and careerists.

Nineteenth-century southern schools were in reality extensions of the home. Decentralized decision-making, characteristic of Victorian American education, meant family control. Mothers taught their children in elementary subjects or delegated the task to older siblings or unmarried aunts. Or several families hired a schoolmistress and underwrote the school. If the school was not "hired out," any self-elected teacher might then contract for her services in a "select school." The teacher hired a room, then visited the neighborhood offering her services. Mrs. Ward and May Woodfine operated such neighborhood schools at Burns Creek and Alfredo, North Carolina, respectively. Neighborhood or "select schools" were sometimes family enterprises. William Siler of North Carolina built a schoolhouse near his home so that his daughter could teach summer sessions.[45] When her father built a schoolhouse on his farm and insisted that she teach, Amanda Jane Cooley resented the decision to force her into a job she did not want. She recognized that her education was unequal to the task. Amanda Cooley never mastered grammar; for example, she wrote in her diary, "I got my arm sprained yesterday so that I cant work and am afraid I shall never write so good any more."[46]

The only supervision of her work as a teacher, however, was from members of her family who occasionally visited the schoolroom. Since Amanda Jane Cooley taught family members, such supervision seemed not at all out of place.[47]

Teachers in select schools and peripatetic teachers were notoriously undereducated, a fact appreciated by Jenny Akehurst, an experienced teacher who escaped teacher overpopulation in the North and came south. She met with rebuffs when she approached prospective parents. Once a planter's wife refused Jenny Akehurst's services saying that she had had enough of inexperienced, "half-handed" teachers. Jenny Akehurst replied that she was a "wholehanded" teacher and resented the insult to her ability. Later Jenny Akehurst had harsh words for uneducated mothers who made decisions about their children's education. She wrote to her future husband, Sylvanus Lines, in 1858:

> You do not know what it is to be a governess in the family of a Georgia planter, whose wife through a *false* education is not capable of giving one word of advice or making one wise suggestion in regard to the training of her own children. . . . [O]ne reared in the halls of fashion and wealth is but poorly fitted for the realities of life.[48]

Jenny Akehurst's view of planter women's lack of education may have been true of a portion of that class; however, since 1800 the South had supported female education. Besides select schools and neighborhood schools, county academies and seminaries enrolled female students. Community subscription and investment, however, supported church-affiliated academies and private schools. Although the schools offered an array of academic subjects including literature, science, languages, and the social sciences, the core of the curriculum remained the study of the Scriptures, bible history, and theology. Women's education, as historian Catherine Clinton has explained, served to uphold class interests. Designed to instill domestic virtue and reinforce women's roles as nurturer and wife, education enhanced women's chances in the marriage market.[49] Yet women appreciated education for its own sake. Mothers encouraged their daughters to take advantage of schooling and even envied their opportunity. Julia A. Conrad's mother cautioned her to "be diligent in [her] studies."[50] And Mary Ann Cobb coaxed her daughter, Matty, to go back to school after the young girl expressed a fear that classmates would ridicule her for her slowness.[51] The promise of success instilled pride in mothers of educated young women. In 1856, when North Carolinian Annie Darden witnessed her daughters' class examination—which was a public recitation in the nineteenth century—she wished she were "young again to share the benefits of this grand school" and hoped her daughters would be "fitted out to a brighter world." Unfortunately, the daughters never graduated.[52] Despite women's pride in their education, few career opportunities existed to advance their status, except as wives.

Teaching remained the major employment of women in the antebellum period. Outstanding graduates of academies sometimes were asked to join the teaching staff. And some teachers, such as Elizabeth Lomax, were invited to head academies. Women also taught in boarding schools and female colleges. Reverend Sidney Bumpas and Fannie Bumpas jointly taught at a Presbyterian school, and the Gastons ran the highly successful Corona Female College in Corinth, Mississippi, from 1857 to 1864. Joseph and Anne Beale Davis administered Wesleyan Female College for three years just prior to the war.[53]

By the end of the Civil War, then, women educated in country academies and colleges and experienced teachers were prepared to continue their teaching to sustain themselves economically. However, because of community resistance, it was not until 1872 that the region adopted a common-school system.[54] The system opened greater opportunities for women to teach in public schools and confirmed the "feminization" of elementary schools, a development that began in the 1830s. Despite gains, the quality and extent of southern women's education was not comparable to the education received by women in the North. A woman's education was considered high in quality only if it provided her with the necessary accomplishments to be a wife and mother. Women, themselves, did not regard an academy education as an end in itself. Few seriously considered a higher education.[55] And though education contributed to southern women's self-confidence and a more positive self-image, the immediate circumstances of war and community prohibitions allowed only gradual change in women's roles. Until the modernization period women could not fulfill the potential of their educations.

In the Civil War era, southern education outfitted women for marginal employment, which did little to encourage autonomy. Furthermore, the sheer effort of survival limited women's efforts toward independence, and this was especially true of women who migrated to urban areas. Men's wages lagged behind soaring wartime inflation, and necessity induced women to take jobs in support of their families. At first, southern women merely tolerated the idea, but circumstance eventually accustomed them to working. One mother, a government clerk herself, expressed a concern about her daughter's job as a clerk: "We had always objected to [our daughter's] applying for an office, because we were afraid of the effect of sedentary employment on her health; but now it seems necessary to us, as the prices of provisions and house-rent have become so very high."[56] When the mother finally resigned herself to necessity, she accepted the idea of independence. "So it seems that the Lord intends us to work for our daily bread, and to be independent," she wrote.[57]

Although southern women characterized their position as independent, their job opportunities left them with little autonomy. Employment did not provide them with independent means. The women in the McGuire family, for example, contributed to family support and thus the daughter could not establish a separate household. Mrs. McGuire's initial monthly salary of $125 was later raised to $250 a month. However, women's salaries were wholly inadequate, considering inflationary consumer prices; shoes cost between $125 and $150 per pair and flour sold for $300 a barrel.[58] Mary Massey, a Civil War historian, has written that "many refugees had to work at any job they could find, and it was not unusual for entire families to seek employment."[59] With the help of her children, Jorantha Semmes plaited hats and sold them at $50 each. She estimated she would earn $2,000 in 1865, while the cost of maintaining her family had risen to $4,800.[60]

Exploitation further reduced women's chances for economic independence. Almost invariably southern women were given menial jobs. In Richmond, for example, middle- and working-class women helped their families to subsist by selling homemade soap and gooseberry wine, while others made pickles and catsup for restaurants. Destitute women picked up what jobs they could; they dyed, spun, and wove wool. The plight of urban women seamstresses was particularly desperate. Victims of the government contract system, they suffered long periods of unemployment when material was unavailable. Sewing jobs were therefore often scarce, and poor women walked miles in search of one. The women of St. Paul's Episcopal Church in Richmond offered sewing jobs to refugee and working-class women, but such opportunities were rare.[61]

Farm women who worked under the contract system fared better than did urban women because food and shelter were available to them. Nevertheless, a Virginia farm woman who sewed clothes in the "put out system" worked for $10 a week, an amount that she divided with her sisters and daughters who assisted her. The farm woman's allotment could not cover her costs even if she did not purchase foodstuffs. The price of muslin alone was $6 to $8 per yard.[62]

Although seamstresses could do little but complain privately about below-subsistence wages, female arsenal workers struck for higher pay in December 1863. The Confederate States Laboratory agreed to pay $5 a day to single women and $7 a day to married women. Not content with this inequity, some three hundred women struck again for equal pay. Unwilling to submit to the women's demands, the government hired three hundred women replacements the next day for the hazardous work. It is clear that the government considered female labor expendable. Any organization that might have developed from this burgeoning labor movement was rendered futile by the precipitous action of Confederate authorities.[63] Thus the alternate experience of southern white women as a marginal labor force was therefore of limited value in offering any degree of women's independence.

When unemployment and inflationary conditions made it nearly impossible to support families, some women took direct action against "extortioners," those whom they felt responsible for their families' plight. Bread riots and women's organized protests against merchants, speculators, and government officials occurred in cities and towns throughout the Confederacy. Mobile, Richmond, Atlanta, Macon, Columbus, Augusta, Salisbury, Jonesville, and High Point all experienced the wrath of organized women. Women organized collectively on behalf of unemployed husbands and starving children. Mobile, Alabama, experienced a violent mob action in September 1863 when a group of women armed with pitchforks and "kitchen utensils" and carrying placards proclaiming "Bread or Blood" marched in the streets assaulting merchants who charged exorbitant prices. The women held their own for most of a day until the Seventeenth Alabama Regiment was called in to restore order. Unable, however, to fire upon "starving wives, mothers, sisters and daughters" of men in service, the regiment returned to their barracks without taking any action against the women. The issue was settled only when officials promised to bring prices under control.[64]

The wives of Tredegar iron workers in Richmond, convinced that the supply of food was inadequate and that prices were exorbitant, met in a neighborhood Baptist church and agreed to carry their protest to Governor John Letcher. When the governor provided no satisfaction, the women, armed with knives, hatchets, and pistols, invaded the commercial district and looted not only food but also clothing and jewelry. Only the intervention of President Jefferson Davis and an armed citizen guard prevented further damage and ended the incident. But the distress of these unfortunate women moved the city council to enact a relief program.[65]

In March 1863, twelve women entered a Whitehall Street store in Atlanta to ask the price of bacon. When the storekeeper replied that it was $1.00 a pound, some of the women responded by holding a gun to his head while another asked how indigent soldiers' wives could pay such inflated prices. Meanwhile, other women helped themselves to approximately $200 worth of supplies.[66] As wives of fighting men, women felt justified in attacking exploitative merchants.

This radical behavior on the part of southern women must be seen in its cultural context. Contemporaries did not interpret the action as a women's protest. Instead they argued that the riots were motivated by unionist sympathies, the innate criminality of the lower classes, and the greed of distillers to confiscate corn. (Suspicion that illegal distilleries competed for scarce grain prompted the last theory.) In all of these cases, observers assumed that various male interests manipulated women to revolt.[67] It is clear that those who commented upon the incidents could not conceive that women were acting on their own. Nevertheless, women did act on their own; they were capable of taking initiative on behalf of their families. The women of Richmond met in a Baptist church, a symbol of the family system in southern society. Most of the women who protested were wives of unemployed iron-workers, desperately fighting to preserve their families from poverty and starvation. The motivating force behind the riots was thus preservation of the family; the action of these women was neither a conscious nor a preconscious feminist protest.[68]

In *The Making of the English Working Class*, E. P. Thompson argues that eighteenth-century food riots were tied to resentment against the market system and were a protest to preserve the old paternalistic moral order, an order that established clear lines of relationships and obligations.[69] Likewise in the new southern urban environment women challenged merchants and the government for unfairly raising prices, scarcity notwithstanding. Clearly, women wished to preserve those family values that supported the rural economic system because their identity was most closely associated with the family system. Bertram Wyatt-Brown suggests, for example, that family meant status among southern lower classes and that the number of children in a family was directly proportional to its status.[70] However, in war-weary Richmond, greater numbers of children led to greater destitution. Thus economic as well as family values changed, leaving urban women struggling to stem the tide.

The wartime experience of Confederate women most clearly demonstrates that the employment of women represented only a temporary gain for women's independence and was elastic in its effect. The two professions closely identified with women's war work—nursing and Civil Service—ended with the war. With the cessation of hostilities, Civil Service jobs were terminated and hundreds of Confederate women copiers and clerks were displaced. The Federal government did employ some southern women during the 1880s, but mostly it gave preference to northern women, war widows, or orphans who claimed that their loyalty entitled them to a position.[71]

In the South nursing was almost wholly a voluntary service. Family members tended the convalescent, and volunteer bands of women organized wayside homes to minister to the disabled while these men awaited railway connections home. One volunteer organization, the Soldier's Home of Montgomery, expanded its effort to establish the Ladies Memorial Hospital, a renowned health-care center for servicemen. Volunteerism did provide women with the opportunity to initiate collective action and exercise managerial skills. Sophie Gilmer Bibb and her associate, Mrs. William Bell, supervised the Ladies' Hospital of Montgomery until 1865, even though it had been taken over by the Confederate authorities. And Harriet Woodhall, a member of the Ambulatory Alabama Hospital Committee, which was organized to follow the army of Tennessee, volunteered her services to institute a field unit but was instead appointed to run a hospital at Okloma, Mississippi, to minister to Alabama troops. Another volunteer, Mary Davis, president of the Florence Military Aid Society, personally transported the wounded to the society's newly established medical facility.[72]

The southern community praised such volunteer work, but it rejected nurses because they represented independence from family ties. Mary Ann Huff, a student of Confederate women's roles in the war, has noted that "except for a few orders of Catholic and Protestant nuns, there were no trained nurses in [Georgia] since female hospital attendants were scorned by 'polite' southern society."[73]

Army leaders also discouraged female nurses and only by sheer determination did women overcome the prohibitions of the military. A few trained nurses worked in the field army, and Phoebe Pember and Ella King Newson were among them. Their training advanced them to supervisory positions in which they managed the volunteers. Massey has estimated that only 3,200 Union and Confederate women were paid nurses. Of that number, however, only a small percentage were southern women. Some southern black women also worked for hospital wages—either as slaves or as free women—to support themselves and their families.[74]

Middle-class white women who volunteered their services at hospitals adapted admirably to wartime conditions, often working under the most shocking circumstances. Sidney Harding, who volunteered as a nurse, reported that in a New Orleans hospital blood-soaked casualties lay unattended in piles of cotton on the floor of the hospital. The stench from the wounded pervaded the rooms.[75] Despite the conditions witnessed by novices, women nurses maintained a sense of calm and efficiency. The volunteer nurse Lucy Wood Butler noted that her fellow workers remained "composed" even when surrounded by the dead and dying.[76] One very young woman who gained considerable experience in a short period of time admitted to a friend, "I can dress amputated limbs now and do most anything in the way of nursing wounded soldiers."[77]

At the end of the war, however, women could not transfer their wartime nursing experience to civilian hospitals. Paid nurses were deactivated and such highly trained and competent women as Kate Cumming and Phoebe Pember were forced to take low-status and low-paying jobs. Phoebe Pember mustered out of service and found employment as a teacher. Sophie Gilmer Bibb, whose talents had helped build the Ladies Memorial Hospital, invested her skills in organizations that provided memorials for the Confederate dead. The professionalization of nursing did not occur until the mid-1880s when Clara Barton established the International Red Cross. Only twenty-two nursing schools existed in the United States until late in the century.[78] Therefore, while the demand for nursing expanded during wartime, nursing did not provide women with a new profession in the postwar South.

Nevertheless, wartime volunteerism offered a variety of experience to women, and women's relief associations contributed significantly to the war effort. These associations followed the traditional pattern of participation by women in emergency relief. Chiefly responsible for supplies, women furnished clothing and linens, but their work was hampered by the lack of a central administrative agency to distribute goods. Women fared better when they controlled a project in a specific area. In Columbia, South Carolina, and Savannah, Georgia, for example, women raised funds for way stations for disabled soldiers, and they ably managed them, offering meals to the stranded men. Women's skill in raising money benefited hospitals, which received medical supplies and other needed help as a result.

Besides engaging in health-related volunteerism, southern women joined together in patriotic efforts. The year before the war a small group of elite women from Lowndes County, Alabama, organized a boycott movement against northern manufactured goods by writing letters to local newspapers urging a boycott. Soon thereafter, the Lowndes Ladies of the South met and passed resolutions condemning abolitionism and calling for a boycott. They criticized the weak efforts of the state Assembly to end trade with the North. Other women of Lowndes County encouraged local merchants to join the boycott. Although the boycott met little response from women, the effort may be seen in the larger context of women's support for secession. For instance, the Montgomery sewing circle made and passed out blue cockades, symbols of secession. The women berated unionist men who refused to wear the symbol. In addition, the Mobile Women's Auxiliary of the Young Men's Secession Association sewed a secession banner and presented it to the association at a gala sponsored by the women.[79]

During the war, women's collective efforts contributed to the protection of port cities. The Ladies' Gunboat Associations of Savannah, Georgia, and Selma, Alabama, solicited funds from other women to build ironclads. However enthusiastic the canvassers, they failed in Selma to collect sufficient funds and donated the amount collected to the military hospitals. The Savannah women were more successful and they outfitted a gunboat.[80] Voluntary societies thus provided valuable organizational experience for southern white women. Nevertheless, as in former wars, the participation of women in the war effort did not necessarily result in civil and political equality.[81] Organized for a temporary exigency, the wartime aid associations did not transform the activity of women into reform activism until late in the century.

Teaching presented the most viable opportunity for women after the war. But the war did not create teaching jobs. Since the middle period of the nineteenth century southern women had been teaching school in ever increasing numbers. College men taught winter sessions, and young women often took over the long summer quarter.[82] Teaching opportunities available to women after the war only reinforced a prewar trend.

The limited autonomy offered to women by education, marginal work, and volunteerism maintained traditional sexual roles for the most part. That white women responded to the crisis in traditional ways is demonstrated not only by urban and farm women but by planters' wives. With the exception of women such as Adele Allston, who alone faced down an aroused plantation community, and the Virginia woman whose punishment of black instigators defused militancy, women suffered from their position as the junior partner in the farm enterprise.[83] Mistresses whose husbands entered military service certainly assumed greater responsibility, but they were aided by overseers, kinsmen, neighbors, or fellow church members in executing the business of the plantations.[84] Such dependence upon male expertise created severe disciplinary problems in white women's dealing with black males.

Although women had some understanding of plantation maintenance, daily management was generally delegated to available men. A mistress's involvement in management was directly proportional to an overseer's competence. If the overseer failed to preserve order, the mistress intervened, but as Catherine Edmondston, a South Carolina planter's wife, noted ruefully, "Master's eye and voice are more potent than Mistress's."[85]

Clarence Lee Mohr, a scholar of Afro-American history, has argued that women's lack of firsthand knowledge of farm work often forced her dependence upon bondmen for expertise and assistance. When black men acted as overseers, in fact, white women experienced a shift in authority. Black men ceased to recognize control by the mistress. Mohr claims that this accounts for white women's complaints about the ungovernability of slaves during the war. Certainly, military and political destabilization affected the mistress-slave relationship but of even more significance was the effort of white women to solve their crisis-related problems in traditional ways, namely, by reliance upon men.[86] Such was the hold of community values that when faced with sudden new responsibilities, women interpreted them only in view of their traditional marital partnership, as evidenced by a South Carolina woman who wrote to her husband in the Confederate Congress, "I tell you candidly this attention to farming is up hill work for me. I can give orders first rate, but when I am not obeyed, I can't keep my temper. . . . I am ever ready to give you a helping hand, but I must say I am heartily tired of trying to manage *free* negroes."[87]

When the blacks were freed and departed from the plantations, white women were forced to redistribute household work and assume domestic chores. White women also had difficulty in adjusting to their changed relationship with black women. Mary Cary Ambler described her loss of control in religious terms:

It may seem strange to some how sad I feel at the breaking of a tie which I have felt from childhood for I do feel an attachment for our servants. [B]ut deep down in my heart there is a heavier . . . anxiety—which I am trying to keep down. I have had to trust to God, gradually has He taught the lesson. [O]ne by one those things to which I looked and trusted have been exposed. I have seen the folly of trusting to any thing on this earth. . . . I feel my utter helplessness.[88]

Although Mary Cary Ambler's attachment to her retainers moved her to wish "God speed" to Martha, her washer woman, and to give her clothes for her journey, at the same time the young woman, along with her sisters, had begged her father not to release the black women and children from the plantation because, as she explained, that would "leave the washing, milking, cooking and cleaning the house to us and we were not quite ready to begin."[89]

Faced with the desertion of their bondwomen, other white women reacted with disillusionment and hostility.[90] The group disloyalty of her servants prompted Catherine Broun, a North Carolina mistress, to remark, "I am beginning to lose confidence *in the whole race*."[91] A young friend wrote to Lise Mitchell that Rose, her valued maid, had left her, and the friend opined that "negroes' hearts were nearly as black as Yankees'."[92] And eighteen-year-old Kate Foster of North Carolina wished her departing bondwomen "good riddance."[93]

The initial novelty of housework soon wore off. Lise Mitchell's friend bragged about the biscuits she made from a recipe supplied her by an Irish neighbor. And she remarked, with a hint of pride, "I ought to be grateful to Rose for leaving for I have gained a great deal of useful knowledge."[94] Light-hearted efficiency gave way to sheer drudgery as white women complained of numbed fingers from sewing and the sheer fatigue of housework.[95]

The Civil War, which shattered existing black-white relationships, exposed the authentic concerns of black women—with their own and their families' welfare. White owners scrutinized their slaves for evidence of a "change," meaning detachment from white interests and authority. When they noticed that "Nelly is not the same" or that "Henny . . . is not the same person that she was," white southerners assumed radical intent—the self-will, self-determination, and self-definition of their servants.[96] In a tone of disgust Kate Foster wrote in her diary, "We think all [the slaves] will go whenever it pleases their 'majesties.'"[97] White mistresses remained impervious to black-kin networks and community bonds that fostered black identity and solidarity and enabled blacks to gain some economic and political advantages. However, freed blacks received these advantages from within the context of a viable white community, whose interests to some extent were supported by external forces of the Union army and the Freedmen's Bureau.

Herbert Gutman and Leon Litwack have argued that black autonomy derived from strong family ties. The desire to reunite families caused black emigration throughout the war and early postwar years, and the black exodus naturally broke many former ties to the white master and mistress. Black labor then forced a redefinition of the work relationship through the work contract. Many contracts were explicit in their insistence that women were to have time off for household duties. And much to the consternation of white employers, many black women refused to work. Lastly, because planters no longer had hegemony over blacks, there were fewer instances of black women's sexual exploitation by white men.[98] All of these elements indicate changes in black behavior that crisis conditions allowed, but the white neighborhood network prevailed, forcing a constriction of black autonomy. Tacit agreement among planters prevented the hiring of another's servants, thus compelling blacks to return to their original masters or starve. And black men who desired that their wives not work for white men found that economic conditions and traditional attitudes that made black women responsible for family support sent them back to work in the fields.[99] White racism, inflamed by black emancipation, retained the perception of black women as nothing but prostitutes, a view that would unite black women into a reform movement later in the century.

The Civil War, then, allowed the free expression of black identity and a greater integration of the black family. Black solidarity that fused into the family culture of the prewar South enabled black labor to win more equitable working conditions through the negotiation of contracts. The continued existence of the white community, however, restricted black gains—whites indirectly forced blacks to remain on the plantation, set limits on wages, compelled black women to work, all the while retaining the racism that enabled the oppressive community dynamic to operate.

Because the white evangelical community continued to survive after the Civil War, traditional roles, both racial and sexual, survived as well. Relationships between men and women and whites and blacks altered slowly in that context. After all, it was the entire southern community that responded to the war crisis—family, kin, and neighbors gave refuge to the displaced and offered encouragement to one another through correspondence. The education of women, so closely identified with the community, offered only marginal employment outside of the family, and entire families worked to support themselves during the war. Reform, therefore, evolved gradually as the ties of church and family vied with the secular forces of modernization in the late nineteenth century.

6. A WATERED GARDEN

... and their soul shall be as a watered garden ...
Jeremiah 31:12

uring the postwar period modernization competed with kinship loyalties as family values attempted to preserve the structure of southern society. But the triumph of modern secular-rational attitudes and behavior, which supported a redirection of capital and labor, the expansion of a railroad network, the improvement of agrarian technology, and the commercialization of agriculture, did not reformulate sexual roles.[1] Despite separation of families southerners continued to maintain family connections. Thus the strength of their kin networks overcame the power of modernizing influences, at least for several decades. Southern families reacted like those in twentieth-century emerging nations, such as Africa and India, whose values and roles still largely conformed to family expectations and needs. Evidence clearly indicates that kin systems dissipate very slowly, and they do not break up immediately as a result of modernization.[2] In the South, then, the impact of modernization upon traditional society was uneven.

As a consequence of the tenacity of the kinship system, leaders of the southern women's reform movement advocated changes that fell within the context of the traditional southern community. Thus temperance viewed as "a maternal struggle" widely appealed to southerners because it implied "womanliness first" and reform second.[3] In the same sense, proponents of women's suffrage adopted "white supremacy" arguments to insure their own enfranchisement and thereby sought to assure their opponents that their vote would not disrupt the southern racial system.

On the other hand, prewar modernizing tendencies did alter somewhat the extent of evangelical social control. Changes in production challenged traditional behavior and contributed to the development of dynamic and achievement-oriented attitudes among certain farmers. Elements of a modern personality are present in the market-directed attitudes of some southern farmers. Specialized market farming in tobacco and grain eventually expanded southern output, while technological improvements of the cotton gin and the reaper radically increased production. Moreover, the campaign for agrarian reform from 1840 to 1860 resulted in the widespread use of commercial fertilizers and the introduction of improved plows and cotton-planting devices. Thus by the time of the war at least one sector of the southern agrarian economy was oriented toward production for the market rather than for mere self-sufficiency. A weakening of traditional behavior associated with the rural community accompanied this economic change. The decline in the number of church trials after 1860 is one clear indication that the fabric of convention had been rent.[4] The disruption of church organization during the war intensified this trend. The decrease in accusations against fellow church members represented a loss of commitment to antebellum community standards. And the resulting modification of church supervision allowed women a more active public role, although that role continued to be defined primarily in domestic terms.

In the postwar period women worked to amortize church debts and rebuild damaged churches. This "domestic reconstruction" grew out of women's experience in antebellum aid societies and solicitation drives. Unlike prewar aid societies that organized for a specific project and then disbanded, however, the postwar societies became a permanent fixture in the late nineteenth-century evangelical church. The same members who had established the aid societies often joined the missionary societies in the 1880s. Yet these societies, which drew their membership from historic neighborhood-kinship groups, enhanced a sense of collective identity among women who participated in various charitable and fund-raising drives. Thus all southern women's reform efforts proceeded from a common source, that is, from the neighborhood-kinship connections that first coalesced in the missionary societies. The Women's Christian Temperance Union (WCTU) recruited from the missionary societies and the traditional family-oriented evangelical churches. The suffrage movement in turn tapped the WCTU for support.

The neighborhood-kinship bond prevailed despite postwar mobility, an example of which can be found in the correspondence of Catherine McFarland. Writing from North Carolina, she informed her Georgia cousin, James McFarland, that his mother's two sisters were still alive. James McFarland responded with great delight and told Catherine of the history of the rest of the family, which was scattered about the South. He mentioned Brother Andrew in Kentucky, Brother John's son in Louisiana, Sister Bitsey and her family in Trout City, Georgia, Sister Mary and Brother Robert in Georgia within two miles of their mother, and sister Jennet in Alabama. Brother Billy, continued McFarland, moved around and was like a "barren fig tree."[5] The McFarlands obviously kept in contact with their family even though it was scattered.

Remaining in contact with relatives gave southerners a sense of well-being. Although Mary Elizabeth Rives knew where her sister lived, postwar conditions prevented any communication with her. The lack of contact deepened her depression. "I am unusually gloomy," she wrote. "[B]eing separated from my relations is almost unbearable; [I have] a sister [who lives] within thirty-five miles, and I can neither see nor hear from her."[6]

Correspondence between relatives not only provided a psychological link

between family members but also allowed them to express religious concerns that affected the family. Secular attitudes usually distracted individuals
from traditional religious obligations, and families therefore frequently reminded their relatives of their Christian duties. For example, a kinswoman
admonished Mrs. Thomas J. Lenoir because she had not baptized her daughter or persuaded her husband to join a church.[7] Similarly, the sisters of Henry
Scudder badgered their brother to repent. Emily Scudder wrote to Henry, "My
dear brother do you ever think you have a precious never dying soul to
save?"[8]

The growth of secularism coincided with the southern perception of decline in postwar piety.[9] Lucy Muse Fletcher attributed religious inertia to the
sufferings of the war. She wrote, "[I]t is painful to see the bitterness of the
religious community. . . . I dread the hardening power of unsanctified afflic-
tion."[10] According to Mary Jeffries Bethell, unresolved tensions caused conflict within the church, a decline in attendance at Sunday services, and a
growing worldliness.[11] Commenting upon postwar trends within the church,
she said: "I feel sad when I look at the church, almost desolate, some of the
members have died, and some backslidden, nearly all of the rest worldly-
minded. Prayer meetings, class meetings, Sunday school, all are broken up
because iniquity abounds."[12] Some observers commented on the dullness of
church life. Among them was Mary Davis Brown, who compared a Presbyterian meeting to a funeral. What the church needed, she said, was a revival, a
"shaking amongst the dry bones of Bershaba [sic]."[13] In a similar complaint,
Mary Jeffries Bethell reported that only eight persons professed their faith and
only three converts joined the church at a camp meeting in North Carolina.[14]

The decline in piety was accompanied by a relaxation of church discipline,
evidenced by the fact that the frequency of church trials declined. Nevertheless, the double standard, an integral part of the enforcement of discipline,
remained in effect in both country and in town churches. In the postwar
period, men were more often accused of lesser offenses such as drinking
and fighting, while women were frequently accused of the grave sin of immorality. Women's immorality, often alleged, was considered the more serious
offense and usually led to expulsion from the church. An example of the
disparity in punishment is evident in the actions of the Mount Olive Baptist
Church between 1866 and 1876. The deacons of that small congregation laid
charges of drunkenness and profanation against six of its male communicants, while it accused three women of abortion, fornication, and adultery,
respectively.[15] Similarly, the Mount Tabor Baptist Church of Murfreesboro,
North Carolina, expelled two women and one man for immoral conduct, but,
after bringing six men before the congregation for drunkenness, forgave
them.[16] Between 1862 and 1872 the First Presbyterian Church in Athens,
Georgia, suspended William E. Jones, an elder, for dereliction of duty and
excluded two women, Mrs. Elisa McDowell for drunkenness and Mrs. Sarah

Weir for "violation of the seventh commandment being the mother of a bastard child."[17]

Although churches in the postwar period continued to follow the pattern of antebellum discipline, they brought fewer charges against their communicants. Thus, in the decade after the war, the Mount Olive Baptist Church and the Mount Tabor Baptist Church recorded only nine cases apiece of disciplinary action. In retrospect, then, increasing secularism, in conjunction with the larger problems of Reconstruction, helped to erode disciplinary zeal and to divert congregations from close supervision of private conduct.

As a result of the decline in disciplinary action and a growing concern for a renewal of spirit within the churches, women became more deeply involved in church activities. The gradual weakening of church discipline allowed for a more flexible interpretation of the woman's role in the church. Likewise, her participation in the reconstruction of the church enhanced her opportunities for leadership. The formation of women's associations is directly attributable to this new image of female church members.

Although women had supported the church in antebellum years through their contributions and fund solicitation, their role became crucial in the lean postwar period. Matilda Ogilvie, for example, labored for eight years to rebuild the burnt-out Broad Run Baptist Church, which was finally completed in 1871.[18] The work of rebuilding the First Baptist Church of Gainesville, Georgia, was largely accomplished through the effort of ten women who organized a society for that purpose. Each member of "the Ladies Benevolent Society" paid one dollar into a fund for the purchase of materials to make bonnets, aprons, and clothing. Profits earned from the sale of these items were then used to secure building materials. In 1873 a new brick church was erected. The First Baptist Church of Marietta, Georgia, likewise benefited from a building fund established by its female members. After their main work was accomplished in 1898, the group reorganized under the name of the Ladies' Aid Society, which supplied shoes to the needy and established a fund for poor children.[19]

In addition to their fund-raising activities, the women of the Central Presbyterian Church of Atlanta held an industrial class in the church basement for the purpose of teaching sewing skills to "less fortunate" women. Various other women's activities continued throughout the latter part of the century. These activities included the teaching of Sunday school classes and arrangements for fairs and bazaars to raise money for charities.[20] Quite clearly, then, women contributed directly to the reconstruction of southern churches, and they extended welfare services not otherwise available in the postwar South.

However, the key organizational activity after the war was missionary work. Support for missionary tasks had declined precipitously during the war. In 1860, Baptist missions had received $40,000 in contributions, but six years later they could claim a mere $7,000 in gifts. By 1867, the amount had increased, but it was still only slightly more than half of the prewar level. Under such difficult financial straits, the Baptist Mission Board naturally supported fewer missionaries during this period. In response to this crisis, a group in Baltimore organized the Women's Mission Union, which was an outgrowth of the Baptist Missionary Society of that city.[21] The Baltimore society sponsored a program of women bible readers in China. Organized by Mrs. Graves, a missionary's wife, the project enabled lay women to enter native women's homes and read Scripture to them. Unfortunately, few women readers volunteered. Undaunted, in 1868 Mrs. Graves assembled a women's meeting in connection with the Southern Baptist Convention; the group then requested volunteer women bible readers.[22]

Although denominational boards and individual churches actively opposed missionary women's meetings, the societies spread, and, from Baltimore to Virginia, South Carolina, Georgia, and Mississippi, they received a substantial amount of money in contributions. Women in South Carolina alone raised $4,000. Lucy Muse Fletcher of North Carolina happily recorded in her diary for April and July of 1869 that she had successfully organized a missionary society. She noted, moreover, that her chief task was to convince members to come to a monthly meeting and to contribute regularly.[23] By 1872, the Baptist Mission Board supported several unmarried women in missionary work from the proceeds of their mite boxes.[24]

The Women's Missionary Union, which established chapters at various churches, superseded the all-male missionary societies. In one case, the Marietta First Baptist Church Missionary Society voted to include women; however, as women became effective organizers within the society, male membership declined. The society's minutes of 5 April 1874 indicate that only a half-dozen men even bothered to make contributions to the society.[25]

Although the missionary movement reinforced southern women's sense of collective identity, traditional patterns of association accounted for women's initial efforts at self-assertion and leadership. Women in general still demonstrated a shyness about public speaking. Azile Simpson, historian of the Central Presbyterian Church in Atlanta, has noted that there were only about six women in her church who would lead public prayer even though the Women's Foreign Missionary Society was well organized by 1881.[26] Perhaps such meekness can be attributed to the familial character of women's relationship to one another, which so closely resembled traditional neighborhood-kinship residence patterns. Traditional kinship patterns may also account for the more conservative values that tended to survive in women's groups. At the turn of the century, individual missionary societies were divided into neighborhood "circle" meetings, which drew their membership from historic neighborhood-kinship groups. This action merely institutionalized what had been the primary pattern of association. For instance, of the fourteen members of the Hephzibah Baptist Church in Augusta, five were of the Rhodes family, two were of the Davis family, and four were of the Casswell family. The high degree of familial relationships is obvious. A similar relationship is evident in the membership list of the Ladies Benevolent and Missionary Society of the First Presbyterian Church in Athens. That list shows that in 1882 fifty-one of ninety members, or 57 percent, shared surnames. Thus, it is clear that even in urban churches, many women belonged to benevolent or missionary societies in which they had relatives or in-laws.[27] Neighborhood kin association adhered to traditional sex role models that urban interchange gradually transformed.

Since the work of the aid and missionary societies was often similar, these two groups either merged or coordinated their efforts. The Ladies Benevolent Society of the First Baptist Church in Gainesville, Georgia, for example, changed its name in 1893 to the Women's Aid Society and expanded its activities to include missionary work. Inspired by the Home Mission's Movement to encourage "Women's Work for Women," the women of the First Presbyterian Church of Athens chartered the Ladies Benevolent and Missionary Society in 1883. According to the constitution of the society, its purpose was "to administer to the necessities of the poor, to assist in the cause of the Missionaries and to encourage all kinds of benevolent work."[28] The society met monthly and its membership dues were used for works of charity. Through papers written by themselves and read before the society, the women of the society stimulated interest in the missionary endeavor. The organization found its strength in mutual supportiveness. Mrs. Howell Cobb, Jr., who chaired the Benevolent Society, hoped to foster such a spirit when she submitted a resolution "that each lady will do something or say something to encourage ourselves and each other in the interest of the society."[29] The Presbyterian Benevolent and Missionary Society later cooperated with the Methodist Ladies Missionary Society of Athens in the support of local orphans.[30]

Shaped by the organization of benevolent and missionary societies, the southern women's network also supported the careers of women missionaries. Women's colleges served as recruitment centers and training grounds for women missionaries. Among the most active institutions in the movement were Richmond Women's College, Judson College, Bessie Tift College, Hollins College, and Greenville College, all of which attracted women who were ready to serve the missionary cause. This movement represented a significant change from the period between 1845 and 1861, when the Southern Baptist Convention sent only twenty-two married women as missionaries to China and sixteen to Africa.[31] The rejection of single women as missionaries in the antebellum period was justified by the Baptist board on the grounds that "if God wanted them [single women], he would have sent them husbands who would take them as helpmates."[32] The sole exception to the board's policy occurred in 1849 when it sent the unmarried Harriet Baker as a missionary to Africa for the purpose of establishing a school for girls. Because of an unfortunate encounter with a mentally unbalanced missionary and later her own physical illness, Sister Baker had to return home after contributing four years of her service. Despite her heroic effort, the board thereafter was reluctant to send women abroad.[33]

Notwithstanding the discrimination against single female missionaries, women's organizations continued to support women's efforts abroad. The Greenville Auxiliary, a missionary society of the First Methodist Church of Greenville, Mississippi, contributed toward the maintenance of girls' colleges and training schools in China. When in 1889 the auxiliary learned that the expansion of Chinese missions necessitated dividing the field into two provinces, its members interpreted the move as a compliment to their work.[34]

Baptist women were energetic promoters of the missionary cause, and in 1884 their convention reported that women had raised $75,000 in the preceding decade. The successful fund-raising efforts of women forced the Baptist Convention to recognize that women were playing a significant role in the missionary movement, even though the denomination persisted in resisting women's efforts to organize. In 1885, the Baptist Convention publicly praised women's efforts, but at the same time it encouraged its female members to report that they were not dissatisfied with the plans or methods of the board. The women complied, for, according to a report of the Committee on Women's Work, they asked that they be allowed to continue working "in a quiet and unostentatious way." Baptist women carefully avoided conflict with Baptist men and did not establish separate women's missionary boards but rather remained under the male-dominated Foreign and Home Missionary Board. Their flexibility allowed them to continue financing such missionary projects as Lottie Moon's Mission Girls' School in China. Their precedent also enabled organized women's groups to promote the cause of single women in the missions.[35]

In the late nineteenth century, women's work in foreign missions thus helped to implement the home mission movement in the Southern Baptist Convention. The efforts of women were recognized in resolutions proposed in the convention in 1884. Joshua Levering of Maryland requested that the Home Mission Board appoint "a competent woman as superintendent of women's work for Home Missions." This female superintendent would visit cities and organize societies, collect and disseminate information, and in general stimulate home mission work.[36] C. D. Campbell of Georgia added a resolution that provided for a woman to superintend "the collection and dissemination of information in regard to the work among the colored population of the South." Both resolutions were referred to the Home Mission Board and approved.[37] The Baptists had come to recognize the strength of women's involvement in missionary work and the formal role of white women in serving poor blacks in the South.

Very early in its history, the Methodist Episcopal church fostered women's missionary efforts. In 1818, New York preachers encouraged auxiliaries to join the New York Missionary and Bible Society. However, not until 1858 did a women's missionary society form on the Lebanon Circuit of the Tennessee Conference. The group organized to support the work of Mrs. J. W. Lambuth, who educated Chinese women and children and trained Chinese women as bible readers. The Civil War disrupted the society's work, but the group reformed in 1874 as the Women's Bible Mission of Nashville. The indomitable Mrs. M. L. Kelley reunited women for the missionary cause.[38] Later in 1878 the Nashville and Baltimore chapters joined under the General Conference as the General Executive Association, which was referred to later as the Woman's Board of Foreign Missions. By 1879, there were 475 auxiliaries of the General Executive Association. Missionary efforts also included the publication of *Women's Missionary Advocate* (1880), which helped to draw women together in foreign and home missionary work.[39]

The energy of the women's Foreign Missionary Society can be seen in the comments of Mrs. F. A. Butler, historian of the society, who said that women wanted their own society because

> [t]hey wished to be legally authorized to equip and send out women as missionaries to fields already occupied by our General Board, to open boarding and day schools, hospitals and homes, [they wished to be part of] buying and building, [they wished to support] missionaries, teachers, physicians, and [contribute to] scholarship, with a *mental reservation to do many un-thought-of things that would surely come to mind later.*[40]

The challenge, risk, and daring of the missionary women became a fixed part of the society by 1910 when it merged with the General Board of Missions. Women then assumed positions within the General Board. Belle H. Bennett was elected secretary of the Women's Missionary Council and coordinated the work of home and foreign missions.[41]

The Woman's Foreign Missionary Society continued to sponsor Mrs. J. W. Lambuth and in addition sent sisters Lochie Rankin and Dora Rankin to China. Laura Haygood of Georgia, sister of Bishop A. G. Haygood, offered her services to the missions in 1884. Laura Haygood had been a teacher and a principal; moreover, she had been an active organizer of the Woman's Home Mission Society of Georgia and also engaged in work among the poor and blacks of Atlanta. She brought the same sense of purpose to foreign and home missionary work. In China, Laura Haygood raised money for the Mc-Tyeire School for Girls and assumed the principalship.[42]

Presbyterian women, hampered by conservative clerical attitudes and policy, did not organize a centralized mission board until the twentieth century. Local societies were organized, however, and they contributed almost one-third of the entire amount collected for the missions. In 1884, women attempted to organize presbyteries, but they were criticized by ministers who feared that such organizations would lead to women's suffrage. Despite the General Assembly's limitation on women's activities within the church, women persevered and formed presbyteries. By 1910, these presbyterial unions could be found in more than 90 percent of the synods. The necessity for centralization, which became apparent by 1912, forced the assembly to recognize the appointment of a woman secretary to coordinate the work of the synodical unions. Historians Lois A. Boyd and P. Douglas Breckenridge point out that southern Presbyterian women's missionary efforts operated as an auxiliary to the General Assembly in contrast with women's missionary efforts in the North, which were autonomous.[43]

Southern white women formed a network of missionary associations that served to support the careers of a few extraordinary women and thereby ultimately established a core for the active reform groups that emerged in the decade of the 1880s. Anne F. Scott has noted that "the public life of nearly every southern woman leader for forty years began in a church society."[44] And since familial relationships structured the church groups and WCTU leaders were almost always affiliated with the evangelical churches, southern women's reform enthusiastically embraced the domestic and maternal aspects of the national women's reform movements.[45]

The WCTU did not penetrate the South until the 1880s, a decade after the temperance crusade had swept through the Midwest, the West, and the Northeast. Traditional southerners associated the WCTU with women's suffrage and thus discouraged acceptance of the union in the region. A Tennessee woman characterized southern prejudices as being "against women doing anything in public and especially opposed to the Women's Temperance Crusade. Particularly is this true of ministers. They quote St. Paul, and tell us we are wonderfully out of our places."[46]

The WCTU gained only a tentative hold in the South in the late 1870s. Its national convention in Baltimore in 1878 planned to gain a southern stronghold, but the movement made no appreciable progress until President Frances Willard and others launched a series of southern campaigns in 1881–82 and 1883. Conscious of "reuniting" the states in a reform cause, Willard's style won her many supporters.[17] She generated enthusiasm as much for her style as for her message. During a WCTU meeting a student in Nashville voiced his appreciation of Willard's speech: "We are naturally so conservative about women, but as Miss Willard stands before us tonight, she is the embodiment of the qualities she said women should possess, 'womanliness first—afterward what you will.' She seems to us so sisterly and so motherly, with a divine mind."[48]

Although suspicious of northern feminism, southern evangelical communities nevertheless welcomed "a maternal struggle" to protect the home against alcohol abuse.[49] Maternalism clearly influenced Rebecca Felton's decision to join the WCTU in 1886. She said, "I joined the WCTU because it represented organized Mother-love as opposed to this liquor curse."[50] Felton appealed to southerners whose family ties had been strained during the war and in the period of growing industrialization. Felton played upon southern fears of family alienation when she warned of the effects of alcohol abuse. In one such address she lamented: "[T]here is no suffering so acute as a mother's anguish . . . [and] grief over a wayward erring daughter, [a daughter] who has cast off from herself every tie of kinship—every obligation of filial duty— and every vestige of self-respect—to throw her destiny into the slums of vice."[51]

Southern women joined the WCTU for much the same reason as northern women did. They organized much later probably because their region did not sufficiently recover from the war until the 1880s and thus had to have time to produce a generation of leisured middle- and upper-class women. By the 1880s, these women could afford to hire servants and were thus freed from domestic chores that kept them from organizing for reform.[52] Increasing educational opportunities also propelled women toward reform "vocations," although some southern WCTU women had careers of their own. Mrs J. L. Lyons of Jacksonville, Florida, had been a missionary; Fannie Griffin of Montgomery, Alabama, served as principal of a public school; and Georgia H. M'Leod headed the Southern Literary Institute for Young Ladies in Baltimore. Sallie Chapin, a novelist, acknowledged that after her husband's death the temperance movement gave her work without which she would have died.[53] Obviously, southern women needed an arena in which to assert themselves.

The WCTU promoted a broad spectrum of public work for women. In the "Do Everything" program, which Frances Willard enthusiastically supported, women worked in areas of welfare, temperance education, and prison and almshouse reform. Because alcohol and drug abuse proved to be more of a social than a moral problem, temperance women soon found themselves moving into related areas such as prison reform and children's education. Rebecca Felton of Georgia and Julia Tutweiller of Alabama fought against the convict-lease system.[54] In 1879, after reading the Georgia General Assembly's report on the problem of children of male guards born to women in prison, Mrs. Felton wrote an article about the plight of female prisoners. As a result, attention was focused on the chairman of the prison reform committee, Bob Alston, who was threatened and ultimately assassinated by supporters of the convict-lease system.[55] When Mrs. Felton presented a WCTU memorial on behalf of a juvenile reformatory, she found that she was the verbal target of the same group. She argued that she was acutely vulnerable because she had no defense, no vote—nothing but "an active pen."[56] Her dilemma was typical: a public life without public voice. Ultimately, then, some moderate members of the WCTU became convinced of the necessity of suffrage for women.

Women reformers, especially suffragists, challenged evangelical, familial assumptions about the place and role of women. Traditional community values decreed that gender determined that the vocation of women was motherhood. Ordained by God, women's domestic role upheld the proper relationship between the sexes—male domination and female submission. Because southern manhood stood ever ready to protect southern womanhood and men had always represented women at the ballot box, any threat to the preordained order undermined the family system, argued the antisuffragists. Male and female fears—men feared loss of control and women feared offending male authority—upheld traditional assumptions. Some women wished to forfeit their right to vote, arguing they had too many rights anyhow, and besides they were too preoccupied by home duties to want to vote.[57]

Traditionalists were concerned that recognition of women's rights would lead to a degeneration of social cohesion. If the family order disintegrated, a heterogeneous mass of individuals would result and formerly dependent individuals, negroes and women, would then claim independence. Any change in voting opened the possibility of black enfranchisement, a threat to white supremacy. And because states' rights protected the grandfather clauses, literacy tests, and property qualifications that disenfranchised blacks, a national suffrage amendment would challenge the southern states' racial order. Consequently, according to traditionalists, loss of dominance by white males led directly to an unnatural state of affairs. The "antis" rejected considerations of democracy or fairness in favor of broad assertions about male power. One opponent of women's suffrage argued that it was "not a question of what women *want* but what they *ought* to have."[58]

Specific male industrialists—brewers and manufacturers, for example—clearly saw the danger of women's reform. Distillers feared that women's suffrage would usher in prohibition. Producers equated suffrage with a labor lobby that would eliminate the cheap labor of children and convicts. More generally, virtuous women's "clean up" of politics threatened the whole system of patronage and campaign funding which could bear little scrutiny. Southern suffragists, therefore, directed their campaign to the issues of women's place, white supremacy, and special interests.[59]

Although suffrage societies had existed in the South as early as 1867, a systematic movement did not appear until the 1880s and then only when suffragists began to tap into the network of the WCTU.[60] Union women politicized by reform slowly entered the suffrage ranks. For example, Belle Kearny claimed that she had been a member of the Prohibition party until she joined the WCTU, but when the latter refused to support women's rights she "felt again the lack of the vote." WCTU member Rebecca Felton declared that "women's suffrage had its inception in the fight against the saloons," and she alleged that anytime she spoke publicly on an issue, she was bitterly attacked. The clergy, she continued, resented her speaking on prohibition, and they objected to her criticism of the convict-lease system.[61] Prohibitions against public speaking by women and their lack of a political voice convinced some women of the necessity of the vote.

Other feminists, like Caroline E. Merrick of New Orleans, decried the lack of civil rights for women. When the women of St. Anna's Asylum of New Orleans witnessed the bequest of one of their patients, they discovered that their signatures were invalid because the law classified women, along with children and the mentally ill, as "incapable" of assuming an independent status. Despite their humiliation, the women were not easily persuaded by Merrick to send a petition to the Constitutional Convention of 1879, called to protest the lack of legal status for women taxpayers. Mississippi and North Carolina women challenged their states' codes, which proscribed married women from owning property.[62]

The stability of community values prevented the suffrage movement from reaching a broad constituency among southern women until 1910. Initially, suffrage leader Laura Clay's intense organizing effort over a seven-year period to form a suffrage organization netted only four hundred women members. However, after 1910, according to Anne Scott, suffrage gained respectability and gave rise to a multiplicity of suffrage organizations. Moreover, Scott argues that at that point the strength of women's organizations emboldened even the timid to demand the vote.[63]

As an embattled minority in the decades between 1880 and 1910, southern suffragists appealed to class and race. Like their northern sisters, southern suffragists argued that "social housekeeping" affirmed the right of virtuous women to vote and supported the idea that marriage was a partnership. The suffragists held that domestic partners should share equally in civic rights. Indeed, women, taxed without representation, claimed the right to vote and denied that antisuffragists had the authority to determine what women wanted.[64]

Suffragists did not foresee a social breakdown; rather, they argued that the vote would enhance the political order. Women's cleanup of "politics as usual" would only benefit the social order, according to suffragist theory. In addition, prosuffrage forces resented laws that were unfair to women and argued that only the vote could change the discrimination within the legal system.[65]

Yet the outstanding argument in favor of women's suffrage was that sheer numbers would protect white superiority in the South and thus ensure the southern balance of power in the nation. Southern suffragists tacitly approved disenfranchisement of blacks by their support of literacy and property qualifications. The strategy, as Paul Fuller suggests, was borrowed from the northern suffragists, Henry Blackwell and Carrie Chapman Catt, who proposed such limitations as a means of blocking the vote of immigrants and black illiterates. In theory, moderate southern suffragists accepted the idea that black women should be allowed to vote, but in reality they placed limitations upon the idea. Although critics noted that many young black women were literate, southern suffragists argued that property qualifications should be added to the franchise.[66]

White racism thus split the woman's reform movement in the South; and in only a few instances did white and black women organize for the purpose of dealing with the concerns of their respective communities. Directed toward the needs of the Afro-American community, the priorities and methods of black women differed appreciably from the goals and strategies of their white counterparts. Initially, missionary experience for black women was made possible by such northern-based groups as the American Board of Commissioners for Foreign Missions, which commissioned black missionary women, and the American Missionary Association, which hired southern black women teachers in the immediate postwar period. Hence, disparate racial experiences made the reform efforts of black women and white women quite different.

The American Board of Commissioners for Foreign Missions endorsed two black women as missionaries—Henrietta Bailey, the wife of missionary Benjamin Forsyth Ousley, and Nancy Jones, an unmarried woman. Both women were born in the South, Bailey in Washington County, Mississippi, and Jones in Hopkinsville, Kentucky, and both had been educated at Fisk University. Sent to Durban, South Africa, in the 1880s, each served a long and distinguished career in the field.[67]

The Southern Presbyterian Church sent a remarkable group of black women missionaries to Africa between 1894 and 1906. At the age of fifty-six, Maria Fearing offered her services to the church and later founded the Pantops Home for Girls. She taught young African women domestic skills and religious discipline. She saw her role as "civilizing and Christianizing" the African people. Lillian May Thomas, who was sent with Maria Fearing on the 1894 mission, later became superintendent of Pantops and set up a day school in Luebo. A third missionary, Lucy Gantt Sheppard, wife of William Sheppard, leader of the Luebo Mission, taught school and trained women in domestic skills. Mrs. Sheppard also organized the first Congo Women's Society in which members of the prayer group engaged in benevolent work. Another missionary, Althea Maria Brown, transcribed the Bakuba language into a written language in addition to her teaching and nursing responsibilities. Finally, Annie Katherine Taylor, who worked at Pantops later became the supervisor of the Maria Carey Home in Ibanche.[68]

Southern black women labored in greater numbers as teachers among the freedmen of the South. The American Missionary Association originally recruited northern teachers, both male and female, black and white, but financial exigencies pressured Charleston administrators Francis L. Cardozo and Thomas W. Cardozo to hire southern black men and women. "We were already on the spot teaching and [southern black teachers] could be employed cheaper than Northern ones," Francis Cardozo, a mulatto, explained.[69] The wages set by Superintendent Thomas Cardozo discriminated against black women. As of January 1865 black women were paid $25 a month while black men received $40 a month. White women were paid between $35 and $40 in contrast to white males who drew $50 a month. In the spring the association lowered the monthly pay of black women to $12 a month. Thomas Cardozo's pay scales reflected the racial and sexual pay differentials that existed throughout the United States during the nineteenth century. Eventually, however, inflation drove up the price of living to three times the wartime level and prompted black women teachers to demand pay at least equal to northern women. The great need for southern black women teachers forced the association's acquiescence.[70]

Francis Cardozo, who succeeded his brother Thomas in August 1865, was criticized for hiring unskilled and undereducated black teachers, but he pleaded to retain them. In a letter to his superior, Reverend S. Hunt, on 13 January 1866, Francis Cardozo argued for retention of the black teachers in spite of past experiences in which a few South Carolina teachers proved incompetent:

> In your letter you refer to the propriety of selecting suitable colored persons for the work and yet the difficulty of finding such. I fully agree with you, I think it far better that no colored persons should engage in this work at all, than to have such as would only disgrace the cause, and retard the progress of their own people, And yet notwithstanding the unfortunate failures in Charleston . . . I entreat you to employ Mr. and Mrs. McR. because *I felt so sure*, and do still feel, that they will *redeem* the failures committed here.[71]

Although Francis Cardozo defended his choice of black teachers by arguing that they were intelligent, he nevertheless assured his superior that black teachers were placed in less responsible positions until they were ready to teach.[72] Presumably, then, by the end of 1866 the native black women employed by the American Missionary Association—among them Catherine Winslow, Amelia Ann Shrewsbury, Harriet Holloway, Rosabella Fields, and Charlotte Johnson—labored in secondary teaching positions.[73] Their presence among the freedmen and freedwomen attracted many willing students. Judging from the plight of Mary Still, a northern-born black woman who taught in South Carolina, the work, which was so exhausting that it was nearly unendurable, was deeply appreciated by the poor black population. She reported to her superior in the spring of 1866 that her school was well-attended, and later she noted that "the people of Beaufort are anxious for me to remain here; a nother [sic] party wants me to go to Florida."[74] Still eventually left the American Missionary Association because of dire poverty. In a last desperate letter to Reverend Hunt, she said, "[P]rudence tells me to go home. It has cost me all of my salary this winter to aid the poor. I am pennyless today."[75]

The dedication of black women teachers to the poor of their own race indicates that they not only desired to work within their own community but also that they were frustrated by the lack of economic opportunities outside the black community. Thus the American Missionary Association opened the profession of teaching to southern black women, but at the same time it exploited their labor. Nevertheless, black women's teaching experience implanted in them an awareness of community need.

None recognized the need more perceptively than the dynamic Nannie Burroughs who headed the women's auxiliary of the National Baptist Convention in 1901. As a worker for the Foreign Mission Board and later corresponding secretary of the women's auxiliary, she shocked the 1901 National Baptist Convention by suggesting that the convention create an educational and training school for black women. The women's auxiliary and later the convention did support her plan but were unable to contribute the $50,000 she requested. Then, against the advice of convention leaders who argued that financial support could be gained only from the white community, Nannie Burroughs canvassed individual members of the black National Baptist Convention for small donations. She succeeded in accumulating enough capital to establish her school in Washington, D.C. In 1909 she assumed the presidency of the school. She had achieved her goal through the small contributions of members of her own black community.[76]

It is clear that the WCTU benefited from the social consciousness generated by the black women's missionary movement. The southern WCTU did not remain a white woman's movement. On her initial southern tour Frances Willard spoke to black audiences at Atlanta and Clark universities, and both Sally Chapin and Georgia M'Leod influenced black women to organize segregated black women's WCTU chapters. Because the national WCTU did not interfere with local organizational preferences, its southern chapters continued to practice segregation. On the other hand, only a few northern unions were integrated at that time.[77]

With the exception of those in Alabama and Georgia, most of the black chapters of the WCTU, known as "#2 Unions," emerged at the turn of the century. Their membership included some very distinguished black women. For example, Mrs. Booker T. Washington served as president of the Alabama chapter of the WCTU #2. Black women's involvement in the WCTU continued to expand and in the 1890s Lucy Simpson Thurman of Michigan served as the national "Superintendent of Colored Work." Thurman viewed the WCTU in the same way as did white women, that is, as a center for training women as leaders.[78]

The activities of women in the black community gave rise to a wide-ranging and successful reform movement. Their awareness of the need to defend their community against lynching prompted an antilynching crusade that eventually transformed black women's organizations into the powerful club movement. The antilynching movement fostered a productive association of black and white women whose united appeal helped to dispel the myth that lynching protected the virtue of white women. An outgrowth of the antilynching crusade, the National Association of Colored Women, coordinated health, welfare, and education projects among affiliated organizations. Its projects included work in reformatories, industrial schools, kindergartens, reading libraries, homes for the aged, and protective homes for "wayward girls."[79]

Black women were active at the local level as well as at the national level. The Atlanta Neighborhood Union, a settlement project, was established by Eugenia Hope in 1908 for the purpose of improving living conditions among urban black families. The organization provided welfare services to a community deprived of any social agencies. Mrs. Hope, the wife of John Hope, president of Morehouse College, responded to the plight of the poor families who settled near the college. She had begun her efforts as a result of a neighborhood crisis, the death of a woman who left behind two small children with no one to care for them. Mrs. Hope called a meeting of her neighbors to discuss methods of dealing with this and other local concerns. The meeting resulted in the formation of the Atlanta Neighborhood Union, chartered in 1911, which divided the city into zones and districts, with presiding officers, workers, and neighbors accepting responsibility for casework in assigned areas. The caseworkers made intensive surveys of the residents of the area and reported on needs and problems. In order to meet welfare needs, the organization collected funds from dues and solicitations. Within a few years, the Atlanta Neighborhood Union could claim responsibility for improved sanitation, schools, health services, playground construction, and crime control.[80]

The Atlanta Neighborhood Union was just one organization that provided a means of dealing with complex changes that occurred among urban black families at the turn of the century. Herbert Gutman has noted that significant changes took place in the southern black urban home between 1880 and 1900. The "kin-related" household remained typical, but the percentage of "male-absent households and subfamilies increased." Eventually, then, the importance of the nuclear household declined, and the augmented or extended household increased.[81]

The leadership of the Atlanta Neighborhood Union evoked the memory of the traditional rural black community. "What did our foreparents do? . . . These people lived their lives in this community—all of [their] network was there," wrote Mrs. Hope, whose guiding principle was "love thy neighbor as thyself." Eugenia Hope recognized that individual need could be met only through a system of relationships or institutions that could respond to human "instincts, impulses, appetites and desires." If, as Mrs. Hope believed, "home is the basis of a people's development," then the lessons of the system—"thrift, law and sacrifice"—were taught there. The benefits of the "organized community", according to Eugenia Hope, were education, home ownership, and prosperity.[82]

The franchise did not play a central role in black women's reform. Although the suffrage movement gained important leaders like Mary Church Terrell, the majority of black women were preoccupied with community concerns. The attitude of Margaret Murray, a reform leader, typified the black woman's reaction to the suffrage movement. She remarked that women's suffrage was right but that "personally it's never kept me awake at night."[83] The insistence upon white supremacy by southern suffragist leaders, such as Belle Kearny and Rebecca Felton, effectively prevented consistent interracial cooperation on the issue of suffrage.

Joint projects did evolve, however. The antilynching campaign recruited both black and white women. For example, the membership of the General Federation of Women's Clubs in Georgia and North Carolina publicly denounced lynching. Women of both races also cooperated in local projects such as the day-care facility for black children sponsored by the Athens Women's Club. White women also responded to appeals from black women for better school facilities.[84] For the most part, however, southern women followed separate racial paths toward reform.

Despite the tragic racial division in the women's reform movement both in the South and in the North, women made remarkable progress through organized effort. Although methods, strategies, and organization differed, in each racial community both black and white women addressed public issues of health, crime, sanitation, lynching, child care, and education. Unfortunately, race and class determined the collective basis of women's identity. Therefore, women's leadership, spawned by missionary societies and the WCTU, could not provide the combined energies needed to accomplish feminist and social goals. The National American Woman's Suffrage Association belatedly recognized the necessity of the black woman's vote just prior to the passage of the Nineteenth Amendment, and systematic attempts to deal with social problems did not mature until the time of the New Deal.

Regardless of the fact that the southern community exercised social control over individual and family behavior for generations, the role of women did not remain static in southern culture. Church reorganization and secular trends adjusted sexual roles within evangelical society so that women were able to assume church and social responsibilities. And, perhaps more significantly, individual black and white women struggled through the conversion experience toward autonomy and self-definition. Moreover, the farm woman who contributed to southern self-sufficiency by accepting the unequal burdens of both household and field responsibilities not only became knowledgeable about the everyday business of the farm but also became capable managers. Black women, caught in a double bind of slavery and evangelical social control, nevertheless resisted white women's authority, and their role in the evangelical discipline at least allowed them a measure of equality within the church. Although the Civil War did not substantially change the position of women, it did demand the exercise of women's managerial and organizational talents.

Yet because southern rural culture discouraged their association, women were able to assert themselves only very gradually. Without a pattern of systematic association, individual victories over repression and discrimination did not restructure the role of women. Traditional attitudes concerning women's domestic role existed simultaneously with acceptance of women's religious and social leadership. Thus changes in sexual roles evolved slowly in the South because modernization never fully displaced the traditional southern community.

outhern communities, like vertebrae, fastened along the spine of the southern region, holding intact the vital cords of social life while supporting the complex tissue of human relationships. In the sensitive area that was the southern evangelical community, any shift or adjustment of relationships alarmed the neighborhood-kin system. Southern women's autonomy, which threatened to alter the nature of relationships, therefore expressed itself in subtle ways, ways that did not destroy the form or the structure of the evangelical community.

Because their lives bound them to kin rather than to each other, women identified most strongly with community rather than with alien women's groups. However, without the organization of independent women's groups, the struggle, the psychic pain of adjusting to or rejecting community relationships, was especially hard for both black and white women. But their struggle and their pain signaled that something was wrong with the system. Southern women in their own way recognized the pressures and sufferings that oppressed them. And, as circumstances changed with modernization, black and white women's reactions to their plight enabled them to transform older neighborhood-kin associations into active reform groups.

The rigid structure of evangelical community, which maintained traditional sexual roles, was consistently challenged and pressured by women struggling against or adjusting to community expectations. In the evangelical neighborhood, women did not always passively submit to the church committee's intervention or to the church's decision concerning their "conduct." Some women rebuffed committee investigation and a noticeable number of women who did not agree with the disciplinary decisions of congregations formed factions that broke away from the church. Ministers served notice to dissident women by consistently warning them against the dangers of factionalism. In addition to their resistance against discipline, women did not peacefully submit to the denial of voting rights and participation in church management. The Baptist church, at least, debated the issue of the vote for women. Nevertheless, the evangelical order prevailed: women did not vote except in Primitive Baptist churches. Furthermore, in matters of sexual misconduct, the church's peremptory response precluded any defense by women. Thus a male hierarchy dominated the church and administered a double standard of judgment and punishment with regard to women.

The evangelical order, then, defined sexual roles and determined the nature of relationships. The rural partnership, which suggests flexibility of role, actually expanded women's work in the field without extending men's work in the household, a condition that indicated women's double burden in the "partnership." Moreover, the executive problems of the planter's wife demonstrate the many difficulties in the subordinate status of women, among which were the limitation in decision-making and the anxiety of overreaching her authority. Not all women lived in a rural partnership. Widows and single women managed plantations and for the most part enjoyed sovereignty over all aspects of plantation business. Some women exercised considerable skill and turned over a handsome profit in their enterprises. Their position, however, was a unique one in the male-dominated society of the Old South. Urban women were economically dependent, but they had greater leisure than did their rural sisters and were able to develop relationships and to organize benevolent societies.

Although traditional sexual roles were generally accepted in the South, evangelical marriage contained within it the expectations of a true union or partnership. Southern women used their influence to draw men into that union, which would have meant husbands' greater domestic responsibility, but their success was, unfortunately, only sporadic. Both women and men accepted the principle of male domestic responsibility, nonetheless.

Community structures that determined sexual roles also shaped the interior life of women. Individual women expressed their unconscious desires and anxieties in the powerful evangelical symbols of conversion and community. These symbols conveyed a sense of self that was constantly renewed and integrated into a society of neighbors and kin. In a society that valued conformity it seems strange that women's struggle toward self-definition and social integration followed no set course. Each woman chose to accept, reject, or modify evangelical precepts according to her own individual need.

The evangelical religious and familial values that pervaded both black and white culture had profound consequences for the formation of Afro-American women's identity. If, as Lawrence Levine contends, culture is a process— and by the time of the Civil War widespread Christian conversion had made very successful advances into slave culture—then it may be assumed that Afro-American culture became increasingly evangelical. The growth of evangelicalism gave Afro-American women greater opportunity for self-definition. Conversion testimony ritually transformed Afro-American women's identities even though it did not change the maternal character of their roles. Ironically, however, because the patriarchy and the Afro-American community valued maternity, opportunities for women's leadership in religion were enhanced. In addition, the powerlessness of slave men and slave women gave both sexes an equal opportunity to exert initiative and leadership. Afro-American culture contributed to black women's confidence in productivity, resistance to oppression, and maintenance of families.

The Civil War did not disturb the kinship systems or greatly alter women's consciousness. The survival of the southern kin network, shown in the demographic recovery after the war, high rates of stability in certain neighborhoods, and refugee patterns prevented any radical shift in women's roles. Even women's education had a limited impact in changing postwar sexual roles because it was controlled by the community and the family. The postwar period, then, was characterized by the continuity of evangelical social order. First of all, career opportunities, such as nursing and the civil service, ended with the war. Second, women's education prepared women for only marginal employment. Factory women, whose labor was exploited, had little defense against the Confederate government, which quashed the women's strike. Third, collective action, such as women's bread riots, demonstrated that when women did act on their own, they acted in behalf of their families. Moreover, plantation mistresses fared no better after the war than before the war. As deputy husbands, they were in no better position and indeed their circumstance worsened with the loss of household help. Furthermore, the continuity of the white kinship system also limited black women's autonomy. Informal neighborhood agreements among whites forced black labor back to the plantations.

The enduring traditional roles only gradually changed with domestic reconstruction and the introduction of modernization in the latter part of the nineteenth century. Modernization resulted in the decline in piety, decrease in church trials, and the acceptance of sexual segregation. However, the maintenance of kin ties meant that modernization would advance unevenly. Because the sexually segregated reform groups recruited people from the traditional neighborhood-kin group, women's association tended to remain conservative or traditionally evangelical on certain issues. The WCTU found widespread support in the South because it stressed familial values—"organized mother love." And the southern women's suffrage movement preserved white supremacy, the social order of the white community. Regardless of intent, however, simply the experience of active social service expanded and altered community perceptions of white women's roles.

The family concerns of black women prompted reform within the Afro-American community. As missionaries and teachers, black women struggled to educate and encourage higher expectations among Afro-Americans. Moreover, the broad spectrum of community concerns, evidenced by women's involvement in the black WCTU groups, antilynching societies, and especially the Atlanta Neighborhood Union led to black women's solidarity.

The southern women's reform movement with a few exceptions followed a biracial pattern until the twentieth century when the antilynching movement drew black and white women together in common cause. Ultimately, then, the evangelical community proscribed reform but could not prevent it.

TABLE 1.1

Type of Offense in Town Churches by Sex, 1830–1889

| | Number | | | Percent | |
| | White | White | Both | White | White |
Type Of Offense	Males	Females	Sexes	Males	Females
Disorderly conduct	94	15	109	87	50
Sexual offenses	14	15	29	13	50
Total	108	30	138	100	100

Sources: Church minutes of First Baptist Church, Fayetteville, First Baptist Church, Raleigh, North Carolina (from the disciplinary cases in Smith, "Church Organization," Appendix IV, pp. 306–8, 317–19); First Presbyterian Church, Athens, Georgia.

TABLE 1.2

*White Male and Female Offenders Accused of
Disorderly Conduct and Sexual Offenses
North Carolina and Georgia Churches, 1830–1889*

| | Number | | | Percent | |
| | White | White | Both | White | White |
Type Of Offense	Males	Females	Sexes	Males	Females
Disorderly conduct	566	132	698	94	56
Sexual offenses	38	103	141	6	44
Total	604	235	839	100	100

Sources: Church minutes of Mount Olive Baptist Church, Alamance County, Cypress Presbyterian Church, Harnett County, North Carolina; Beaverdam Baptist Church, Wilkes County, Bark Camp Baptist Church, Burke County, Cabin Creek Baptist Church, Jackson County, Georgia; First Presbyterian Church, Athens, Georgia; and C. V. Smith's nine North Carolina Baptist churches: First Baptist Church, Fayetteville, First Baptist Church, Raleigh, Red Bark, Hepzibah, Wheely's, Mt. Pisgah, Jersey, Island Ford, Three Forks.

TABLE 1.3

Charges against Offenders by Sex:
North Carolina and Georgia Churches, 1830–1889

	Number			Percent	
Charges against Offenders	White Males	White Females	Both Sexes	White Males	White Females
Single Charges	132	76	208	73	86
Multiple Charges	49	12	61	27	14
Total	181	88	269	100	100

Sources: Church minutes of Mount Olive Baptist Church, Alamance County, Cypress Presbyterian Church, Harnett County, North Carolina; Beaverdam Baptist Church, Wilkes County, Bark Camp Baptist Church, Burke County, Cabin Creek Baptist Church, Jackson County, Georgia; First Presbyterian Church, Athens, Georgia.

TABLE 1.4

White Male and Female Offenders Forgiven or Acquitted
for Disorderly Behavior or Sexual Misconduct:
North Carolina and Georgia Churches, 1830–1889

	Number			Percent	
Offenders	White Males	White Females	Both Sexes	White Males	White Females
Forgiven	59	14	73	33	16
Not Forgiven	122	74	196	67	84
Total	181	88	269	100	100

Sources: Church minutes of Mount Olive Baptist Church, Alamance County, Cypress Presbyterian Church, Harnett County, North Carolina; Beaverdam Baptist Church, Wilkes County, Bark Camp Baptist Church, Burke County, Cabin Creek Baptist Church, Jackson County, Georgia; First Presbyterian Church, Athens, Georgia.

TABLE 1.5
Type of Punishment Administered to White Male and Female Offenders for Sexual Misconduct: North Carolina and Georgia Churches, 1830–1889

| | Number | | | Percent | |
	White Males	White Females	Both Sexes	White Males	White Females
None	2	1	3	17	4
Suspension or Exclusion	10	26	36	83	96
Total	12	27	39	100	100

Sources: Church minutes of Mount Olive Baptist Church, Alamance County, Cypress Presbyterian Church, Harnett County, North Carolina; Beaverdam Baptist Church, Wilkes County, Bark Camp Baptist Church, Burke County, Cabin Creek Baptist Church, Jackson County, Georgia; First Presbyterian Church, Athens, Georgia.

TABLE 1.6
Restoration of White Male and Female Offenders by Sex: North Carolina and Georgia Churches, 1830–1889

| | Number | | | Percent | |
Restoration	White Males	White Females	Both Sexes	White Males	White Females
Restored	24	6	30	13	7
Not Restored	157	82	239	87	93
Total	181	88	269	100	100

Sources: Church minutes of Mount Olive Baptist Church, Alamance County, Cypress Presbyterian Church, Harnett County, North Carolina; Beaverdam Baptist Church, Wilkes County, Bark Camp Baptist Church, Burke County, Cabin Creek Baptist Church, Jackson County, Georgia; First Presbyterian Church, Athens, Georgia.

TABLE 4.1

Black Male and Female Offenders Accused of
Disorderly Conduct and Sexual Offenses:
North Carolina and Georgia Churches, 1830–1865

Type Of Offense	Number			Percent	
	Black Males	Black Females	Both Sexes	Black Males	Black Females
Disorderly conduct	19	11	30	86	69
Sexual offenses	3	5	8	14	31
Total	22	16	38	100	100

Sources: Church minutes of Mount Olive Baptist Church, Alamance County, Cypress Presbyterian Church, Harnett County, North Carolina; Beaverdam Baptist Church, Wilkes County, Bark Camp Baptist Church, Burke County, Cabin Creek Baptist Church, Jackson County, Georgia; First Presbyterian Church, Athens, Georgia.

N O T E S

Abbreviations Used in the Notes

DiU	Dillard University, New Orleans, La.
DU	Duke University, Durham, N.C.
GDAH	Georgia Department of Archives and History, Atlanta, Ga.
GHS	Georgia Historical Society, Savannah, Ga.
LC	Library of Congress, Washington, D.C.
LSU	Louisiana State University, Baton Rouge, La.
NCC UNC	North Carolina Collection, University of North Carolina, Chapel Hill, N.C.
NCSA	North Carolina State Archives, Raleigh, N.C.
RC	Radcliffe College, Cambridge, Mass.
SCC USC	South Caroliniana Collection, University of South Carolina, Columbia, S.C.
SCHS	South Carolina Historical Society, Charleston, S.C.
SHC UNC	Southern Historical Collection, University of North Carolina, Chapel Hill, N.C.
TU	Tulane University, New Orleans, La.
UGA	University of Georgia, Athens, Ga.
VHS	Virginia Historical Society, Richmond, Va.
VSL	Virginia State Library, Richmond, Va.

Introduction

1. Owsley, *Plain Folk*; Kenzer, "Portrait of a Southern Community"; Anderson, *Family Structure*; Rosenberg and Anspach, *Working Class Kinship*.

2. Smith-Rosenberg, "The Female World."

3. Cott, *The Bonds of Womanhood*; Berg, *The Remembered Gate*.

4. Cott, *The Bonds of Womanhood*, p. 98.

5. Ibid., p. 201.

6. Ibid., pp. 201–4.

7. Berg, *The Remembered Gate*, pp. xi, 148, 170.

8. Smith, "Church Organization."

Chapter 1

1. Howell Cobb Correspondence, UGA.

2. Burke, *Reminiscences*, p. 97; Hop-

ley, *Life in the South*, 1:56; Amelia Jane
Akehurst Diary, 22 Feb. 1857, UGA.

3. Burke, *Reminiscences*, p. 27.

4. Amanda Jane Cooley Roberts Diary,
2 July 1843, VHS; Fannie Page Hume
Diary, 8 Jan. 1860, SHC UNC; Amelia
Jane Akehurst Diary, 22 Feb. 1857, 14
Mar. 1858, UGA; Annie Darden Diary, 8
Oct. 1855, NCSA.

5. Anne Beale Davis Diary, 9 Feb. 1851,
SHC UNC.

6. Maria Bryan Harford to Julia A.
Cumming, 8 Oct. 1840, Hammond-Bryan-
Cumming Family Correspondence, SCC
USC; Susan L. Brown to John B. Miller,
13 Jan. 1843, Miller-Furman-Dabbs
Family Papers, SCC USC; Miss Weisiger
Diary, 22 Dec. 1844, VSL.

7. Sarah A. Lamar to John B. Lamar, 24
Mar. 1841, Howell Cobb Correspondence, UGA.

8. Burke, *Reminiscences*, pp. 236–37;
Mary Ann Lamar to Mary Ann Cobb,
Sept. 1848, Howell Cobb Correspon-
dence, UGA; Hessie to Mary Ann Cobb, 6
Oct. 1849, Howell Cobb Correspon-
dence, UGA.

9. Anne Beale Davis Diary, 28 Oct.
1838, SHC UNC.

10. Miss Weisiger's Diary, 19 Mar., 4
Aug. 1842, VSL.

11. 16 Sept. 1833, Howell Cobb Correspondence, UGA.

12. H. A. Cobb to Sarah Lamar, 30
Sept. 1845, Howell Cobb Correspondence, UGA.

13. S. R. Cobb to Mary Ann Cobb, 22
Oct. 1846, Howell Cobb Correspondence, UGA.

14. L. Rutherford to Howell and Mary
Ann Cobb, 2 Jan. 1848, Howell Cobb
Correspondence, UGA.

15. Mathilda Todd DeVan Memorial, 10
July 1865, TU.

16. Annie Darden Diary, 10 Feb. 1855,
NCSA.

17. Cott, *The Bonds of Womanhood*,
p. 3.

18. Smith-Rosenberg, "Beauty, the
Beast," pp. 197–221; Cott, *The Bonds of
Womanhood*; Berg, *The Remembered
Gate*; Ryan, "The Power of Women's Networks," pp. 66–85. Both Nancy Cott and
Mary Ryan explore the more complex
ambiguities associated with the relationship between women's organization and
the reform movement.

19. Cott, *The Bonds of Womanhood*,
p. 3; Berg, *The Remembered Gate*;
Smith-Rosenberg, "Beauty, the Beast."

20. Mathews, *Religion in the Old
South*, p. 110.

21. For an understanding of the limitations upon antebellum agrarian productivity, urban growth, an integrated market
system, and "modern" attitudes toward
fertility, see Hilliard, *Hog Meat and Hoecake*; Weaver, *Mississippi Farmers*; Russel, "The Effects of Slavery," pp. 112–26;
Wright, *The Political Economy of the Cotton South*; McDonald and McWhiney,
"The South from Self-Sufficiency,"
pp. 1095–1119; Huffman, Jr., "Town and
Country in the South," pp. 366–81; Rindfuss, "Changing Patterns of Fertility in the
South," pp. 621–35; Vinovskis, "Socio-
economic Determinants of Interstate Fertility," pp. 375–96.

22. Mathews, *Religion in the Old
South*, pp. 1–80; see also Schneider,
"Kinship, Community," pp. 155–74, for a
discussion of the relationship between
bloodline and locality; Boles, "Evangelical Protestantism"; Boles, *The Great Revival*.

23. *Plain Folk*, pp. 62, 66, 70. See also
Matthews, *Neighbor and Kin*, pp. 3–4;
Brown, "Social Class, Intermarriage,"
pp. 232–33.

24. Cypress Presbyterian Church Minutes, NCSA; United States Census Reports, Harnett and Cumberland counties,

1830–80, LC and on microfilm, UGA; Tax Lists, Harnett County, 1837–47, NCSA; Marriage Records, Harnett County, 1800–80, NCSA; Ross, *The Cape Fear*, pp. 47–53.

25. Owsley, *Plain Folk*, pp. 62, 63, 70, 94; Matthews, *Neighbor and Kin*; Hendrix, "Kinship and Economic-Rational Migration," pp. 534–43; Hendrix, "Kinship, Social Class," pp. 399–409; Brown, "Social Class, Intermarriage," pp. 232–42; Brown et al., "Kentucky Mountain Migration," pp. 48–69; Schwarzweller et al., *Mountain Families in Transition*. The names on the membership lists of the Mount Olive Baptist Church, Alamance County, correlated with identical names on the United States census reports of 1830–1880 (multiple identical names were eliminated), demonstrating that church members resided in Alamance, Rockingham, Guilford, Randolph, Chatham, Wake, Orange, and Granville counties.

26. "Patterns of Crisis," pp. 524–43.

27. To Elizabeth J. Holmes Blanks, n.d., Elizabeth J. Holmes Blanks Correspondence, DU.

28. Wyatt-Brown, "The Ideal Typology," pp. 1–29.

29. Laura Norwood to Louisa S. Lenoir, 8 Aug. 1839 (?), Lenoir Family Papers, SHC UNC.

30. Lizzie Graves to Sarah Jones Lenoir, 11 Mar. 1851, Lenoir Family Papers, SHC UNC; Julia Picking to Eliza Myra Lenoir, 15 May 1834, Lenoir Family Papers, SHC UNC; Henrietta Spencer [niece] to Sarah B. Evans, 12 Sept. 1842, Nathaniel Evans and Family Papers, LSU; S. B. Evans to Gabriel Adams, 5 Jan. 1843, Nathaniel Evans and Family Papers, LSU; S. B. Thomas to S. B. Evans, 6 June 1843, Nathaniel Evans and Family Papers, LSU.

31. Martha Foster Crawford Diary, 9

Sept. 1849, DU.

32. Ibid., 13 Nov. 1847, DU.

33. Fannie Page Hume Diary, 24 July 1860, SHC UNC.

34. Mary Telfair to Mary Few, 30 Mar. [no year], Telfair Family Papers, GHS.

35. Louisa Lord Correspondence, 11 June 1853, SCHS.

36. *Family Structure*, p. 509.

37. Wallman, "Kinship, Anti-kinship," pp. 331–41. Recent studies show rural migrants maintained contact with urban kin for aid and job information; Anderson, *Family Structure*; Anderson, "Family, Household, and the Industrial Revolution," pp. 59–75; Hareven, ed., *Family and Kin*; Hareven, "The Dynamics of Kin."

38. Suggested by Shulman, "Life Cycle Variations," pp. 817–18.

39. Kissinger, *The Sermon on the Mount*, p. 38; Wadsworth, "God and Man Are Co-Workers," pp. 106–7; Mallary, "The Doctrine of Election," Sermon XIV; Boswell, "Salvation in Its Individual Relations." For the importance of the Sermon on the Mount in the training of southern children, see Susan Davis Nye Hutchinson Diary, 1 Dec. 1833, 6 Dec. 1840, NCSA.

40. *Religion in the Old South*, pp. 40, 2–5, 39–46, 65, 240. See also Mary Davis Brown Diary, 6 Oct. 1855, SCC USC; Anne A. Turner Diary, 20 Mar. 1832, DU; Miss Weisiger Diary, 11 July 1843, VSL; Julia A. Hawes to Louisa L. Lenoir, 15 July 1844, Lenoir Family Papers, SHC UNC; Mathilda Todd DeVan Memorial, 1868, TU; Harriott Cheves to Susan Middleton, 1 Apr. 1862, Cheves Collection, SCHS; L. Rutherford to Howell and Mary Ann Cobb, 19 Mar. 1848, Howell Cobb Correspondence, UGA.

41. S. Myra Cox Smith Diary, 6 Apr. 1852, Somerville-Howorth Collection, RC; Anne Beale Davis Diary, 16 Feb.

1851, 7 Aug. 1851, 18 June 1857, 17 Jan. 1859, SHC UNC.

42. Lizzie Graves to Sarah Jane Lenoir, 11 Sept. 1854, Lenoir Family Papers, SHC UNC.

43. Anne Turner Diary, 26 Aug. 1868, DU.

44. "Articles of Faith," adopted 7 Feb. 1828, Beaver Dam Baptist Church Minutes, VSL.

45. Battle Run Baptist Church Minutes, 7 Mar. 1835, VSL.

46. Beaver Dam Baptist Church Minutes, 7 Feb. 1828, VSL.

47. Ryan, "The Power of Women's Networks," pp. 71-72.

48. Green River Baptist Association Minutes, p. 5., NCSA.

49. Sweet, *Methodism in American History*, pp. 110ff., 253; Smith, "Church Organization," pp. 74-75, 139; Thompson, *Presbyterians in the South*, 1:77; *The Constitution of the Presbyterian Church* (1833).

50. Beaver Run Baptist Church "Rules of Decorum," VSL; see also "Articles of Faith," adopted 7 Feb. 1828, Beaver Dam Baptist Church Minutes, VSL; Green River Baptist Church Circular Letter, 1848, NCSA; White Oak Primitive Baptist Church Minutes, 7 May 1854, NCSA; Mount Olive Baptist Church "Rules of Decorum," NCSA.

51. Smith, "Church Organization," p. 139.

52. *The Doctrines and Discipline of the Methodist Episcopal Church* (1840), pp. 92-94; *The Doctrines and Discipline of the Methodist Episcopal Church* (1866), pp. 124-29; Mell, *Corrective Church Discipline*.

53. Smith, "Church Organization," pp. 52-53, 117, 128.

54. Wheeler's Primitive Baptist Church Minutes, NCC UNC; Red Banks Primitive Baptist Church Minutes, NCSA.

55. Beaver Run Baptist Church Minutes, Aug. 1834, VSL; Pleasant Union Christian Church Records, pp. 10-12, SHC UNC; Chapel Hill Presbyterian Church Records, p. 62, SHC UNC; Worrell, *Review of Corrective Church Discipline*, pp. 208-9.

56. Worrell, *Review of Corrective Church Discipline*, pp. 209-16.

57. Pleasant Union Christian Church Records, SHC UNC; Broad Run Baptist Church Minutes, VHS.

58. Smith, "Church Organization," pp. 304-41; Kenzer, "Portrait of a Southern Community."

59. Broad Run Baptist Church Minutes, 12 July, 9 Aug., 13 Dec. 1828, VSL; Occoquam Virginia Baptist Church Minutes, 3 Aug. 1827, May 1831, VHS; Cabin Creek Baptist Church Minutes, 3 June 1838, GDAH.

60. Pleasant Grove Primitive Baptist Church Minutes, Jan., Mar. 1851, 10 Aug. 1832, NCSA.

61. Cabin Creek Baptist Church Minutes, 3 June 1848, GDAH.

62. Wheeler's Primitive Baptist Church Minutes, Aug., Sept. 1839, NCC UNC.

63. Pleasant Grove Primitive Baptist Church Minutes, Feb.-June 1846, NCSA.

64. Ibid., May 1847, NCSA.

65. Smith, "Church Organization," p. 203.

66. Byrd Presbyterian Church Minutes, 11 Oct. 1829, VSL.

67. Ibid.

68. Ibid.

69. Bark Camp Baptist Church Minutes, 22 May 1836, GDAH.

70. Beaverdam Baptist Church Minutes, 15 Apr. 1865, GDAH.

71. Cabin Creek Baptist Church Minutes, 6 July 1844, GDAH.

72. Mount Olive Baptist Church Minutes, Sept. 1849, NCSA.

73. Wheeler's Primitive Baptist Church

Minutes, July 1834, NCC UNC.

74. Pleasant Grove Primitive Baptist Church Minutes, Dec. 1838, NCSA.

75. Wheeler's Primitive Baptist Church Minutes, May 1831, Mar. 1849, NCC UNC; Pleasant Grove Primitive Baptist Church Minutes, Apr. 1846, NCSA.

76. *The Doctrines and Discipline* (1840), pp. 87–88.

77. Hopley, *Life in the South*, 1:26; Monumental Methodist Church Trustee Minutes, 25 May 1835, VSL; *The Doctrines and Discipline* (1866), p. 93; Emory, *History of the Discipline*, pp. 183–87; Annie to Sarah J. Lenoir, 13 June 1849, Lenoir Family Papers, SHC UNC; Fannie Page Hume Diary, 11 Jan. 1860, SHC UNC; Anne Beale Davis Diary, 29 May 1839, SHC UNC; Louisa Norwood to Capt. Thomas J. Lenoir, 10 May 1858, Lenoir Family Papers, SHC UNC.

78. Martha Foster Crawford Diary, 15 Sept. 1850, 6 Oct. 1850, 21 Apr. 1852, 14 May 1852, 19 May 1852, 4 June 1852, DU; Miss Weisiger Diary, 4 May 1843, VSL; Frances (Fannie) Moore Webb Bumpas Diary, pp. 12–13, 15–16, 18, 23, SHC UNC.

79. Miss Weisiger Diary, 4 May 1843, VSL.

80. For evidence of female prayer meetings see Frances Ann Bernard Capps Diary, 5 Nov. 1844, 26 Aug. 1845, 17 Mar. 1856, VHS; Sermon Delivered at the Funeral of Evelina H. Smith Comstock, Nellie Nugent Somerville Collection, RC; Anne Beale Davis Diary, 26 Aug. 1838, SHC UNC.

81. Monumental Methodist Church Minutes, p. 120, VSL; Bethel Church Class Records, 1842–49, VSL; Alexander Circuit, Alexander County Records, 1837–1922, NCSA; Miss Weisiger Diary, 11 Oct. 1845, VHS; S. Myra Cox Smith Diary, 13 May 1852, 22 Nov. 1854, Somerville-Howorth Collection, RC; Frances (Fannie) Moore Webb Bumpas reported a Young Ladies Class in her diary, 3 Apr. 1846.

82. Ella Gertrude Clanton Thomas Diary, 4 June 1864, DU.

83. Miss Weisiger Diary, 6 Oct. 1842, VSL.

84. Frances (Fannie) Moore Webb Bumpas Diary, p. 8, SHC UNC; Miss Weisiger Diary, 15 Jan., 17 July, 3 Sept. 1843, VSL; Mary Ann Lamar to Mary Lamar Peter, undated, Howell Cobb Correspondence, UGA; Cory, "Temperance and Prohibition."

85. "Minutes of the Charleston Baptist Association at the 82nd Anniversary at Beulah Church," 3–6 Nov. 1832, p. 13, SCC USC; Brummitt, *Looking Backward*, p. 11; Athens First Presbyterian Church Minutes, GDAH.

86. Henry, "The Female Laborer in the Vineyard: Funeral Discourse, Occasioned by the Death of Miss Elizabeth Robertson"; Second Presbyterian Church, Charleston, 26 August 1827, p. 9, TU.

87. Henry, "The Female Laborer in the Vineyard," pp. 9–10.

88. Thompson, *Presbyterians in the South*, 1:289, 292; Royall, *Mrs. Royall's Southern Tour*, 2:20; Eliza J. Grantlang to Mary Ann Lamar, 31 May 1833, UGA; Independent Presbyterian Church of Savannah Church Records, 20 Apr. 1853, GHS; Brummitt, *Looking Backward*, p. 11.

89. C. Parnell to George J. M. David, 10 Nov. 1833, Hooker Collection, RC; Eliza J. Grantlang to M. A. Lamar, 31 May 1833, Howell Cobb Papers, UGA.

90. Shiloh Baptist Association Minutes, 26 Mar. 1852, VSL; Anna Lesesne Diary, 14 Jan. 1836, SCHS; Trinity and Cumberland Methodist Church Minutes (Board of Stewards), vol. 4, 2 July 1866, SCHS; Reveille Church Minutes (Board), pp. 12, 22, 25, VSL; Monumental Methodist Church, "History of Monumental Church," by Rev. W. Edwards, p. 94, VSL.

Chapter 2

1. Spruill, *Women's Life and Work*, p. 81; Owsley, *Plain Folk*, p. 35. For an examination of the myth see Taylor, *Cavalier and Yankee*, pp. 162–65.

2. Gray, *History of Agriculture*, 2:811; Bonner, *A History of Georgia Agriculture*, pp. 74, 78; Weaver, *Mississippi Farmers*, pp. 45, 49, 62, 93, 95; Hilliard, *Hog Meat and Hoecake*, p. 105; McDonald and Mc-Whiney, "The South," pp. 1096, 1105–7.

3. Hilliard, *Hog Meat and Hoecake*, pp. 24, 210; Bonner, *History of Georgia*, p. 74; Wright, *The Political Economy*, pp. 63, 71.

4. Wright, *The Political Economy*, p. 45.

5. Earle and Hoffman, "The Foundation of the Modern Economy," pp. 1055–94.

6. Tryon, *Household Manufacturing in the United States*, p. 297; Pessen, "How Different," p. 1125; Spruill, *Women's Life and Work*, pp. 80–83; Berkin and Norton, *Women of America*, pp. 37–39.

7. *Women's Life and Work*, p. 81.

8. Ibid., p. 82.

9. *Plain Folk*, p. 35.

10. Carr and Walsh, "The Planter's Wife," p. 70.

11. *Reminiscences of Georgia*, p. 21.

12. Olmsted, *Journey in the Back Country*, 1:154; Trollope, *Domestic Manners*, 1:43.

13. *Journey in the Back Country*, 1:221.

14. *Reminiscences*, p. 208.

15. *Journey in the Back Country*, 1:221.

16. Mary M. Carr Diary, 22 June 1861, DU.

17. Dick, *The Dixie Frontier*, pp. 144, 190; Tryon, *Household Manufacturing*, p. 299; Elisha Cain to Mary Telfair, 20 Nov. 1836, Telfair Family Papers, GHS.

18. Olmsted, *Journey in the Back Country*, 1:154–55.

19. Burke, *Reminiscences*, p. 208; Tryon, *Household Manufacturing*, pp. 296–97.

20. *Reminiscences*, p. 209.

21. Olmsted, *Seaboard Slave States*, 2:141, 190; Elisha Cain to Mary Telfair, 20 Nov. 1836, Telfair Family Papers, GHS.

22. Mendell and Hosmer, *Notes of Travel*, pp. 251–52; Burke, *Reminiscences*, pp. 23–25.

23. See Ulrich, *Good Wives*, p. 47.

24. Burke, *Reminiscences*, pp. 23–25.

25. Olmsted, *Seaboard Slave States*, 2:42.

26. Eaton, *The Growth of Southern Civilization*, p. 190.

27. Bremer, *Homes of the New World*, p. 366; Burke, *Reminiscences*, pp. 25, 178, 208; Olmsted, *Seaboard Slave States*, 2:9; Trollope, *Domestic Manners*, 2:43; Mendell and Hosmer, *Notes of Travel*, pp. 128, 175, 250.

28. Dick, *The Dixie Frontier*, p. 300.

29. Polly M. Summey to Salina Louise Lenoir, 2 Dec. 1835, Lenoir Family Papers, SHC UNC.

30. Julia Picking to Eliza Myra Lenoir, 15 May 1834; Lizzie Graves to Sarah J. Lenoir, 11 March 1851, 8 Sept. 1855, Lenoir Family Papers, SHC UNC; Amanda Jane Cooley Roberts Diary, 4 May 1845, 31 Mar. 1849, VHS; Olmsted, *Journey in the Back Country*, 1:154–55.

31. *Homes of the New World*, p. 366.

32. E. A. McKay to Mary Ann Cobb, 22 July 1846, Howell Cobb Correspondence, UGA.

33. Carr and Walsh, "The Planter's Wife," pp. 55–86.

34. McWhiney, *Southerners*, pp. 10, 12; Eaton, *Growth of Southern Civilization*, pp. 33–40; Owsley, "The Pattern of Migration," pp. 147–76.

35. Olmsted, *Journey in the Back*

Country, 2:32–33.

36. McWhiney, *Southerners*, p. 11.

37. For a discussion of the work roles of planters' wives see Scott, *The Southern Lady*, pp. 28–33.

38. Scott, *The Southern Lady*, p. 31.

39. Clinton, *The Plantation Mistress*, p. 21.

40. Ibid., p. 18.

41. Mrs. William B. Taliaferro Diary, 4, 5 Dec. 1861, VHS; Martha Varnier Diary, 5 Jan. 1859, VSL; Edmondston, "Journal of a Secesh Lady," pp. 4, 23; Sara R. Cobb to Mary Ann Cobb, 2 Nov. 1840, Howell Cobb Correspondence, UGA; Elizabeth Baldwin Wiley Harris Diary, 29 Sept. 1863, DU; Annie Darden Diary, 16, 20, 25 Jan. 1855, NCSA.

42. Sally Nivison Lyons Taliaferro Diary, Memorandum for 1861, VHS.

43. Ibid.

44. Edmondston, "Journal of a Secesh Lady," pp. 1–10.

45. Annie Darden Diary, undated, NCSA, pp. 2–3, 7, 8, 15, 27, 39, 54.

46. Meta Morris Grimball Diary, undated, p. 5, SHC UNC.

47. Scott, *The Southern Lady*, pp. 50–51.

48. Mary Ann Cobb to Howell Cobb, 8 Dec. 1848, Howell Cobb Correspondence, UGA.

49. Mary Ann Cobb to Howell Cobb, 7 Dec. 1849, Howell Cobb Correspondence, UGA.

50. Howell Cobb to Mary Ann Cobb, 6 May 1846, Howell Cobb Correspondence, UGA.

51. Edmondston, "Journal of a Secesh Lady," p. 143.

52. Ulrich, *Good Wives*, pp. 9, 36.

53. Newspaper clipping, 1848 (?), SHC UNC.

54. Ulrich, *Good Wives*, p. 37.

55. Howell Cobb to Mary Ann Cobb, 16, 24, 29 May 1846; Mary Ann Cobb to

David Gibson, 9 Oct. 1839; Howell Cobb to Mary Ann Cobb, 23 Apr. 1839, Howell Cobb Correspondence, UGA.

56. Anne DeWolf Middleton to Nathaniel Russell Middleton, 17 Aug. 1853, Nathaniel Russell Middleton Papers, SCHS.

57. Mary Ann Cobb to Howell Cobb, 24 July 1846, Howell Cobb Correspondence, UGA.

58. Mary Ann Cobb to Howell Cobb, Sept. 1846, Howell Cobb Correspondence, UGA.

59. Lee & Hardy to Nancy Pinson, 26 Nov., 29 Dec. 1836, 10 Feb., 10, 28 Mar., 22 Apr. 1837, Nancy Pinson Papers, LSU.

60. Watkins & Linton to Sarah B. Evans, 22 Nov., 29 Dec. 1830, 6, 14 Feb., 9 May, 22 June 1831, Nathaniel Evans and Family Papers, LSU.

61. A. H. Urquhart to Margaret Telfair, 1 July 1836, 23 Mar. 1838, Telfair Family Papers, GHS; A. H. Urquhart to Mary Telfair, 7 Mar. 1838, Telfair Family Papers, GHS; Elisha Cain to Mary Telfair, 20 Nov. 1836, 30 Dec. 1836, Telfair Family Papers, GHS; James Gunnelly to Mary Telfair, 2 Apr. 1836, 10 Dec. 1833, Telfair Family Papers, GHS; Joseph Gunnelly to Mary Telfair, 11 Jan. 1835, Telfair Family Papers, GHS; Jon Hollander to S. B. Evans, 22 Dec. 1842, 1 June 1847, May–Dec. 1848, 9 Dec. 1842, Sara B. Evans Papers, LSU; Susan M. Heriot to J. B. Miller, 23 Jan. 1840, 30 Nov., 29 Dec. 1839, Miller-Furman-Dabbs Family Papers, SCC USC; Harriott Warren to John B. Miller, 6 Sept. 1844, 28 Feb. 1850, Miller-Furman-Dabbs Family Papers, SCC USC; F. A. Goodwin to John B. Miller, 10 Nov. 1847, Miller-Furman-Dabbs Family Papers, SCC USC; Eleanor Spann to John B. Miller, 12 Nov. 1838, Miller-Furman-Dabbs Family Papers, SCC USC.

62. See Thomas Bishop and Sons, 1861–86 Accounts, E. P. Bishop Collection, UGA; James Kirksey Daybook,

1837–40, UGA; Everett Daybook (General Merchant) Account Books, 1848–51,UGA.

63. *Homes of the New World*, pp. 279–80, 336–37.

64. Ibid., p. 337.

65. *Notes of Travel*, p. 124.

66. Ibid.

67. Herman, "Loving Courtship," pp. 329–35.

68. Scott, *The Southern Lady*, pp. 29, 43; Mary Telfair to Mary Few, 5 Apr. 1837, Telfair Family Papers, GHS; Amelia Jane Akehurst Lines Diary, 1, 6, 8, 10 Sept. 1859, UGA.

69. Amanda Jane Cooley Roberts Diary, 23 Mar. 1845, VHS.

70. Martha Foster Crawford Diary, Oct. 1847, DU.

71. Mary Ann Cobb to Howell Cobb, 19 Dec. 1838, Howell Cobb Correspondence, UGA.

72. Mary Ann Cobb to Hessie, 13 Aug. 1852, Howell Cobb Correspondence, UGA.

73. Waddy Butler to Lucy Wood, 29 Sept. 1860, Lucy Wood Butler Correspondence, SHC UNC.

74. Sidney D. Bumpas to Frances (Fannie) Moore Webb, 4 Jan. 1842, Bumpas Collection, SHC UNC.

75. Welter, "The Cult of True Womanhood," pp. 151–74.

76. *The Doctrines and Discipline*, p. 113.

77. Elizabeth Lindsay Lomax Diary, 11 Apr. 1848, VHS.

78. Ibid.

79. *The Constitution of the Presbyterian Church*, p. 520.

80. Anne Turner Diary, 15 Apr. 1832, 19 Apr. 1835, DU.

81. 2, 23 July 1860, Somerville-Howorth Collection, RC.

82. 18 Feb. 1856, Lenoir Family Papers, SHC UNC.

83. "Journal of a Secesh Lady," p. 174.

84. Frances (Fannie) Moore Webb Bumpas Diary, 1 Mar. 1842, SHC UNC.

85. 11 June 1845, Nathaniel Russell Middleton Papers, SCHS.

86. Mat [Jones] to Julia Jones, 25 June 1863, Beverly Jones Family Papers and Books, SHC UNC.

87. Lucilla McCorkle Diary, 1 May 1850, SHC UNC.

88. Mary Ann Cobb to Howell Cobb, 8 Jan. 1850, Howell Cobb Correspondence, UGA.

89. Howell Cobb to Mary Ann Cobb, 14 Jan. 1847, Howell Cobb Correspondence, UGA.

90. Clinton, *The Plantation Mistress*, p. 136.

91. Lucilla McCorkle Diary, undated [1850?], SHC UNC.

92. Mary Ann Cobb to Howell Cobb, 5 Feb. 1850, Howell Cobb Correspondence, UGA.

93. Anne DeWolf Middleton to Nathaniel Russell Middleton, 17 Aug. 1853, SCHS.

94. Howell Cobb to Mary Ann Cobb, 20 July 1846, Howell Cobb Correspondence, UGA.

95. Mary Ann Cobb to Howell Cobb, 13 Jan. 1847, Howell Cobb Correspondence, UGA.

96. Howell Cobb to Mary Ann Cobb, 18 Jan. 1847, Howell Cobb Correspondence, UGA.

97. Howell Cobb to Mary Ann Cobb, 31 Jan. 1847, Howell Cobb Correspondence, UGA.

98. Howell Cobb to Mary Ann Cobb, 25 Jan. 1850, Howell Cobb Correspondence, UGA.

99. Cornelia Lenoir to Walter Lenoir, Mar. [1858?], Lenoir Family Papers, SHC UNC.

100. Mary Ann Cobb to Howell Cobb, 9 Nov. 1842, Howell Cobb Correspondence, UGA.

Chapter 3

1. For a discussion of role, culture, and community and their relationship to the unconscious see Schneider, "Kinship, Community, and Locality," pp. 155–74; Matthews, *Neighbor and Kin*, p. 9; Ulrich, *Good Wives*, p. 5; Nye, *Role Structure*, pp. 4–7; Rossi, "On the Assumptions of Structural Analysis," p. 5; Lévi-Strauss, *The Elementary Structures of Kinship*, p. 496.

2. Douglas, *Implicit Meanings*, p. 153.

3. See Geertz's hermeneutic concept in "From the Native's Point of View," pp. 480–92.

4. See Cott, *The Bonds of Womanhood*, pp. 126–59, and Welter, "The Feminization of American Religion," pp. 88–129, on the dual implications of evangelical religion for women.

5. Suggested by Douglas, "Social and Religious Symbolism of the Léle," p. 12.

6. Amelia Jane Akehurst Diary, 24 Mar. 1857, 21 Oct. 1857, 11 Jan. 1858, UGA; Anna Maria Akehurst Diary, 15 Feb. 1859, 12 July 1858, UGA; Lines, *To Raise Myself a Little*, pp. 4, 38, 57, 75.

7. Anna Maria Akehurst Diary, 29 July 1860, UGA.

8. Ibid., 1 Jan. 1863, 20 Feb. 1864, 24 Oct. 1864, 2 Sept. 1866.

9. Lines, *To Raise Myself a Little*, p. 83.

10. Anna Maria Akehurst Diary, 24, 29 Mar., 2 Apr., 2 Sept. 1866; 19 July 1868 (copy of a letter to Mary Bosy), 27 Oct. 1870, UGA.

11. Ibid., 3 Jan. 1870, 27 Oct. 1870,UGA.

12. Ibid., 27 Oct. 1870, UGA.

13. Welter, "The Cult of True Womanhood," pp. 151–74; Cott, *Bonds of Womanhood*, chap. 2.

14. Cott, *Bonds of Womanhood*, pp. 91, 127–28.

15. Anna Maria Akehurst Diary, 11 July 1870, UGA.

16. Jung, *Psychology and Alchemy*, p. 420.

17. Anna Maria Akehurst Diary, 10 Aug. 1870, 14 Apr. 1872, UGA.

18. Isaiah 27:3.

19. I am indebted to Pattie Buice for suggesting the biblical citations. Jeremiah 17:7–8.

20. Anna Maria Akehurst Diary, 11 July 1870, UGA.

21. Ibid., 27 Feb. 1871, UGA.

22. Ibid.

23. Victorian women slept together as a common practice when husbands left on business or when women visited.

24. Anna Maria Akehurst Diary, 31 Mar. 1871.

25. Paul Freeman suggested this interpretation.

26. I am indebted to Pattie Buice for this interpretation.

27. Anna Maria Akehurst Diary, 2 July 1871, UGA.

28. Ibid.

29. Ibid.

30. Ibid.

31. Ibid.

32. Ibid.

33. Ibid.

34. Ibid., 9 July 1871, UGA.

35. Ibid., 12 Nov.1871, 24 Dec. 1871, UGA.

36. Ibid., 31 Mar. 1872, UGA.

37. Ibid., undated, 1872, UGA.

38. Frances Ann Bernard Capps Diary, 13 Aug. 1840, VHS.

39. Ibid., 15 Aug. 1840, VHS.

40. Ibid., 17, 24, 26–27, 30 Aug. 1840, VHS.

41. Ibid., 31 Aug. 1840, VHS.

42. Ibid., 6 Sept. 1841, VHS.

43. Ibid., 10 Aug. 1843, VHS.

44. Ibid., 20 June 1849, 9 Sept. 1857, VHS.

45. Ibid., 24 Aug. 1845, VHS.

46. Ibid., 31 Jan. 1850, VHS.

47. Ibid., 1 Feb. 1850, VHS.

48. Amanda Virginia Edmonds Chappelear Diary, 24 May 1857, 9, 12, 14, 27 Aug. 1857, 29 Feb. 1859, 7 Nov. 1858, 29 Sept. 1859, VHS.

49. Ibid., 13 May 1858, VHS.

50. Ibid., 6 Feb. 1859, VHS.

51. Ibid.

52. See also Gregory of Nyssa, *The Life of Moses*, pp. 123–25.

53. Pattie Buice suggested this interpretation.

54. Jung, *Psychology and Religion*, p. 508.

Chapter 4

1. Johnson, *God Struck Me Dead*, p. 161.

2. Ibid., p. 153.

3. Ibid., p. 154.

4. Ibid., pp. 153–54, 159.

5. Ibid., p. 156.

6. Ibid.

7. Ibid., pp. 156–57.

8. Kenzer, "Portrait of a Southern Community," pp. 38–39; see also Gutman, *The Black Family*.

9. Raboteau, *Slave Religion*, pp. 44–92, 132, 175–76; Levine, *Black Culture*, p. 23; Blassingame, *The Slave Community*, pp. 162–64.

10. For a discussion of the relationship between identity, ritual, and community see Shorter, "Symbolism, Ritual and History," pp. 139–49; Turner, "Ritual Symbolism," pp. 79–95; Raboteau, *Slave Religion*, p. 35. Recent scholarship that examines the nature of ideology within culture includes Althusser, *For Marx*; Althusser, *Lenin and Philosophy*; Jameson, *The Political Unconscious*.

11. *Roll, Jordan, Roll*, p. 162.

12. Levine, *Black Culture*, p. 32.

13. Rahner, *Foundations of Christian Faith*, pp. 36–42.

14. Genovese, *Roll, Jordan, Roll*, pp. 163, 181.

15. "Symbolism, Ritual and History," p. 140.

16. Ibid.

17. "You Must Die This Day," Johnson, *God Struck Me Dead*, p. 63.

18. Ibid., p. 64.

19. "Pray a Little Harder," ibid., p. 127.

20. "More Than a Conqueror," ibid., p. 171.

21. "Everthing Just Fits," ibid., p. 115.

22. Zahan, *The Religion, Spirituality*, p. 45.

23. Ibid., pp. 54–55.

24. Gutman, *The Black Family*, pp. 124, 142, 188–89.

25. Owens, *This Species of Property*, pp. 40–41.

26. A rhythmic dance and song, performed in the leader-response style of spirituals in order to effect conversion. For further information see Raboteau, *Slave Religion*, pp. 62–73; Levine, *Black Culture*, pp. 37–38, 165.

27. Raboteau, *Slave Religion*, p. 268.

28. Ibid., pp. 267–68; Johnson, *God Struck Me Dead*, p. 123.

29. "Time Brought You to This World," [Johnson], "God Struck Me Dead," p. 102, DiU.

30. Johnson, *God Struck Me Dead*, p. 59.

31. "I Came from Heaven and Now Return," [Johnson], "God Struck Me Dead," p. 24, DiU.

32. Johnson, *God Struck Me Dead*, p. 170.

33. "I Am as Old as God," [Johnson], "God Struck Me Dead," p. 37, DiU.

34. Johnson, *God Struck Me Dead*, p. 58.

35. Rawick, *The American Slave*, 18:162–63.

36. Ibid., vol. 3, pt. 3, p. 254.

37. Johnson, *God Struck Me Dead*, p. 63.

38. Ibid., p. 65.

39. Ibid., p. 59.

40. Ibid., p. 65.

41. Ibid., p. 100.

42. Ibid., p. 114.

43. Ibid., p. 100.

44. Ibid., p. 11.

45. Ibid., p. 94.

46. "The Loveliest Singing in the World," [Johnson], "God Struck Me Dead," p. 14, DiU.

47. Johnson, *God Struck Me Dead*, pp. 66, 94.

48. "Hewn from the Mountains of Eternity," [Johnson], "God Struck Me Dead," p. 102, DiU.

49. Johnson, *God Struck Me Dead*, p. 96.

50. "Loveliest Singing in the World," [Johnson], "God Struck Me Dead," p. 15, DiU.

51. "I Am as Old as God," [Johnson], "God Struck Me Dead," p. 37, DiU.

52. Johnson, *God Struck Me Dead*, p. 68.

53. *Homes of the New World*, p. 393; Albert, *The House of Bondage*, pp. 9, 11.

54. Johnson, *God Struck Me Dead*, p. 75.

55. Ibid., p. 62.

56. Rawick, *The American Slave*, 18:210.

57. Albert, *House of Bondage*, pp. 31, 97.

58. Rawick, *The American Slave*, vol. 3, pt. 3, p. 260.

59. Ibid., vol. 12, pt. 1, p. 181.

60. Miss Abby Diary, 28 May [no year], UGA.

61. *A Theological Anthropology*, pp. 24–25.

62. *African Religions and Philosophy*, pp. 5, 17, 25; Mbiti, *New Testament Eschatology*, pp. 24–25, 30.

63. *The Religion*, p. 45.

64. *New Testament Eschatology*, p. 168.

65. *A Theological Anthropology*, p. 28.

66. Chapel Hill Presbyterian Church Records (1845–85), 16 Aug. 1860, p. 64, SHC UNC; see also the admittance of black women, pp. 86–87.

67. Broad Run Baptist Church Minutes, 9 Jan. 1836, VHS; Trinity Methodist Church Society Records, 1826–57, 1 July 1833, SCHS.

68. Gutman, *The Black Family*, pp. 70–72.

69. Ibid., p. 72.

70. Beaverdam Baptist Church Minutes, 20 Feb. 1841, GDAH.

71. Ibid., 4 Mar. 1841.

72. Mohr, "Slavery in Oglethorpe County," p. 11.

73. Ibid., p. 7.

74. See Scott, *The Southern Lady*, pp. 4–21.

75. Raboteau, *Slave Religion*, pp. 55–74; Levine, *Black Culture*, p. 33; Mathews, *Religion in the Old South*, pp. 185–236.

76. Douglas, *Natural Symbols*, p. 34.

77. "My Mother," p. 242.

78. Archibald Williams Account Book, 30 Dec. 1845, UGA; Mary Carr Diary, 21 Mar. 1860, DU; Rawick, *The American Slave*, 18:30; Rawick, *The American Slave*, vol. 12, pt. 1, p. 113, vol. 12, pt. 2, pp. 148, 289; Olmsted, *Journey in the Seaboard States*, 2:11; Blassingame, *Slave Testimony*, p. 563; Bonner, *History of Georgia Agriculture*, p. 191; Jones, "My Mother," pp. 236–53; White, "Ain't I a Woman?" pp. 12–19.

79. Rawick, *The American Slave*, vol. 12, pt. 1, p. 175, vol. 12, pt. 2, p. 149.

80. Ibid., vol. 1, pt. 3 supplement, p. 38; Miller, "Dear Master," p. 184; Lerner, *The Grimké Sisters*, p. 37.

81. Finch, *An Englishwoman's Experience*, p. 294; Rawick, *The American Slave*, 18:276; ibid., vol. 12, pt. 1, p. 243.

82. Anna Maria Akehurst, draft of letter

to an editor, undated, Akehurst-Lines Papers, UGA.

83. Albert, *House of Bondage*, p. 64.

84. Rawick, *The American Slave*, 18:199.

85. Ibid., vol. 6, pt. 1 supplement, p. 88; Miller, "Dear Master," p. 184.

86. Laura Beecher Comer Diaries, 2 Jan. 1862, SHC UNC.

87. Blassingame, *Slave Testimony*, p. 138.

88. Rawick, *The American Slave*, 18:276–82.

89. Blassingame, *Slave Testimony*, pp. 263, 266.

90. Rawick, *The American Slave*, 18:134.

91. Ibid., p. 277.

92. Mary Ann Cobb to Howell Cobb, 3, 6 July 1851, Howell Cobb Correspondence, UGA; Rawick, *The American Slave*, vol. 15, pt. 1, p. 16; ibid., 18:134.

93. Anna Maria Akehurst, draft of a letter to an editor, undated, Akehurst-Lines Papers, UGA.

94. Rawick, *The American Slave*, 18:277.

95. Johnson, *God Struck Me Dead*, p. 137.

96. Ibid., p. 284.

97. Ibid., p. 286.

98. Ibid., p. 284.

99. Ibid., p. 162.

100. Miller, "Dear Master," pp. 221, 239–40.

101. Blassingame, *Slave Testimony*, p. 87.

102. Ibid., p. 87n.

103. Rawick, *The American Slave*, vol. 3, pt. 1 supplement, pp. 28, 35; vol. 12, pt. 1, pp. 75, 156, 175, 168; vol. 12, pt. 2, p. 149; vol. 2, pt. 1, p. 1; vol. 3, pt. 3, p. 249; "Sixty-Five Years a 'Washer and Ironer,'" [Johnson], "God Struck Me Dead," DiU; Jones, "My Mother," pp. 240, 244.

104. White, "Ain't I," p. 22; Jones, "My Mother," p. 251.

105. Jones, "My Mother," p. 252.

106. Ibid.

107. *Reminiscences*, pp. 229–30.

108. Blassingame, *Slave Testimony*, p. 118.

109. Rawick, *The American Slave*, 18:9; Griffiths, *Autobiography*, p. 40; Owens, *This Species of Property*, p. 111.

110. Adele Allston Vanderhorst Diary, 28 Sept. 1863, SCHS.

111. Rawick, *The American Slave*, 18:9.

112. Johnson, *God Struck Me Dead*, pp. 132–33.

113. Griffiths, *Autobiography*, p. 319.

114. Ibid., pp. 356, 386, 387, 390, 397. For an understanding of the constricted life of an urban slave see chap. 2 of Robert S. Starobin's *Industrial Slavery in the Old South*.

115. As quoted by Gutman, *The Black Family*, p. 197; see also p. 217.

116. Albert, *House of Bondage*, pp. 7–8.

117. Johnson, *God Struck Me Dead*, p. 130.

118. Griffiths, *Autobiography*, pp. 13, 52.

119. See Mathews, *Religion in the Old South*, pp. 169–77, for a discussion of evangelical obligations to slaves.

120. Rawick, *The American Slave*, vol. 12, pt. 1, p. 234.

121. Elizabeth Virginia Lindsay Lomax Diary, 21 Sept. 1850, VHS.

122. Caroline Homassel Thornton Diary, 19 Sept. 1856, VHS.

123. Mary Ann Cobb to Howell Cobb, 22 Jan., 6 Feb., 14 Dec. 1843, Howell Cobb Correspondence, UGA.

124. Amanda Virginia Edmonds Chappelear Diary, 14 June 1859, VHS.

125. "Stayed with Her People," [Johnson], "God Struck Me Dead," pp. 196–97, DiU.

126. Scott, "Women's Perspective," pp. 154–55.

127. Ibid., 155, 157; Scott, *The Southern Lady*, pp. 48–49.

128. Ella Gertrude Clanton Thomas Diary, 23 Sept. 1864, 9 Oct. 1865, DU; Massey, "The Making of a Feminist," pp. 8–9.

129. *A Woman's Wartime Journal*, pp. 13–14.

130. Lucy Wood Butler to Waddy Butler, 21 Jan. 1861, Lucy Wood Butler Correspondence, SHC UNC.

131. Hall, *The Aristocratic Journey*, p. 209.

132. Catherine Broun Diary, 18 Dec. 1863, SHC UNC.

133. *Homes of the New World*, p. 276.

134. Scott, *The Southern Lady*, p. 51.

135. Chesnut, *A Diary from Dixie*, p. 49.

136. Scott, *The Southern Lady*, p. 51.

137. Ibid.

138. Griffiths, *Autobiography*, p. 364; Litwack, *Been in the Storm So Long*, p. 110.

139. Mary Wallace Jones to George Jones, 5 Jan. 1850, Jones Family Papers, GHS; Bill of Sale, 11 Apr. 1845, Proctor Family Papers, LSU; Sarah R. Cobb to Mary Ann Cobb, 26 Apr. 1842, 29 Jan. 1843, Howell Cobb Correspondence, UGA; S. A. Rees to John B. Lamar, 31 Oct. 1852, Howell Cobb Correspondence, UGA.

140. Miss Abby Diary, undated, UGA.

141. Rawick, *The American Slave*, 18:17, 117, 156.

142. Edmondston, "Journal of a Secesh Lady," p. 242.

143. Rawick, *The American Slave*, vol. 3, pt. 3, p. 125; vol. 2, pt. 2, p. 342; see also Sidney Harding Diary, Mar.–Dec. 1864, p. 8, LSU.

144. Rawick, *The American Slave*, vol. 3, pt. 3, p. 125.

145. Brent, *Incidents in the Life*, p. 49.

146. Laura Beecher Comer Diaries, 5 Jan. 1862, SHC UNC.

147. Ibid., 14 Feb. 1862, SHC UNC.

Chapter 5

1. Hopkins, "Occupational and Geographical Mobility," pp. 200–213; Worthman, "Working-Class Mobility," pp. 172–213; Barney, "Patterns of Crisis," pp. 524–43; Huffman, "Town and Country," pp. 366–81; Roberson, "Social Mobility," pp. 135–45; Wiener, "Planter Persistence and Social Change," pp. 235–60. McGuire, *Diary of a Southern Refugee*, pp. 21–22; Massey, *Refugee Life*, pp. 24–29, 32; Susan Middleton to Harriott Cheves, 15 Feb. 1862, 2 Mar. 1862, Cheves Collection, SCHS; Fannie Page Hume Diary, 16–17 Mar. 1862, 13 Aug. 1862, SHC UNC. See mother-daughter correspondence in the Wayne-Stites-Anderson Family Papers, 5 Nov. 1861, 4 July 1863, GHS.

2. Gillespie, *Psychological Effects of War*; Freud and Burlingham, *War and Children*; Waller, *War and the Family*; Fraser, *Children in Conflict*; Purdue, *Slavery and the Evolution of Cherokee Society*.

3. *Victims*; Miss Abby Diary, undated, UGA; Edmondston, "Journal of a Secesh Lady," pp. 37–38; Sterkx, *Partners in Rebellion*, p. 52; Craven, *The Growth of Southern Nationalism*, pp. 335–38; Thomas, *The Confederate Nation*, p. 234.

4. Loewenberg, "The Psychohistorical Origins," pp. 1457–1502.

5. Vinovskis, "Socioeconomic Determinants of Interstate Fertility Differentials," pp. 375–96.

6. *A History of the United States*, pp. 50–51.

7. Higgs, "Mortality in Rural America,"

pp. 178, 182–91; Meeker, "The Improving Health of the United States," pp. 353–73.

8. *America and the Gilded Age*, p. 11.

9. "Portrait of a Southern Community," p. 129.

10. Hilliard, *Hog Meat and Hoecake*, p. 11; Pessen, "How Different," p. 1135.

11. Hopkins, "Occupational and Geographical Mobility," pp. 200–213; Worthman, "Working-Class Mobility," pp. 172–213.

12. "Town and Country in the South," p. 372.

13. "Planter Persistence and Social Change," pp. 235–60.

14. "Portrait of a Southern Community," pp. 127–29.

15. *Family Structure*.

16. Hendrix, "Kinship, Social Class and Migration," pp. 399–409; Hendrix, "Kinship and Economic-Rational Migration," pp. 534–43; Rosenberg and Anspach, *Working Class Kinship*, pp. 110, 131–33; Nye, *Role Structure*.

17. *Neighbor and Kin*.

18. Massey, *Refugee Life*, pp. 15–16, 19, 21–22, 60.

19. McGuire, *Diary of a Southern Refugee*, p. 22.

20. Massey, *Refugee Life*, pp. 24, 29; Susan Middleton to Harriott Cheves, 16 Feb. 1862, 2 Mar. 1862, Cheves Collection, SCHS.

21. Fannie Page Hume Diary, 16–17 Mar. 1862, 13 Aug. 1862, SHC UNC; Elizabeth [?] to Jane [?], 28 Oct. 1864, Mary DeSaussure Fraser Papers, DU; Massey, *Refugee Life*, p. 32; Eliza Frances Andrews, *The War-Time Journal*, p. 19.

22. Massey, *Refugee Life*, pp. 13, 69–70, 83.

23. McGuire, *Diary of a Southern Refugee*, pp. 168, 200.

24. Massey, *Refugee Life*, p. 16.

25. Ibid., p. 68.

26. Ibid., pp. 150–51.

27. Sidney Harding Diary, 5 Sept. 1863, 10 Mar., 10–21 Dec. 1864, pp. 8, 71, 75, LSU.

28. Massey, *Refugee Life*, pp. 70, 116–19.

29. Lise Mitchell to Cousin Annie, 20 Aug. 1862, Lise Mitchell Papers, TU; M. to Leize [Lise] Mitchell, 27 Feb. 1863, Lise Mitchell Papers, TU.

30. Massey, *Refugee Life*, p. 152.

31. Ibid., p. 120.

32. R. E. James to Mary DeSaussure Fraser, 28 Dec. 1864, Mary DeSaussure Fraser Papers, DU.

33. Millie Gwyn to Sarah J. Lenoir, 14 June 1862, Lenoir Family Papers, SHC UNC.

34. Jettie [Jeannette Levingston] to Julia A. Jones, 15 Oct. 1861, Beverly Jones Collection, SHC UNC.

35. Martha [?] to Julia A. Jones, 1863?, Beverly Jones Collection, SHC UNC.

36. Minerva [?] to Julia A. Jones, 30 July 1864, Beverly Jones Family Papers and Books, SHC UNC.

37. Susan Middleton to Harriott Cheves, 2 Mar. 1862, 16 Feb. 1862, Cheves Collection, SCHS.

38. Susan Middleton to Harriott Cheves, 22 Feb. 1862, ibid.

39. Harriott Cheves to Susan Middleton, 10/12 Oct. 1863, ibid.

40. Susan Middleton to Harriott Cheves, 4 Jan. 1864, ibid.

41. Clinton, *The Plantation Mistress*, pp. 123–25.

42. *Strictures on the Modern System*, p. 14.

43. *A Vindication*, p. 265.

44. Norton, *Liberty's Daughters*, pp. 274–75.

45. Clifford, "Saints, Sinners and People," p. 259; Clifford, "Home and School," pp. 10–11, 13; Katz, *Education in American History*; Mary W. Cobb to Mary Ann Cobb, 24 Jan. 1842, Howell

Cobb Correspondence, UGA; Clinton, "The Plantation Mistress," pp. 109–10; Aunt Adelaide to Mary Gash, 28 Mar. 1851, Mary Gash and Family Papers, NCSA; A. W. Siler to Uncle Gash, 23 Mar. 1847, Mary Gash and Family Papers, NCSA.

46. Amanda Jane Cooley Diary, 20 Feb. 1842, VHS.

47. Ibid., 11 Jan. 1846, 18 Jan. 1846.

48. Jennie Akehurst to Sylvanus Lines, 17 Feb. 1858, Akehurst-Lines Papers, UGA.

49. Clinton, *The Plantation Mistress*, p. 131; Clinton, "The Plantation Mistress," pp. 105–7.

50. [?] to Julia A. Conrad, 19 Mar. 1838, Beverly Jones Family Papers and Books, SHC UNC.

51. Mary Ann Cobb to Howell Cobb, 17 July 1846, Howell Cobb Correspondence, UGA.

52. Annie Darden Diary, 18 Apr. 1856, NCSA.

53. Gray, "Corona Female College," pp. 129–34; Frances (Fannie) Moore Webb Bumpas Diary, pp. 36, 51–52, SHC UNC; Mary Ann Lenoir to Mother, 28 Feb. 1836, Lenoir Family Papers, SHC UNC; Sarah C. Ferrell to Mary Ann Lamar, 15 Jan. 1833, Howell Cobb Correspondence, UGA; Unidentified Friend to Julia A. Conrad, 1840?, SHC UNC; Stephenson, "The Davises, the Southalls," pp. 257–79.

54. Orr, *A History of Education*, p. 216.

55. Clinton, *The Plantation Mistress*, pp. 136–37.

56. McGuire, *Diary of a Southern Refugee*, p. 298.

57. Ibid.

58. Ibid., pp. 196, 252.

59. Massey, *Refugee Life*, p. 172.

60. Ibid., pp. 172–73.

61. McGuire, *Diary of a Southern Refugee*, pp. 196–97, 244; Massey, *Bonnet Brigades*, p. 146; Wasdell, *St. Paul's Church*, 1:181; *Richmond Daily Examiner*, 29 May 1862.

62. Massey, *Bonnet Brigades*, pp. 146–47; McGuire, *Diary of a Southern Refugee*, p. 173.

63. Massey, *Bonnet Brigades*, pp. 147–48.

64. Sterkx, *Partners in Rebellion*, p. 146.

65. Thomas, *The Confederate State of Richmond*, pp. 117–22; Thomas, *The Confederate Nation*, pp. 202–5.

66. Huff, "The Role of Women," pp. 68–69.

67. McGuire, *Diary of a Southern Refugee*, pp. 202–3, 345; Sally to Sarah J. Lenoir, 22 Jan. 1865, Lenoir Family Papers, SHC UNC.

68. According to Mary P. Ryan, "The Power of Women's Networks," historians must recognize that women's agency has not always been directed toward autonomy but rather has been subjected to "the constraints, ironies, and contradictions that confront[ed] human beings in the past" and continue to challenge humanity into the future (p. 66). Thus southern women's mob action analyzed in light of its purpose—to preserve family order—did not primarily contribute to feminist ends or women's power and freedom.

69. Pp. 62–68.

70. Wyatt-Brown, "The Ideal Typology," p. 15.

71. Massey, *Bonnet Brigades*, p. 341.

72. Sterkx, *Partners in Rebellion*, pp. 114, 117–18.

73. Huff, "The Role of Women," p. 29.

74. Massey, *Bonnet Brigades*, pp. 48, 52; Pember, *A Southern Woman's Story*.

75. Sidney Harding Diary, Mar.–Dec. 1864, LSU.

76. Lucy Wood Butler Diary, 21 July 1861, SHC UNC.

77. Jane Smith to Janie Robeson, 12 Apr. 1865, Lenoir Family Papers, SHC UNC.

78. Massey, *Bonnet Brigades*, pp. 351–52.

79. Sterkx, *Partners in Rebellion*, pp. 23–28.

80. Ibid., pp. 102–3; Huff, "The Role of Women," pp. 45–46.

81. Smith, *Daughters of the Promised Land*, pp. 57–76; Wilson, "The Illusion of Change," pp. 117–36; Kerber, *Women of the Republic*, pp. 119; see also Ryan, *Womanhood in America*, pp. 119, 187–88.

82. Orr, *A History of Education*, p. 90.

83. Litwack, *Been in the Storm So Long*, pp. 209–11.

84. Isabella McNeill to K. M. McNeill, 5 July 1861, 13 Aug. 1861, Harnett County Papers, SHC UNC; Clinton, "The Plantation Mistress," p. 287.

85. Edmondston, "Journal of a Secesh Lady," p. 250.

86. "Georgia Blacks during Secession," pp. 164–79.

87. Quoted from Litwack, *Been in the Storm So Long*, p. 11.

88. Mary Cary Ambler Stribbling Diary, 23 Apr. 1862, VSL.

89. Ibid.

90. Sally Armstrong Diary, 29 Apr. 1863, VHS; Mrs. T. J. Johnson to daughter, 14 July 1863, Wayne-Stites-Anderson Papers, GHS.

91. Catherine Broun Diary, 1 May 1864, SHC UNC.

92. M. to Leize [Lise] Mitchell, 27 Feb. 1863, Lise Mitchell Papers, TU.

93. Kate D. Foster Diary, 28 July 1863, DU.

94. M. to Leize [Lise] Mitchell, 27 Feb. 1863, Lise Mitchell Papers, TU.

95. Litwack, *Been in the Storm So Long*, pp. 354–59.

96. Ibid., pp. 332, 348.

97. Kate D. Foster Diary, 30 July 1863, DU.

98. Gutman, *The Black Family*, pp. 363–431; Litwack, *Been in the Storm So Long*, pp. 230–45, 300–304, 341.

99. Litwack, *Been in the Storm So Long*, p. 344, 350; Pleck, "A Mother's Wages," pp. 381–86.

Chapter 6

1. For a discussion of modernization and its uneven effects upon family structure see Brown, *Modernization*, pp. 114–15; Vaghefi, "A Micro-Analysis Approach," pp. 181–97; Stearns, "Modernization and Social History," pp. 189–209; Chekki, *Modernization and Kin Network*.

2. Tessler and Hawkins, "Acculturation, Socio-Economic Status, and Attitude Change," pp. 473–95; Brown, *Modernization*, pp. 114–15; Bohmer, "Modernization, Divorce and the Status of Women," pp. 81–90; Chekki, *Modernization and Kin Network*, pp. 60, 152–55.

3. Bordin, *Woman and Temperance*, p. 3; Gordon, *Woman Torch Bearers*, p. 22.

4. Bonner, *A History of Georgia Agriculture*, pp. 93–98, 188; Gray, *History of Agriculture*, 2:811. In "Church Organization," Smith comments on the high rate of church trials during the 1830s (p. 204).

5. Catherine McFarland Papers, undated, GHS.

6. Mary Elizabeth Rives Diary, 26 June 1865, LSU.

7. S. L. L. to Mrs. Thomas J. Lenoir, 18 Aug. 1868, Lenoir Family Papers, SHC UNC.

8. Emily Scudder to Henry Scudder, 5 Jan. 1869, 8 Jan. 1872, Henry Scudder Papers, GHS; Mary L. Magie to Henry Scudder, 13 Jan. 1872, Henry Scudder Papers, GHS.

9. Carter, *A Spiritual Crisis*; Garrison, *March of Faith*; Schlesinger, *A Critical Period in American Religion*; Moseley, *A Cultural History*.

10. Lucy Muse Walton Fletcher Diary, Sept. 1865 (?), DU.

11. Mary Jeffries Bethell Diary, 7 Aug. 1865, 29 Mar. 1866, 10 Oct. 1866, 30 Aug. 1867, SHC UNC.

12. Ibid., 7 Aug. 1865, SHC UNC.

13. Mary Davis Brown Diary, 4 Oct. 1867, SCC USC.

14. Mary Jeffries Bethell Diary, 30 Aug. 1867, SHC UNC.

15. Mount Olive Baptist Church Minutes, 1866–76, NCSA.

16. Mount Tabor Baptist Church Minutes, 1865–70, NCSA.

17. First Presbyterian Church (Athens, Georgia) Minutes, 6 Feb., 9, 13 Mar. 1870; 24, 30 Nov. 1862; 12 Dec. 1866, 19 Jan. 1867.

18. Broad Run Baptist Church Minutes, 1866, p. 69, VHS.

19. Johnson, "The Missionary Society," pp. 1–2; Marietta First Baptist Church Ladies Aid Society Minutes, 8 May 1898, GDAH.

20. Central Presbyterian Church, "Women's Work in the Central Presbyterian Church" [by Azile Simpson],GDAH; Trinity and Cumberland Methodist Church Minutes of the Board of Stewards, vol. 4, 2 July 1866, SCHS; Laura Beecher Comer Diary, vol. 2, 31 Mar. 1867, SHC UNC; Elizabeth Ellis Munford to Etta Wythe Munford, 25 Mar. 1889, Munford Family Papers, VHS; Sarah Ervin McIver Diary, 29 Jan. 1880, SHC UNC; Pleasant Union Christian Church Records, 3 Oct. 1891, SHC UNC.

21. Heck, *In Royal Service*, pp. 74, 85, 89, 93–94; Tupper, *The Foreign Missions of the Southern Baptist Convention*, pp. 90–91.

22. Heck, *In Royal Service*, p. 94.

23. Lucy Muse Walton Fletcher Diary, 4 Apr. 1869, July 1869, DU.

24. Heck, *In Royal Service*, pp. 96–103.

25. Marietta First Baptist Church Missionary Society Minutes, Feb. 1870, 5 May 1870, 1 Jan. 1871, 6 Mar. 1872, 5 Apr. 1874, p. 31, 2 Dec. 1874, GDAH.

26. "Women's Work," p. 1.

27. First Baptist Church (Gainesville, Georgia) Missionary Society Minutes, p. 4,GDAH; Hephzibah Baptist Church Women's Missionary Society Minutes, 9 Aug. 1884, GDAH; First Presbyterian Church (Athens, Georgia) Ladies Benevolent Society Minutes, pp. 1, 50–55, 140–43, UGA.

28. First Baptist Church (Gainesville, Georgia) Minutes, p. 2, GDAH; First Presbyterian Church (Athens, Georgia) Ladies Benevolent Society Minutes and Constitution, p. 45, UGA.

29. First Presbyterian Church (Athens, Georgia) Ladies Benevolent Society Minutes, pp. 9–10.

30. Ibid., p. 14.

31. Heck, *In Royal Service*, pp. 74, 85.

32. Ibid., p. 86.

33. Ibid., pp. 86–87; Tupper, *The Foreign Missions*, p. 91.

34. Greenville Auxiliary of the First Methodist Episcopal Church (Greenville, Mississippi), 24 Feb. 1879, 7 Apr. 1880, 2 Dec. 1881, Apr. 1882, 2 Mar. 1883, 7 Sept. 1883, Mar. 1884, 4 Dec. 1885, 28 Nov. 1887, 23 July 1889, Sept. 1889, Somerville-Howorth Collection, SL.

35. Southern Baptist Convention, *Proceedings* (Baltimore), 1884, Appendix B II; Southern Baptist Convention, *Proceedings* (Augusta), 1885, p. 31; Southern Baptist Convention, *Proceedings* (Memphis), 1889, Appendix A; Foreign Missions Board, *44th Annual Report of the Foreign Missions Board*, p. xxxix.

36. Southern Baptist Convention, *Pro-*

ceedings (Baltimore), 1884, p. 17.

37. Ibid.

38. Cannon, *History of Southern Methodist Mission*, pp. 40–41, 72–73.

39. Ibid., pp. 74–75.

40. Ibid., p. 77.

41. Ibid., pp. 77–80.

42. Ibid., pp. 108–10.

43. *Presbyterian Women in America*, pp. 207–24.

44. Scott, *The Southern Lady*, p. 141.

45. See Giele, "Social Change in the Feminine Role"; Bordin, *Woman and Temperance*, pp. 163, 168–70.

46. Bordin, *Woman and Temperance*, p. 52.

47. Ibid., pp. 76–78.

48. Gordon, *Woman Torch Bearers*, p. 22.

49. Bordin, *Woman and Temperance*, p. 3.

50. "I Come Before You to Remind You that Women Have Rights," p. 11, Rebecca Felton Papers, UGA.

51. "Respected Audience . . . of Christian Women," p. 14, Rebecca Felton Papers, UGA.

52. Bordin, *Woman and Temperance*, pp. 10–12.

53. Willard, *Woman and Temperance*, pp. 555–58.

54. Scott, *The Southern Lady*, p. 148.

55. Felton, *Country Life in Georgia*, pp. 284–85.

56. Ibid., p. 286.

57. Scott and Scott, *One Half the People*, p. 4; Kraditor, *The Ideas*, pp. 12–14; Taylor, "The Woman Suffrage Movement in Texas," p. 199; Taylor, "The Woman Suffrage Movement in Mississippi," pp. 4, 5; Taylor, *The Woman Suffrage Movement in Tennessee*, p. 80.

58. Kraditor, *The Ideas*, pp. 17–18, 20; Taylor, "The Woman Suffrage Movement in North Carolina," pp. 53–54; Taylor, "A Short History of the Woman Suffrage

Movement in Tennessee," p. 207; Scott and Scott, *One Half the People*, p. 26.

59. Scott and Scott, *One Half the People*, pp. 25–26.

60. Stanton, Anthony, and Gage, *The History of Woman Suffrage*, 3: 818.

61. "Women's Suffrage Had Its Inception in This Fight against Saloons," Rebecca Felton Papers, UGA; Felton, *Country Life*, pp. 296, 286; Kearney, *A Slaveholder's Daughter*, p. 188.

62. Stanton, Anthony, and Gage, *History of Woman Suffrage*, 3:789, 806, 825; Fuller, *Laura Clay*, p. 40.

63. Scott, *The Southern Lady*, pp. 179–80.

64. Rebecca Felton, "Why Women Should Have the Ballot," p. 1, Rebecca Felton Papers, UGA; Taylor, "The Woman Suffrage Movement in North Carolina," p. 54; Taylor, "The Woman Suffrage Movement in Texas," p. 199.

65. Taylor, "The Woman Suffrage Movement in Arkansas," pp. 27–28; Taylor, "The Woman Suffrage Movement in Texas," p. 199.

66. Rebecca Felton, "A Few Plain Facts . . ." and "My Reasons for Claiming the Ballot Privilege . . . ," Rebecca Felton Papers, UGA; Fuller, *Laura Clay*, pp. 63–65.

67. Vinton Index to American Board of Commissioners for the Foreign Missions Collection, vol. 39, Congregational Library, Boston; Ousley, "Native Helpers at Mound Bayou, Mississippi," undated, p. 1, DiU.

68. Jacobs, "Their 'Special Mission,'" p. 155; Shaloff, *Reform in Leopold's Congo*, p. 40; Edmiston, "Maria Fearing," pp. 291–95.

69. Francis L. Cardozo to William E. Whiting, 13 Jan. 1865, American Missionary Association Correspondence, DiU; Thomas W. Cardozo to William E. Whiting, 11 Apr. 1865, American Missionary Association Correspondence,

DiU; Francis L. Cardozo to S. Hunt, 10 Oct. 1865, 9 Dec. 1865, American Missionary Association Correspondence, DiU.

70. F. L. Cardozo to Reverend S. Hunt, 18 Oct. 1865, American Missionary Association Correspondence, DiU; Thomas W. Cardozo to William E. Whiting, 11 Apr. 1865, American Missionary Association Correspondence, DiU.

71. American Missionary Association Correspondence, DiU.

72. Ibid.

73. Francis Cardozo to S. Hunt, 3 Nov. 1866, American Missionary Association Correspondence, DiU.

74. Mary Still to S. Hunt, 25 Mar. 1866, 28 Mar. 1866, American Missionary Association Correspondence, DiU.

75. Mary Still to S. Hunt, 25 Mar. 1866, American Missionary Association Correspondence, DiU.

76. Pelt and Smith, *The National Baptists*, pp. 105–6, 141–44.

77. Bordin, *Woman and Temperance*, p. 83.

78. Hays, *Heritage of Dedication*, pp. 163–75; Bordin, *Woman and Temperance*, p. 84.

79. Lansman, "With an Army of Organized Women," pp. 29–44. See Hall, *Revolt against Chivalry*, for a discussion of twentieth-century cooperation. Lerner, *The Majority Finds Its Past*, p. 85.

80. Mrs. John B. Hope, obituary in the *Atlanta University Bulletin* (Dec. 1947), p. 26; Walter Chivers, "A Report of Results Gained through Cooperative Efforts of College Neighbors," Personal File, Mrs. John B. Hope, Atlanta Neighborhood Union Papers, Atlanta University; "An Experiment in Community Welfare" and "The History of the Neighborhood Union," Box 1, Atlanta Neighborhood Union Papers, Atlanta University.

81. Gutman, *The Black Family*, pp. 447–48.

82. "Thy Neighbor as Thyself," "Revelation of Jesus," "The Highest Development of Civilization . . . ," "Human Beings Are Complex Centers of Instincts . . . ," Mrs. Hope's Memoranda for Speeches, 1919–24, Box 5, Atlanta Neighborhood Union Papers, Atlanta University.

83. Lansman, "With an Army," p. 123.

84. Ibid., p. 147.

BIBLIOGRAPHY

Manuscripts and Typescripts

Athens, Georgia
Special Collections, University of Georgia Library
  Miss Abby Diary
  Anna Maria Akehurst Diary
  Akehurst-Lines Papers
  E. P. Bishop Collection
  Howell Cobb Correspondence
  Cobb-Erwin-Lamar Collection
  Cobb Family Papers
  Everett Daybook (General Merchant)
  Rebecca Felton Papers
  Rebecca Felton and William Felton Collection
  First Presbyterian Church. Ladies Benevolent Society. Minutes and Constitution.
  Charles Colcock Jones Collection
  James Kirksey Daybook (General Merchant)
  Amelia Jane Akehurst Lines Diary
  Archibald Williams Account Book

Atlanta, Georgia
Georgia Department of Archives and History
  Bark Camp Baptist Church, Burke County. Minutes.
  Beaverdam Baptist Church, Wilkes County. Minutes.
  Bethel Baptist Church, Dooley County, Vienna. Women's Missionary Union. [List of] Presidents and Membership.
  Cabin Creek Baptist Church, Jackson County. Minutes.
  Central Presbyterian Church, Atlanta. "Women's Work in the Central Presbyterian Church, 1858–1933," by Azile Simpson; also on microfilm.
  Doraville Association of the Reformed Presbyterian Church, Doraville. Ladies Benevolent Society Minutes.
  First Presbyterian Church, Athens. Minutes.
  First Baptist Church, Gainesville. Missionary Society of the First Baptist Church. Minutes.
  Hephzibah Baptist Church, Augusta. Women's Missionary Society. Minutes.
  Island Creek Baptist Church, Carr's Station. Washington Baptist and Mission Society. Minutes.
  Johnson, Allie. "The Missionary Society of the First Baptist Church, Fifty-Eight Fruitful Years, 1896–1954." Microfilm.
  Marietta First Baptist Church, Cobb County. Ladies Aid Society. Minutes.
  _____. Missionary Society. Minutes.

———. "Twenty-fifth Anniversary Minutes and History of the Women's Auxiliary of the Synod of the Georgia Presbyterian Church, United States."
Special Collections, Atlanta University Library
  Atlanta Neighborhood Union Papers

Baton Rouge, Louisiana
Department of Archives and Manuscripts, Louisiana State University Library
  Mary Bateman Diary
  Nathaniel Evans and Family Papers
  Sara B. Evans Papers
  Sidney Harding Diary
  Eliza A. Magruder Diary
  Nancy Pinson Papers
  Proctor Family Papers
  Mary Elizabeth Rives Diary

Boston, Massachusetts
The Congregational Library
  Vinton Index to American Board of Commissioners for the Foreign Mission Collection.

Cambridge, Massachusetts
Arthur and Elizabeth Schlesinger Library, Radcliffe College
  Lucy Parker Chamberlain Collection
  Somerville-Howorth Collection
Houghton Library, Harvard University
  American Board of Commissioners for Foreign Missions Correspondence.

Chapel Hill, North Carolina
North Carolina Collection, University of North Carolina Library
  Wheeler's Primitive Baptist Church, Person County. Minutes.
Southern Historical Collection, University of North Carolina Library
  Alamance Cotton Mill Records
  Barkley Family Papers
  Bear Creek Baptist Church Records
  Mary Jeffries Bethell Diary
  Catherine Broun Diary
  Bumpas Papers
  Frances (Fannie) Moore Webb Bumpas Diary
  Lucy Wood Butler Papers
  Chapel Hill Presbyterian Church Records, Orange County
  Elizabeth Collier Diary
  Laura Beecher Comer Diaries
  Julia A. Conrad Papers
  Anne Beale Davis Diary
  Grace B. Elmore Diary

Meta Morris Grimball Diary
Harnett County Papers
Fannie Page Hume Diary
Susan Davis Nye Hutchinson Diary
Beverly Jones Family Papers and Books
Le Conte and Furman Family Papers
Lenoir Family Papers
Lucilla McCorkle Diary
Sarah Ervin McIver Diary
Mary Fries Patterson Diaries
Pleasant Union Christian Church Records, Harnett County.
Yadkin Baptist Church Records

Charleston, South Carolina
South Carolina Historical Society
  Allston-Pringle-Hill Papers
  Cheves Collection
  Anna Lesesne Diary
  Louisa Lord Correspondence
  Nathaniel Russell Middleton Papers
  Protestant Episcopal Female Domestic Missionary Society. Account Books.
  Trinity and Cumberland Methodist Church. Minutes of the Board of Stewards.
  Trinity Methodist Church. Minutes Books.
  Trinity Methodist Church Society Records.
  Adele Allston Vanderhorst Diary

Columbia, South Carolina
South Caroliniana Collection, University of South Carolina Library
  Mary Davis Brown Diary
  Hammond-Bryan-Cumming Family Correspondence
  McKissick Family Correspondence
  Miller-Furman-Dabbs Family Papers

Durham, North Carolina
Manuscript Division, William R. Perkins Library, Duke University
  Elizabeth J. Holmes Blanks Correspondence
  Mary M. Carr Diary
  Martha Foster Crawford Diary
  Lucy Muse Walton Fletcher Diary
  Kate D. Foster Diary
  Mary DeSaussure Fraser Papers
  Mary Jane Fraser Diary
  Elizabeth Baldwin Wiley Harris Diary
  Ella Gertrude Clanton Thomas Diary
  Anne A. Turner Diary

New Orleans, Louisiana
Amistad Research Center
   American Missionary Association Correspondence
   [Clifton H. Johnson, ed.] "God Struck Me Dead." Social Science Documents.
   Ousley, Henrietta B. "Native Helpers at Mound Bayou, Mississippi." Pamphlet of the
     American Missionary Society.
Manuscripts Section, Howard-Tilton Memorial Library, Tulane University
   Acklen Family Papers
   Mathilda Todd DeVan Memorial
   Hodges Family Papers
   Charles Colcock Jones Papers
   Lise Mitchell Papers
   Ogden Family Papers

Raleigh, North Carolina
North Carolina State Archives
   Alexander Circuit (Methodist), Alexander County. Class Lists.
   John Heritage Bryon Collection
   Centre Presbyterian Church, Robeson County. Minutes.
   Thurmond Chatham Papers
   Cypress Presbyterian Church, Harnett County. Minutes.
   Annie (Nannie) Darden Diary
   Leonidas Polk Denmark Collection
   First Presbyterian Church, Beaufort County. Minutes.
   First Presbyterian Church, Morganton, Burke County. Morganton Female Working
     Society. Minutes.
   Flat River Primitive Baptist Church. Minutes.
   Mary Gash and Family Papers
   Green River Baptist Association, Rutherford County. Minutes.
   Edward Jones Hale Papers
   Susan Davis Nye Hutchinson Diary
   Marriage Records, Alamance, Orange, Cumberland, and Harnett counties.
   Mount Olive Baptist Church, Alamance County. Minutes.
   Mount Tabor Baptist Church, Murfreesboro, Hertford County. Minutes.
   Patterson Papers
   Pleasant Grove Primitive Baptist Church, Reidsville, Caswell County. Minutes.
   Reavis Family Papers
   Red Banks Primitive Baptist Church, Pitt County. Minutes.
   Tax Lists, Harnett County, 1837–47.
   Trinity Missionary Baptist Church, Caswell County. Minutes.
   Capus M. Waynich Collection
   White Oak Primitive Baptist Church, Jones County. Minutes.
   William-Dameron Family Papers
   Wills and Estates, Alamance County
   Jonathan Worth Papers

Richmond, Virginia
Virginia Historical Society
  Sally Armstrong Diary
  Broad Run Baptist Church, Fauquier County. Minutes.
  Lucy Wood Butler Diary and Correspondence
  Frances Ann Bernard Capps Diary
  Chamberlayne Family Papers
  Amanda Virginia Edmonds Chappelear Diary
  Fryingpan Baptist Church, Fairfax County. Minutes.
  Elizabeth Virginia Lindsay Lomax Diary
  Munford Family Papers
  Occoquam Baptist Church. Minutes.
  Amanda Jane Cooley Roberts Diary
  Sally Nivison Lyons Taliaferro Diary
  Caroline Homassel Thornton Diary
  Susan Elizabeth Gordon Webb Diary
Department of Archives, Virginia State Library
  Battle Run Baptist Church, Culpepper County. Minutes.
  Battle Run Baptist Church, Rappahannock County. Records.
  Beaver Dam Baptist Church, Isle of Wight County. Minutes.
  Beaver Run Baptist Church, Isle of Wight County. Minutes.
  Bethel Methodist Church, Brunswick County. Class Records.
  Byrd Presbyterian Church, Goochland County. Minutes.
  Harriette Cary Papers
  Jane Gibbs Diary
  Monumental Methodist Church, Portsmouth. "History of Monumental Church" [by
      Rev. W. Edwards].
  Monumental Methodist Church, Portsmouth. Trustee Minutes.
  Munford Family Papers
  New Concord Presbyterian Church, Campbell County. Minutes.
  Reveille Methodist Church, Richmond. Board Minutes.
  Shiloh Baptist Association, Charlotte County. Minutes.
  Kate S. Sperry Diary
  Mary Cary Ambler Stribbling Diary
  Martha Varnier Diary
  Miss Weisiger Diary

Savannah, Georgia
Georgia Historical Society
  Jones Family Papers
  Catherine McFarland Papers
  Henry Scudder Papers
  Telfair Family Papers
  Wayne-Stites-Anderson Family Papers

Washington, D.C.
Manuscript Division, Library of Congress
  Judith Page Rives Autobiography
  United States Census Reports, 1830–80: for Georgia: Burke, Jackson, and Wilkes
      counties, and the city of Athens; for North Carolina: Alamance, Chatham,
      Cumberland, Granville, Guilford, Harnett, Orange, Randolph, Rockingham,
      and Wake counties, and the cities of Fayetteville and Raleigh. These reports
      are available on microfilm at the University of Georgia Library, Athens,
      Georgia.

Published Narratives, Diaries, Travelogues, and Histories of Women

Albert, Octavia V. Rogers. *The House of Bondage: Charlotte Brooks and Other Slaves*.
    New York, 1890.
Andrews, Eliza Frances. *The War-Time Journal of a Georgia Girl*. Edited by Spencer
    Bidwell King, Jr. Atlanta: Cherokee Publishing Co., 1976.
Botume, Elizabeth Hyde. *First Days amongst the Contrabands*. Boston: Lee and Shep-
    ard Publishers, 1893.
Bremer, Fredrika. *Homes of the New World*. Translated by Mary Howitt. New York:
    Harper Brothers, 1853.
Brent, Linda [Harriet G. Jacobs]. *Incidents in the Life of a Slave Girl*. Boston, 1861.
Burke, Emily P. *Reminiscences of Georgia*. Oberlin, Ohio: J. M. Fitch, 1850. In *History
    of Women*. New Haven, Conn.: Research Publications, 1975. Microfilm.
Chesnut, Mary Boykin. *A Diary from Dixie*. Edited by Ben Ames Williams. Boston:
    Houghton Mifflin Co., 1949.
Edmondston, Catherine Ann Devereux. "Journal of a Secesh Lady": *The Diary of Cath-
    erine Ann Devereux Edmondston, 1860–1866*. Edited by Beth H. Crabtree and
    James W. Patton. Raleigh: Division of Archives and History, Department of Cul-
    tural Resources, 1979.
Felton, Rebecca Latimer. *Country Life in Georgia: In the Days of My Youth*. 1919. Re-
    print. New York: Arno Press, 1980.
Finch, Marianne. *An English-woman's Experience in America*. New York: Negro Uni-
    versities Press, 1969.
Gay, Mary Ann Harris. *Life in Dixie during the War: 1861–1862–1863–1864–1865*. 4th
    ed. Atlanta: Forte and Davis, 1901.
Griffiths, Mattie. *Autobiography of a Female Slave*. New York: Redfield, 1857.
Hall, Mrs. Basil. *The Aristocratic Journey*. New York: G. P. Putnam's Sons, 1931.
Hopley, Catherine. *Life in the South*. 2 vols. London: Chapman and Hall, 1863.
Johnson, Clifton H., ed. *God Struck Me Dead*. Boston: Pilgrim Press, 1969.
Kearney, Belle. *A Slaveholder's Daughter*. New York: Abbey Press, 1900.
Kemble, Frances Anne. *Journal of a Residence on a Georgian Plantation in 1838–
    1839*. Edited by John A. Scott. New York: Alfred A. Knopf, 1961.
Leigh, Francis Butler. *Ten Years on a Georgia Plantation since the War*. 1883. Reprint.
    New York: Negro Universities Press, 1969.

Lines, Amelia Akehurst. *To Raise Myself a Little: The Diaries and Letters of Jennie, a Georgia Teacher, 1851–1886*. Edited by Thomas Dyer. Athens: University of Georgia Press, 1982.

McDonald, Cornelia. *A Diary with Reminiscences of the War and Refugee Life in the Shenandoah Valley, 1860–1865*. Nashville: Cullom and Gertner, 1934.

[McGuire, Judith]. *Diary of a Southern Refugee by a Lady of Virginia*. New York, 1868.

McGuire, Judith. *Diary of a Southern Refugee*. 3d ed. Richmond, 1889.

Mendell, Miss, and Hosmer, Miss. *Notes of Travel and Life*. New York, 1854.

Miller, Randall M., ed. *"Dear Master": Letters of a Slave Family*. Ithaca: Cornell University Press, 1978.

More, Hannah. *Strictures on the Modern System of Female Education*. London: A. Straham, 1801.

Pember, Phoebe Yates. *A Southern Woman's Story*. New York: G. W. Carleton and Co., 1879.

Pierce, Bishop. "Why Women Should Be Well Educated." Edited by Atticus Haygood. Nashville: Southern Methodist Publishing House, 1886.

Royall, Ann. *Mrs. Royall's Southern Tour*. Washington, 1831.

Stanton, Elizabeth Cady; Anthony, Susan B.; and Gage, Joclyn, eds. *History of Women Suffrage*. Vol. 3. Rochester, N.Y., 1881.

Trollope, Frances. *Domestic Manners of the Americans*. 2 vols. New York: Dodd, Mead and Co., 1894.

Tyler Ronnie C., and Murphy, Lawrence R., eds. *The Slave Narratives of Texas*. Austin: Encino Press, 1974.

Willard, Frances. *Woman and Temperance*. Hartford, Conn.: Park Publishing Co., 1883.

Wollstonecraft, Mary. *A Vindication of the Rights of Woman*. New York: Reprint. W. W. Norton and Co., 1967.

Published Sermons and Church Documents

Beckwith, John Watrous. *Sermons*. Manuscript Division, University of Georgia, Athens.

Boswell, Thomas L. "Salvation in Its Individual Relations." *The Methodist Pulpit South*. Washington, 1859.

The Constitution of the Presbyterian Church. Philadelphia: Presbyterian Board of Education, 1833.

The Doctrines and Discipline of the Methodist Episcopal Church. New York: T. Mason and G. Lane, 1840.

The Doctrines and Discipline of the Methodist Episcopal Church, South. Nashville: A. H. Redford, 1866.

The Doctrines and Discipline of the Methodist Episcopal Church, South. Nashville: Southern Methodist Publishing House, 1878.

Emory, Roberts. *History of the Discipline of the Methodist Episcopal Church*. New York: G. Lane and P. P. Sandford, 1844.

Hawley, Bostwick. *Manual of Methodism*. New York: Phillips and Hunt, 1879.

Haygood, Atticus G. *Bishop Pierce's Sermons and Addresses*. Nashville: Southern Methodist Publishing House, 1886.

————. *Sermons and Speeches*. Nashville: Southern Methodist Publishing House, 1883.

Henry, T. Charlton. *The Female Laborer in the Vineyard: Funeral Discourse, Occasioned by the Death of Miss Elizabeth Robertson*. [Preached in the Second Presbyterian Church, Charleston, 26 August 1827.] Charleston: Observor Office Press, 1827.

Kollock, Henry. *Sermons on Various Subjects*. 4 vols. Savannah: S. C. and I. Schenck, 1822.

Mallary, C. D. "The Doctrine of Election," Sermon XIV, *Sermons of Reverend C. D. Mallary*. In *The Georgia Pulpit: Or Ministers' Yearly Offering*, edited by Robert Fleming. Richmond, 1847.

Mell, P. H. *Corrective Church Discipline*. Athens, Georgia: E. D. Stone Press, 1912.

Peterson, P. A. *Hand-Book of Southern Methodism*. Richmond: J. W. Fergusson and Son, 1883.

Riley, B. F. *A History of the Baptists in the Southern States East of the Mississippi*. Philadelphia: American Baptist Publication Society, 1898.

Rogers, E. P. "Death, the Christian's Gain: A Sermon." First Presbyterian Church, Augusta, April 30, 1848. Rare Books Room, University of Georgia, Athens.

Southern Baptist Convention. *Proceedings*. Baltimore, 1884.

————. Augusta, 1885.

————. Memphis, 1889.

Tupper, H. A. *The Foreign Missions of the Southern Baptist Convention*. Philadelphia: American Baptist Publication Society, 1889.

Wadsworth, Edward. "God and Man Are Co-Workers in the Salvation of the Soul." In *The Methodist Pulpit South*, edited by William T. Smithson. Washington: William T. Smithson, 1859.

Wasdell, Elizabeth Wright. *St. Paul's Church*. 2 vols. Richmond, n.d.

Worrell, A. A. *Review of Corrective Church Discipline*. Nashville: Southwestern Publishing House, 1860.

Unpublished Secondary Sources

Boles, John B. "Evangelical Protestantism in the Old South: From Religious Dissent to Cultural Dominance." Paper read at the Tenth Annual Chancellor's Symposium in Southern History, 4 October 1984, University of Mississippi, University, Mississippi.

Clinton, Catherine. "The Plantation Mistress: Another Side of Southern Slavery, 1780–1835." Ph.D. dissertation, Princeton University, 1980.

Cory, Earl Wallace. "Temperance and Prohibition in Antebellum Georgia." Master's thesis, University of Georgia, 1961.

Giele, Janet Zollinger. "Social Change in the Feminine Role: A Comparison of Women's Suffrage and Woman's Temperance, 1870–1920." Ph.D. dissertation, Radcliffe College, 1961.

Huff, Mary Ann. "The Role of Women in Confederate Georgia." Master's thesis, Emory University, 1967.

Kenzer, Robert Charles. "Portrait of a Southern Community, 1849–1881: Family, Kinship and Neighborhood in Orange County, North Carolina." Ph.D. dissertation, Harvard University, 1982.

Lansman, Jeanne Milligan. "With an Army of Organized Women: The Club Movement among Black Women in the United States, 1895 to 1920." Master's thesis, University of Georgia, 1982.

Mohr, Clarence Lee. "Georgia Blacks during Secession and Civil War, 1859–1865." Ph.D. dissertation, University of Georgia, 1975.

_____. "Oglethorpe County, Georgia during the Formation Period, 1773–1830." Master's thesis, University of Georgia, 1970.

Scott, Anne. "Are We the Women Our Grandmothers Were?" Keynote Address at the Atlanta Historical Society Symposium, "From Myth to Modern Times." Spelman College, November 4, 1980.

Smith, Cortland Victor. "Church Organization as an Agency of Social Control: Church Discipline in North Carolina, 1800–1860." Ph.D. dissertation, University of North Carolina, 1966.

White, Deborah. "Ain't I a Woman?" Ph.D. dissertation, University of Illinois, Chicago Circle, 1978.

Books and Articles

Althusser, Louis. *For Marx*. Translated by Ben Brewster. New York: Pantheon Books, 1969.

_____. *Lenin and Philosophy and Other Essays*. Translated by Ben Brewster. New York: Monthly Review Press, 1971.

Altman, Leon L. *The Dream in Psychoanalysis*. New York: International Universities Press, 1975.

Anderson, Michael. "Family, Household, and the Industrial Revolution." In *The American Family in Social-Historical Perspective*, edited by Michael Gordon. New York: St. Martin's Press, 1973.

_____. *Family Structure in Nineteenth-Century Lancashire*. Cambridge: Cambridge University Press, 1971.

Balthasar, Hans Urs von. *A Theological Anthropology*. New York: Sheed and Ward, 1967.

Barney, William L. "Patterns of Crisis: Alabama White Families and Social Change, 1850–1870." *Sociology and Social Research* 63 (April 1979): 524–43.

Bayliss, John F., ed. *Black Slave Narratives*. London: Macmillan Co., 1970.

Berg, Barbara J. *The Remembered Gate: Origins of American Feminism*. New York: Oxford University Press, 1978.

Berkin, Carol Ruth, and Norton, Mary Beth. *Women of America: A History*. Boston: Houghton Mifflin Co., 1979.

Blassingame, John W. *The Slave Community: Plantation Life in the Antebellum South*. New York: Oxford University Press, 1979.

————, ed. *Slave Testimony: Two Centuries of Letters, Speeches, Interviews, and Autobiographies*. Baton Rouge: Louisiana State University Press, 1977.

Boardman, Fon W., Jr. *America and the Gilded Age, 1876–1900*. New York: Henry Z. Walch, 1972.

Bogue, Donald J. *The Population of the United States*. Glencoe, Ill.: Free Press, 1959.

Bohmer, Carol. "Modernization, Divorce and the Status of Women: Le Tribunal Bobodioulass." *African Studies Review* 23 (September 1980): 81–90.

Boles, John B. *The Great Revival, 1787–1805*. Lexington: University Press of Kentucky, 1972.

Bonner, James C. *A History of Georgia Agriculture, 1732–1860*. Athens: University of Georgia Press, 1964.

Bontemps, Arna. *Great Slave Narratives*. Boston: Beacon Press, 1969.

Bordin, Ruth. *Woman and Temperance: The Quest for Power and Liberty, 1873–1900*. Philadelphia: Temple University Press, 1981.

Boyd, Lois A., and Brackenridge, R. Douglas. *Presbyterian Women in America: Two Centuries of a Quest for Status*. Westport, Conn.: Greenwood Press, 1983.

Brown, James Stephen. "Social Class, Intermarriage, and Church Membership in a Kentucky Community." *American Journal of Sociology* 59 (September 1951): 232–42.

————; Schwarzweller, Harry K.; and Mangalam, Joseph J. "Kentucky Mountain Migration and the Stem Family: An American Variation on a Theme by LePlay." *Rural Sociology* 28 (Spring 1963): 48–69.

Brown, Richard D. *Modernization: The Transformation of American Life, 1600–1865*. New York: Hill and Wang, 1976.

Brummitt, Stella Wyatt. *Looking Backward, Thinking Forward: The Jubilee History of the Women's Home Missionary Society of the Methodist Episcopal Church*. Cincinnati, 1830.

Caligar, Leopold, and May, Rollo. *Dreams and Symbols: Man's Unconscious Language*. New York: Basic Books, 1968.

Cannon, James M., III. *History of Southern Methodist Missions*. Nashville: Cokesbury Press, 1926.

Carr, Lois Green, and Walsh, Lorena S. "The Planter's Wife: The Experience of White Women in Seventeenth-Century Maryland." In *Our American Sisters: Women in American Life and Thought*, edited by Jean E. Friedman and William G. Shade. 3d ed. Lexington, Mass.: D. C. Heath and Company, 1982.

Carter, Paul. *A Spiritual Crisis of the Gilded Age*. De Kalb: Northern Illinois University Press, 1971.

Cash, W. J. *The Mind of the South*. New York: Vintage Books, 1941.

Chekki, Danesh A. *Modernization and Kin Network*. Leiden: E. J. Brill, 1974.

Chesser, Barbara E. "Comment on Naomi Goldenberg's 'A Feminist Critique of Jung.'" *Signs: Journal of Women in Culture and Society* 3 (Spring 1978): 721–24.

Clifford, Geraldine Joncich. "Home and School in Nineteenth-Century America: Some Personal History Reports from the United States." *History of Education Quarterly* 18 (Spring 1978): 10–11.

————. "Saints, Sinners, and People: A Position Paper on the Historiography of American Education." *History of Education Quarterly* 15 (Fall 1975): 259.

Clinton, Catherine. *The Plantation Mistress: Woman's World in the Old South*. New
    York: Pantheon Books, 1982.
Cott, Nancy F. *The Bonds of Womanhood: "Women's Sphere" in New England, 1780–
    1835*. New Haven: Yale University Press, 1977.
———. "Divorce and the Changing Status of Women in Eighteenth-Century Massa-
    chusetts." *William and Mary Quarterly* 33 (October 1976): 586–614.
Craven, Avery O. *The Growth of Southern Nationalism*. Baton Rouge: Louisiana State
    University Press, 1953.
Dick, Everett. *The Dixie Frontier: A Social History*. New York: Alfred A. Knopf, 1948.
Donald, David Herbert. *Liberty and Union*. Boston: Little, Brown and Co., 1978.
Douglas, Ann. "Heaven Our Home: Consolation Literature in the Northern United
    States, 1830–1880." *American Quarterly* 26 (December 1974): 496–515.
Douglas, Mary. *Implicit Meanings: Essays in Anthropology*. London: Routledge and
    Kegan Paul, 1975.
———. *Natural Symbols: Explorations in Cosmology*. New York: Pantheon Books,
    1970.
Drabek, Thomas E.; Key, William H.; Erickson, Patricia E.; and Crowe, Juanita L. "The
    Impact of Disaster on Kin Relationships." *Journal of Marriage and the Family* 37
    (August 1975): 481–94.
Earle, Carville, and Hoffman, Ronald. "The Foundation of the Modern Economy: Agri-
    culture and the Costs of Labor in the United States and England, 1800–1860."
    American Historical Review 85 (December 1980): 1055–94.
Easterlin, Richard A. "Factors in the Decline of Farm Family Fertility in the United
    States: Some Preliminary Research Results." *Journal of American History* 63 (De-
    cember 1976): 600–614.
Eaton, Clement. *The Growth of Southern Civilization, 1790–1860*. New York: Harper
    and Row, 1961.
Edinger, Edward F. "Psychotherapy and Alchemy I. Introduction." *Quadrant* 11 (Sum-
    mer 1978): 5–27.
———. "Psychotherapy and Alchemy II. Calcinatio." *Quadrant* 11 (Summer 1978):
    28–37.
———. "Psychotherapy and Alchemy III. Solutio." *Quadrant* 11 (Winter 1978): 63–85.
Edmiston, Althea B. "Maria Fearing." In *Informal Sketches of Seven Women Mission-
    aries of the Presbyterian Church, U.S.* Compiled by Hallie Paxson Winsborough,
    edited by Sarah Lee Vinson Timmons. Atlanta: Committee on Women's Work,
    1937.
Fraser, Morris. *Children in Conflict*. London: Secker Warburg, 1973.
Freud, Anna, and Burlingham, Dorothy T. *War and Children*. New York: Medical War
    Books, 1943.
Friedman, Jean E., and Shade, William G., eds. *Our American Sisters: Women in
    American Life and Thought*. 3d ed. Lexington, Mass.: D. C. Heath and Co., 1982.
Fuller, Paul E. *Laura Clay and the Woman's Rights Movement*. Lexington: University
    Press of Kentucky, 1975.
Garrison, Winfred E. *March of Faith: The Story of Religion in America since 1865*.
    1933. Reprint. Westport, Conn.: Greenwood Press, 1983.
Geertz, Clifford. "From the Native's Point of View: On the Nature of Anthropological

Understanding." In *Symbolic Anthropology: A Reader in the Study of Symbols and Meanings*, edited by Janet L. Solgin, David D. Kennitzer, and David M. Schneider. New York: Columbia University Press, 1977.

Genovese, Eugene. *Roll, Jordan, Roll: The World the Slaves Made*. New York: Vintage Books, 1976.

Gillespie, H. D. *Psychological Effects of War on Citizen and Soldier*. New York: W. W. Norton and Co., 1942.

Goldenberg, Naomi R. "A Feminist Critique of Jung." *Signs: Journal of Women in Culture and Society* 2 (Winter 1976): 433–49.

————. "Reply to Barbara Chesser's Comment on 'A Feminist Critique of Jung.'" *Signs: Journal of Women in Culture and Society* 3 (Spring 1978): 724–27.

Gordon, Elizabeth Putnam. *Woman Torch Bearers: The Story of the Women's Christian Temperance Union*. Evanston, Ill.: National Women's Temperance Union Publishing House, 1924.

Gray, Lewis Cecil. *History of Agriculture in the Southern United States to 1860*. 2 vols. 1933. Reprint. Gloucester, Mass.: Peter Smith, 1958.

Gray, Ricky Harold. "Corona Female College (1857–1864)." *Journal of Mississippi History* 42, no. 2 (May 1980): 129–34.

Gregory of Nyssa, Saint. *The Life of Moses*. New York: Paulist Press, 1978.

Greven, Philip. *The Protestant Temperament*. New York: Alfred A. Knopf, 1977.

Gutman, Herbert G. *The Black Family in Slavery and Freedom, 1750–1925*. New York: Pantheon Books, 1976.

Hall, Jacquelyn Dowd. *Revolt against Chivalry: Jesse Daniel Ames and the Women's Campaign against Lynching*. New York: Columbia University Press, 1979.

Hall, James A. *Clinical Uses of Dreams: Jungian Interpretation and Enactments*. New York: Grune and Stratton, 1977.

Hareven, Tamara K. "The Dynamics of Kin in an Industrial Community." In *Turning Points: Historical and Sociological Essays on the Family*, edited by John Demos and Sarane Spence Boocock. Chicago: University of Chicago Press, 1978.

————, ed. *Family and Kin in Urban Communities, 1700–1930*. New York: New Viewpoints, 1977.

Hays, Agnes Subbs. *Heritage of Dedication*. Evanston, Ill.: Signal Press, 1973.

Heck, Fanny. *In Royal Service*. Richmond: L. H. Jenkins, 1913.

Hendrix, Lewellyn. "Kinship and Economic-Rational Migration: A Comparison of Micro and Macro-level Analyses." *Sociological Quarterly* 16 (Autumn 1975): 534–43.

————. "Kinship, Social Class and Migration." *Journal of Marriage and Family* 41 (May 1979): 399–409.

Herman, Sondra R. "Loving Courtship or the Marriage Market? The Ideal and Its Critics, 1871–1911." In *Our American Sisters: Women in American Life and Thought*, edited by Jean E. Friedman and William G. Shade. 3d ed. Lexington, Mass.: D. C. Heath and Co., 1982.

Higgs, Robert. "Mortality in Rural America, 1879–1920: Estimates and Conjectures." *Explorations in Economic History* 10 (Winter 1973): 177–95.

Hilliard, Sam Bowers. *Hog Meat and Hoecake: Food Supply in the Old South, 1840–1860*. Carbondale: Southern Illinois University Press, 1972.

Hopkins, Richard J. "Occupational and Geographical Mobility in Atlanta, 1870–1896."

Journal of Southern History 34 (May 1968): 200–213.

Huffman, Frank J., Jr. "Town and Country in the South, 1850–1880: A Comparison of Urban and Rural Social Structures." *South Atlantic Quarterly* 76 (Summer 1977): 366–81.

Idowu, E. Bolaji. *African Traditional Religion: A Definition*. London: SCM Press, 1973.

Ironmonger, Elizabeth Hogg, and Phillips, Pauline Landrum. *History of the Women's Christian Temperance Union of Virginia*. Richmond: Cavalier Press, 1958.

Jacobson, Paul H. "An Estimate of the Expectation of Life in the United States in 1850." *Millbank Memorial Fund Quarterly* 35 (April 1957): 197–201.

Jameson, Fredric. *The Political Unconscious: Narrative as a Socially Symbolic Act*. Ithaca: Cornell University Press, 1981.

Johnson, Clifton H., et al. *God Struck Me Dead*. Philadelphia: Pilgrim Press, 1969.

Jones, Jacqueline. " 'My Mother Was Much of a Woman': Black Women, Work and the Family under Slavery." *Feminist Studies* 8, no. 2 (Summer 1982): 235–69.

Jones, Katherine M. *Heroines of Dixie*. New York: Bobbs-Merrill Co., 1955.

Jung, Carl G. *Aion: Researches into the Phenomenology of the Self*. Translated by R. F. C. Hull. In *Collected Works of Carl G. Jung*, vol. 9. New York: Pantheon Press, 1959.

———. *Collected Papers on Analytical Psychology*. Translated by Constance E. Long. New York: Moffat Yard and Co., 1917.

———. *Dreams*. Translated by R. F. C. Hull. Princeton: Princeton University Press, 1974.

———. *Man and His Symbols*. New York: Dell Publishing Company, 1964.

———. *Psychology and Alchemy*. Translated by R. F. C. Hull. 2d ed. Princeton: Princeton University Press, 1968.

———. *Psychology and Religion: West and East*. Translated by R. F. C. Hull. 2d ed. Princeton: Princeton University Press, 1969.

———. *The Symbolic Life*. Vol. 18. Translated by R. F. C. Hull. Princeton: Princeton University Press, 1976.

Katz, Michael B. *Education in American History*. New York: Praeger, 1973.

Kerber, Linda K. *Women of the Republic: Intellect and Ideology in Revolutionary America*. Chapel Hill: University of North Carolina Press, 1980.

Kissinger, Warren S. *The Sermon on the Mount: A History of Interpretation and Bibliography*. Metuchen, N.J.: Scarecrow Press, 1975.

Kraditor, Aileen S. *The Ideas of the Woman Suffrage Movement, 1890–1920*. New York: Anchor Books, 1971.

Kren, George M., and Rappoport, Leon. "Clio and Psyche." *Journal of Psychology* 1 (September 1973): 151–63.

Leach, Edmund. "Levi-Strauss in the Garden of Eden: An Examination of Some Recent Developments in the Analysis of Myth." *Transactions of the New York Academy of Sciences* 23 (1960): 386–96.

Lebsock, Susan. *Free Women of Petersburg*. New York: W. W. Norton and Co., 1983.

Lerner, Gerda. *The Grimké Sisters from South Carolina: Rebels against Slavery*. Boston: Houghton Mifflin Co., 1967.

———. *The Majority Finds Its Past: Placing Women in History*. New York: Oxford University Press, 1979.

Levine, Lawrence W. *Black Culture and Black Consciousness: Afro-American Folk*

Thought from Slavery to Freedom. New York: Oxford University Press, 1977.

Lévi-Strauss, Claude. *Myth and Meaning*. Toronto: University of Toronto Press, 1978.

———. *Structural Anthropology*. Translated by Claire Jacobson and Brooke Grundfest Schoepf. New York: Basic Books, 1963.

———. "The Structural Study of Myth." *Journal of American Folklore* 68 (1955): 428–44.

Lichtman, Allan J., and Challinor, Joan R., eds. *Kin and Communities: Families in America*. Washington, D.C.: Smithsonian Institution Press, 1979.

Litwack, Leon F. *Been in the Storm So Long: The Aftermath of Slavery*. New York: Alfred A. Knopf, 1979.

Loewenberg, Peter. "The Psychohistorical Origins of the Nazi Youth Cohort." *American Historical Review* 76 (December 1971): 1457–1502.

Loveland, Anne C. *Southern Evangelicals and the Social Order, 1800–1860*. Baton Rouge: Louisiana State University Press, 1980.

McDonald, Forrest, and McWhiney, Grady. "The South from Self-Sufficiency to Peonage: An Interpretation." *American Historical Review* 85 (December 1980): 1095–1119.

McPherson, James M. *Ordeal by Fire: The Civil War and Reconstruction*. New York: Alfred A. Knopf, 1982.

McWhiney, Grady. *Southerners and Other Americans*. New York: Basic Books, 1973.

Massey, Mary Elizabeth. *Bonnet Brigades*. New York: Alfred A. Knopf, 1966.

———. "The Making of a Feminist." *Journal of Southern History* 39 (February–November 1973): 809.

———. *Refugee Life in the Confederacy*. Baton Rouge: Louisiana State University Press, 1964.

Mathews, Donald G. *Religion in the Old South*. Chicago: University of Chicago Press, 1977.

Matthews, Elmora. *Neighbor and Kin: Life in a Tennessee Ridge Community*. Nashville: Vanderbilt University Press, 1965.

Mbiti, John S. *African Religions and Philosophy*. New York: Frederick A. Praeger, 1969.

———. *Concepts of God in Africa*. New York: Frederick A. Praeger, 1970.

———. *New Testament Eschatology in an African Background*. New York: Oxford University Press, 1971.

Meeker, Edward. "The Improving Health of the United States, 1850–1915." *Explorations in Economic History* 9 (Summer 1972): 353–73.

Mohr, Clarence Lee. "Slavery in Oglethorpe County, Georgia, 1773–1865." *Phylon* 23 (Spring 1972): 11.

Morley, John. *Death, Heaven and the Victorians*. London: Studio Vista, 1971.

Moseley, James C. *A Cultural History of Religion in America*. Westport, Conn.: Greenwood Press, 1981.

Norton, Mary Beth. *Liberty's Daughters: The Revolutionary Experience of American Women, 1750–1800*. Boston: Little, Brown and Co., 1980.

Nye, F. Ivan. *Role Structure and Analysis of the Family*. Beverly Hills: Sage Publications, 1976.

Oberholtzer, Ellis Paxson. *A History of the United States since the Civil War*. 5 vols. 1917. Reprint. New York: Negro Universities Press, 1969.

Olmsted, Frederick Law. *A Journey in the Back Country*. 2 vols. New York: G. P. Putnam's Sons, 1907.

———. *A Journey in the Seaboard Slave States*. 2 vols. New York: G. P. Putnam's Sons, 1904.

Orr, Dorothy. *A History of Education in Georgia*. Chapel Hill: University of North Carolina Press, 1950.

Owens, Leslie Howard. *This Species of Property*. New York: Oxford University Press, 1976.

Owsley, Frank L. "The Pattern of Migration and Settlement of the Southern Frontier." *Journal of Southern History* 9 (1945): 147–76.

———. *Plain Folk of the Old South*. Chicago: Quadrangle Books, 1949.

Paludan, Philip. *Victims: A True Story of the Civil War*. Knoxville: University of Tennessee Press, 1981.

Pessen, Edward. "How Different from Each Other Were the Antebellum North and South?" *American Historical Review* 85 (December 1980): 1125.

Pleck, Elizabeth H. "A Mother's Wages: Income Earning among Married Italian and Black Women, 1896–1911." In *A Heritage of Her Own*, edited by Nancy F. Cott and Elizabeth H. Pleck. New York: Simon and Schuster, 1979.

Purdue, Theda. *Slavery and the Evolution of Cherokee Society, 1540–1866*. Knoxville: University of Tennessee Press, 1979.

Raboteau, Albert J. *Slave Religion: The Invisible Institution in the Antebellum South*. New York: Oxford University Press, 1978.

Rahner, Karl. *Foundations of Christian Faith: An Introduction to the Idea of Christianity*. Translated by William V. Dych. New York: Seabury Press, 1978.

Rawick, George P., ed. *The American Slave: A Composite Autobiography*. 1941. Reprint. 19 vols. Westport, Conn.: Greenwood Press, 1972.

Rindfuss, Donald R. "Changing Patterns of Fertility in the South: A Social-Demographic Examination." *Social Forces* 57, no. 2 (December 1978): 621–35.

Roberson, Nancy. "Social Mobility in Ante-Bellum Alabama." *Alabama Review* 13 (January 1960): 135–45.

Rosenberg, George S., and Anspach, Donald F. *Working Class Kinship*. Lexington, Mass.: Lexington Books, 1973.

Ross, Malcolm. *The Cape Fear*. New York: Holt Rinehart and Winston, 1965.

Rossi, Ino, and Contributors. *The Logic of Culture: Advances in Structural Theory and Methods*. South Hadley, Mass.: J. F. Bergin Publishers, 1982.

Roth, Robert J. "Josiah Royce and Salvation Philosophy." In *American Religious Philosophy*. New York: Harcourt, Brace and World, 1967.

Royce, Josiah. "Individual Experience and Social Experience as Sources of Religious Insight." In *The Basic Writings of Josiah Royce*, edited by John J. McDermott. Chicago: University of Chicago Press, 1969.

Russel, Robert R. "The Effects of Slavery upon Nonslaveholders in the Antebellum South." *Agricultural History* 15 (1941): 112–16.

Ryan, Mary P. *Cradle of the Middle Class: The Family in Oneida County, New York, 1790–1865*. New York: Cambridge University Press, 1981.

———. "The Power of Women's Networks: A Case Study of Female Moral Reform in Antebellum America." *Feminist Studies* 5 (Spring 1979): 66–85.

———. *Womanhood in America*. New York: New Viewpoints, 1975.

Saum, Lewis O. "Death in the Popular Mind of Pre–Civil War America." *American Quarterly* 26 (December 1974): 477–95.

Schlesinger, Arthur M. *A Critical Period in American Religion, 1875–1900*. Philadelphia: Fortress Press, 1967.

Schneider, David M. "Kinship, Community, and Locality in American Culture." In *Kin and Communities: Families in America*, edited by Allan J. Lichtman and Joan R. Chalinor. Washington, D.C.: Smithsonian Institution Press, 1979.

Schwarzweller, Harry K.; Brown, James S.; and Mangalam, Joseph J. *Mountain Families in Transition*. College Park: Pennsylvania State University Press, 1971.

Scott, Anne F. "The 'New Woman' in the New South." *South Atlantic Quarterly* 65 (Autumn 1962): 473–83.

———. *The Southern Lady: From Pedestal to Politics, 1830–1930*. Chicago: University of Chicago Press, 1970.

———. "Women's Perspective on the Patriarchy in the 1850s." *Journal of American History* 61 (June 1974).

———, and Scott, Andrew Mackay. *One Half the People: The Fight for Woman Suffrage*. Champaign and Urbana: University of Illinois Press, 1982.

Shorter, Aylward. "Symbolism, Ritual, and History: An Examination of the Work of Victor Turner." In *Historical Study of African Religion*, edited by L. O. Rouger and I. N. Kimambo. London: Heinemann, 1972.

Shulman, Norman. "Life Cycle Variations in Patterns of Close Relationships." *Journal of Marriage and the Family* 37 (November 1975): 817–18.

Smith, Henry Nash. *Virgin Land: The American West as Symbol and Myth*. New York: Vintage Books, 1950.

Smith, Page. *Daughters of the Promised Land: Women in American History*. Boston: Little, Brown and Co., 1970.

Smith-Rosenberg, Carroll. "Beauty, the Beast, and the Militant Woman: A Case Study in Sex Roles and Social Stress in Jacksonian America." In *A Heritage of Her Own*, edited by Nancy F. Cott and Elizabeth H. Pleck. New York: Simon and Schuster, 1979.

———. "The Female World of Love and Ritual: Relations between Women in Nineteenth-Century America." In *The American Family in Social-Historical Perspective*, edited by Michael Gordon. New York: St. Martin's Press, 1978.

Spruill, Julia Cherry. *Women's Life and Work in the Southern Colonies*. 1938. Reprint. New York: W. W. Norton and Co., 1972.

Stannard, David E. *The Puritan Way of Death: A Study in Religion, Culture and Social Change*. New York: Oxford University Press, 1977.

Starobin, Robert S. *Industrial Slavery in the Old South*. New York: Oxford University Press, 1970.

Stearns, Peter N. "Modernization and Social History: Some Suggestions and a Muted Cheer." *Journal of Social History* 14 (Winter 1980): 189–209.

Stekel, William. *The Interpretation of Dreams*. New York: Washington Square Press, 1967.

Stephenson, William E. "The Davises, the Southalls, and the Founding of Wesleyan Female College, 1854–1859." *North Carolina Review* 58 (July 1980): 257–79.

Sterkx, H. E. *Partners in Rebellion: Alabama Women in the Civil War*. Rutherford, N.J.: Fairleigh Dickinson University Press, 1970.

Sweet, William Warren. *Methodism in American History*. New York: Abingdon Press, 1954.

Taylor, A. Elizabeth. "A Short History of the Woman Suffrage Movement in Tennessee." *Tennessee Historical Quarterly* 2 (September 1943): 195–215.

_____. "The Woman Suffrage Movement in Arkansas." *Arkansas Historical Quarterly* 15 (Spring 1956): 17–52.

_____. "The Woman Suffrage Movement in Mississippi, 1870–1920." *Journal of Mississippi History* 30 (1968): 1–34.

_____. "The Woman Suffrage Movement in North Carolina, Part 1." *North Carolina Historical Review* 38 (January 1961): 45–62.

_____. *The Woman Suffrage Movement in Tennessee*. New York: Bookman Associates, 1957.

Taylor, William R. *Cavalier and Yankee: The Old South and American National Character*. Cambridge, Mass.: Harvard University Press, 1979.

Tessler, Mark A., and Hawkins, Linda L. "Acculturation, Socio-Economic Status, and Attitude Change in Tunisia: Implications for Modernization Theory." *Journal of Modern African Studies* 17 (1979): 473-95.

Thernstrom, Stephen, and Knights, Peter R. "Men in Motion: Some Data and Speculations about Urban Population Mobility in Nineteenth-Century America." In *Anonymous Americans*, edited by Tamara Hareven. Englewood Cliffs, N.J.: Prentice-Hall, 1971.

Thomas, Emory M. *The Confederate Nation, 1861–1865*. New York: Harper and Row, 1979.

_____. *The Confederate State of Richmond: A Biography of the Capitol*. Austin: University of Texas Press, 1971.

Thompson, E. P. *The Making of the English Working Class*. New York: Vintage Books, 1966.

Thompson, Ernest Trice. *Presbyterians in the South*. 3 vols. Richmond: John Knox Press, 1963.

Thompson, Mildred C. *Reconstruction in Georgia: Economic, Social, Political, 1865–1872*. New York: Columbia University Press, 1915.

Thompson, Warren S., and Whelpton, P. K. *Population Trends in the United States*. New York: McGraw-Hill Book Co., 1933.

Tryon, Rolla Milton. *Household Manufacturing in the United States, 1640–1860: A Study in Industrial History*. Chicago: University of Chicago Press, 1917.

Turner, Victor W. "Ritual Symbolism, Morality, and Social Structure among the Ndembu." In *African Systems of Thought*. New York: Oxford University Press, 1965.

Tyrrell, Ian R. "Drink and Temperance in the Antebellum South: An Overview and Interpretation." *Journal of Southern History* 48 (November 1982): 485–570.

Ulanov, Anne Bedford. *The Feminine in Jungian Psychology and in Christian Theology*. Evanston, Ill.: Northwestern University Press, 1971.

Ulrich, Laurel Thatcher. *Good Wives: Image and Reality in the Lives of Women in Northern New England, 1650–1750*. New York: Alfred A. Knopf, 1982.

Vaghefi, M. Reza. "A Micro-Analysis Approach to Modernization Process: A Case Study of Modernity and Traditionalism Conflict." *International Journal of Mid-Eastern Studies* 12 (September 1980): 181–97.

Vinovskis, Maris A. "Socioeconomic Determinants of Interstate Fertility Differentials in the United States in 1850 and 1860." *Journal of Interdisciplinary History* 6 (Winter 1976): 375–96.

Waller, Willard. *War and the Family*. New York: Dryden Press, 1940.

Wallman, Sandra. "Kinship, Anti-kinship: Variation in the Logic of Kinship Situations." *Journal of Human Evolution* 4 (1975): 331–41.

Weaver, Herbert. *Mississippi Farmers, 1850–1860*. Nashville: Vanderbilt University Press, 1945.

Welter, Barbara. "The Cult of True Womanhood, 1820–1860." *American Quarterly* 18 (Summer 1966): 151–74.

————. "The Feminization of American Religion." In *Dimity Convictions: The American Woman in the Nineteenth Century*. Athens: Ohio University Press, 1976.

Whitmont, Edward C. "Reassessing Femininity and Masculinity: A Critique of Some Traditional Assumptions." *Quadrant* 13 (Fall 1980): 109–22.

Wiener, Jonathan M. "Planter Persistence and Social Change: Alabama, 1850–1870." *Journal of Interdisciplinary History* 7 (Autumn 1976): 235–60.

Wiley, Bell Irvin. *The Plain People of the Confederacy*. 1943. Reprint. Gloucester, Mass.: Peter Smith, 1971.

Wilson, Joan Hoff. "The Illusion of Change: Women and the American Revolution." In *Our American Sisters: Women in American Life and Thought*, edited by Jean E. Friedman and William G. Shade. 3d ed. Lexington, Mass.: D. C. Heath and Co., 1982.

Worthman, Paul B. "Working-Class Mobility in Birmingham, Alabama, 1880–1914." In *Anonymous Americans*, edited by Tamara Hareven. Englewood Cliffs, N.J.: Prentice-Hall, 1971.

Wright, Gavin. *The Political Economy of the Cotton South: Household Markets and Wealth in the Nineteenth Century*. New York: W. W. Norton and Co., 1978.

Wright, Louis B. "The Colonial Search for a Southern Eden." In *Three Lectures on the Dancy Foundation*. University: University of Alabama Press, 1953.

Wrigley, Edward A. *Nineteenth-Century Society: Essays in the Use of Quantitative Methods for the Study of Social Data*. Cambridge, England: Cambridge University Press, 1972.

Wyatt-Brown, Bertram. "The Ideal Typology and Antebellum Southern History: A Testing of a New Approach." *Societas* 5 (Winter 1975): 1–29.

Zahan, Dominique. *The Religion, Spirituality, and Thought of Traditional Africa*. Chicago: University of Chicago Press, 1979.

I N D E X